Japanese History and Folktales

An Enthralling Exploration of Japan's Past and Legends, Tracing the Rise of Empires, the Age of the Samurai, and the Myths That Shaped a Nation

© **Copyright 2025 - All rights reserved.**

The content contained within this book may not be reproduced, duplicated, or transmitted without direct written permission from the author or the publisher.

Under no circumstances will any blame or legal responsibility be held against the publisher, or author, for any damages, reparation, or monetary loss due to the information contained within this book, either directly or indirectly.

Legal Notice:

This book is copyright protected. It is only for personal use. You cannot amend, distribute, sell, use, quote, or paraphrase any part, or the content within this book, without the consent of the author or publisher.

Disclaimer Notice:

Please note the information contained within this document is for educational and entertainment purposes only. All effort has been executed to present accurate, up-to-date, reliable, and complete information. No warranties of any kind are declared or implied. Readers acknowledge that the author is not engaging in the rendering of legal, financial, medical, or professional advice. The content within this book has been derived from various sources. Please consult a licensed professional before attempting any techniques outlined in this book.

By reading this document, the reader agrees that under no circumstances is the author responsible for any losses, direct or indirect, that are incurred as a result of the use of the information contained within this document, including, but not limited to, errors, omissions, or inaccuracies.

Free limited time bonus

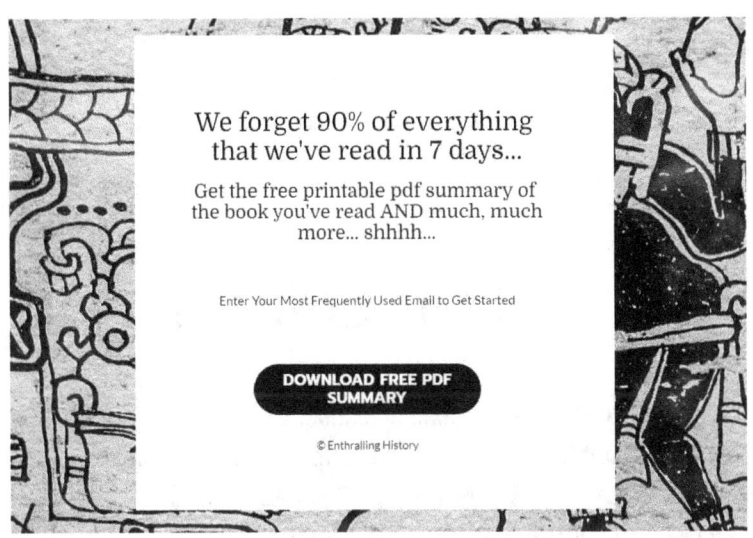

Stop for a moment. We have a free bonus set up for you. The problem is this: we forget 90% of everything that we read after 7 days. Crazy fact, right? Here's the solution: we've created a printable, 1-page pdf summary for this book that you're reading now. All you have to do to get your free pdf summary is to go to the following website:
https://livetolearn.lpages.co/enthrallinghistory/

Or, Scan the QR code!

Once you do, it will be intuitive. Enjoy, and thank you!

Table of Contents

PART 1: HISTORY OF JAPAN 1
    INTRODUCTION 3
    CHAPTER 1: EARLY JAPANESE KINGDOMS 5
    CHAPTER 2: THE IMPERIAL GOLDEN AGE 14
    CHAPTER 3: THE RISE OF THE SAMURAI 23
    CHAPTER 4: THE KAMAKURA CONFLICT 34
    CHAPTER 5: THE ASHIKAGA ERA 41
    CHAPTER 6: THE SENGOKU PERIOD 53
    CHAPTER 7: THE PEACEFUL EDO PERIOD 65
    CHAPTER 8: THE MEIJI TRANSFORMATION 75
    CHAPTER 9: THE SHŌWA ERA 83
    CHAPTER 10: MODERN JAPAN 95
    CONCLUSION 103
PART 2: JAPANESE FOLKTALES AND LEGENDS 107
    INTRODUCTION 109
    CHAPTER 1: TALES FROM ANCIENT TIMES 111
    CHAPTER 2: TALES OF THE KAMI 122
    CHAPTER 3: THE SAMURAI SPIRIT 135
    CHAPTER 4: FOLKTALES OF LOVE AND DESTINY 146
    CHAPTER 5: YOKAI AND SUPERNATURAL CREATURES 157
    CHAPTER 6: SEA WHISPERS AND RIVER SONGS 171
    CHAPTER 7: ADVENTURES AND LEGENDS IN THE WILD 182
    CHAPTER 8: GHOST TALES 194

CHAPTER 9: WISDOM OF THE ELDERS 203
CHAPTER 10: KEY SYMBOLS OF JAPANESE FOLKLORE 211
CONCLUSION 215
HERE'S ANOTHER BOOK BY ENTHRALLING HISTORY THAT YOU MIGHT LIKE 217
FREE LIMITED TIME BONUS 218
WORKS CITED 219
IMAGE SOURCES 224

Part 1: History of Japan

An Enthralling Journey Through Ancient Japanese Empires, the Shogunate Era, Cultural Renaissance, and Modern Period

Introduction

In 1944, anthropologist Ruth Benedict was given the task of explaining Japanese culture and society to an American audience. The two countries were locked in the Pacific theater of World War II. Because of this, Benedict could not travel to Japan. She was not an expert on Japan, but she was open-minded and determined to provide a well-balanced view. The result was a book, *The Chrysanthemum and the Sword*, which many still hail as a work of brilliance in comparative cultural studies. As Benedict explained, it was incredibly difficult for the Western mind to grasp the Japanese worldview. One way is to study the complicated history of this archipelago.

A short anecdote from Benedict's book can serve as a starting point of sorts. During the war, there were Japanese broadcasts about a Japanese air force captain who returned from battle, counted the number of planes that had returned, and then filed his report with his commanding officer. As soon as he had turned in his report, he dropped dead at the headquarters. It was discovered that he had been killed by a bullet wound he had suffered during battle. His body was already ice-cold. It was not the hero-pilot who had filed his report but rather his spirit, which had lingered to finish his duties.

"To Americans, of course, this is an outrageous yarn, "Benedict explained. "But educated Japanese did not laugh at this broadcast."[i] For

---

[i] Benedict, Ruth. *The Chrysanthemum and the Sword: Patterns of Japanese Culture*. Houghton Mifflin, 2005.

the average Japanese, this exemplified the nature of the war, which the Americans failed to grasp. For them, it was about American materialism and capitalism against Japanese spiritualism.

Japan's entry into World War II was driven primarily by imperial ambitions, economic pressures, and strategic considerations, particularly the need to secure access to vital natural resources in Southeast Asia. Japanese propaganda framed the conflict as a civilizational struggle between Western materialism and Eastern spiritualism, which served to justify military expansion.

Some contemporary Westerners may only know Japan by anime, Hello Kitty, and Nintendo, but they miss the context of Japan's current form by ignoring the story of a nation that has conquered and been conquered, a place of endless beauty and brutal warfare. Japan has long defied the Western view that Europe and its colonies dominated world history. This book will help you begin to understand the complexities of Japanese history, from the first humans who called Japan home to the current concerns of the modern Japanese citizen.

Chapter 1: Early Japanese Kingdoms

Many, especially the Japanese people themselves, have wondered when their society began. When did some of the key components of Japanese culture get their start? Rice paddy farming, Shinto beliefs, and a society based on a clear hierarchical structure all seem to have begun around 300 or 400 BCE after the Yayoi people moved into the area. Previously, there had been the Jōmon culture of hunter-gatherers, which had been living on the Japanese islands since 14,000 BCE.

The accepted wisdom is that tens of thousands of years ago, when parts of Japan were still connected to the Asian mainland due to lower sea levels, early humans crossed into what would be the nation of Japan. These humans, like all other humans of the time, relied on hunting and foraging for subsistence. They lived in settlements, but there was something distinctive about these people: they made pottery.

The term "Jōmon" actually means corded pottery, which is the identifier for these unnamed and somewhat mysterious people. The story goes that the Jōmon were conquered and replaced by the Yayoi people, who also came from the mainland (China, Korea, or both). They brought rice farming and bronze tools with them. But this story has been questioned recently.

Accelerator mass spectrometry (AMS) dating completed in the past ten years has shown that the Yayoi people came to Japan in 900 BCE, five hundred years earlier than archaeologists previously thought. This means that the Yayoi and Jōmon people lived in Japan simultaneously. The implication is that the Yayoi violently conquered their new neighbors at an unbelievable speed, but this is a problematic explanation.

Some Yayoi pottery shows a mix of Jōmon styles and techniques alongside new forms brought in by migrants, which suggests that the two groups interacted and blended. DNA taken from remains at Jōmon and Yayoi sites both showed similarities with modern Japanese. This means that the Jōmon certainly didn't die out since their genetics carried on into modern-day populations.

This upending of ideas that were well established created an uproar in Japan, where the past remains a large part of the present. Japan is one of the most well-excavated countries in the world, with thousands of active sites being worked on every year. The Japanese held that the beginning of the Yayoi was the beginning of Japan, so questioning the date and how it happened was hard for the public to accept.

The Jōmon were not part of that tradition. They had lived in Japan, and they had particularly sophisticated pottery for the period. Many Jōmon burials have been found with artifacts such as combs, lacquerware, and small figurines. They had large settlements, but some archaeologists think the Jōmon might have faced real food shortages in certain regions, especially away from the coast, where seasonal changes made it harder to get enough to eat. Others argue they had a pretty stable diet overall, but it probably depended a lot on where they lived and what they had access to. For the most part, they lacked agriculture and metal tools, which allowed the Yayoi population to expand across the archipelago. This population growth, conservative Japanese historians say, is what led to the creation of the Japanese state.

However, modern research indicates that the Yayoi did not conquer the Jōmon and displace them. Instead, small groups of newcomers from the mainland arrived in Japan with new technology, and the Jōmon grew to accept these changes. Over hundreds of years, the two groups were blended into one until a new culture, called the Yayoi, could be identified as being distinct from the previous Jōmon.

With this out of the way, we can say that Japanese history begins with the Jōmon period, which started in 14,000 BCE, at the earliest. It seems that the Jōmon began making pottery in about 13,000 to 11,000 BCE, though this is still uncertain, as the pottery itself cannot be dated—only organic remains near the pottery can be.

It is believed that the creation of pottery reflects a more sedentary lifestyle. This lifestyle change might have come from the end of the Pleistocene Epoch around 11,700 years ago. Large game went extinct on the islands, so the people had to rely more on foraging, especially nuts from deciduous trees. This led to a need to process and store food, which, in turn, led to the creation of pottery.

The Jōmon lived in pit houses and used stone tools to dig out their houses and to work the wood that they used to cover their homes. They began to live more sedentary lifestyles, but this does not mean they collectively abandoned nomadic practices. They had large living sites that consisted of ten houses or more, but they also might have only used them for part of the year. These people cultivated some plants, but these appear not to have made up a large portion of their diet. They grew a wide range of crops, such as buckwheat, bottle gourd, and hemp.

Jōmon pottery is of interest to prehistorians worldwide. The pottery is identifiable, but it changed over time and in different geographical regions. The debate continues as to whether the Jōmon people discovered or were introduced to pottery. The dates given to many finds in Japan appear earlier than those found in China, which leads some to question the accepted theory that the Jōmon learned pottery-making from Chinese migrants. The stylistic commonalities in the pottery in certain areas have led researchers to believe that the Jōmon lived in tribes or similar societal structures.

The Jōmon period is exceptionally long, so it is broken up into various phases, though these phases cannot be clearly defined and are sometimes specific to a certain region. At times, the Jōmon lived in substantial dwellings in large settlements, though over time, some of those populations seem to have declined and were replaced by smaller huts. The Jōmon built large wooden structures, possibly even multi-story ones, and engaged in limited cultivation. They built stone circles and wooden post structures. Some alignments in those monuments suggest they had a sense of seasonal change or solar movement—hints of what you might call a rudimentary calendar.

One of the most intriguing types of Jōmon artifacts that have been found is the lacquerware items. Today, lacquer is harvested from domesticated trees. Each tree produces only a small amount of raw lacquer per year—often much less than 0.1 liters. Lacquer trees in the wild produce even less, which suggests that the Jōmon cultivated lacquer trees for their needs. Given that the trees must mature for eight to ten years before they can be harvested, this hints at well-planned cultivation.

The Jōmon mixed the lacquer with the oil from the egoma (or shiso) plant. They used two types of material to color the lacquer red: hematite and cinnabar. Black coloring was likely obtained using iron compounds. Wooden vessels and textiles were lacquered, and their appearance is only found in relatively wet sites that preserved this material.

Jōmon hunters developed bows and created pit traps to catch wild boar. They domesticated dogs and were skilled fishermen. Despite all of their advances, Jōmon skeletal remains suggest that many people suffered high mortality and possibly nutritional stress. In the Late Jōmon period, small quantities of grain have been found in pottery, but it was not until the arrival of farming populations from the Korean Peninsula in the early 1st millennium BCE that the people of Japan began to engineer their environment for agriculture.

This marks the beginning of the Yayoi period, which lasted from about 300 BCE to 300 CE. Yayoi agriculture in the early phase included cereals, such as buckwheat and barley, particularly in southern Kyūshū, though wet-rice cultivation soon became more important. The more predictable yields of these crops helped farming spread rapidly. This, in turn, led to higher birth rates and longer life expectancy, fueling a population increase across the Japanese islands. Over time, rice paddies with irrigation systems replaced or supplemented earlier dry-field cultivation, thus offering a more dependable food base.

By year 0, the Yayoi population is sometimes speculated to have reached several hundred thousand, though estimates vary. Chinese sources used the name "Wa" (or "Wo") to refer broadly to the peoples of Japan, and they engaged in trade—likely via Korean outposts—with mainland China and Korea. Some Japanese goods, including rice, might have been exchanged, and Chinese and Korean products likewise entered the archipelago. During the middle and late Yayoi period, rice increasingly became the dominant crop in many regions.

At the Yayoi site of Itazuke in Fukuoka Prefecture, evidence such as rice field remains, storage pits, dog bones, and deer or boar bones suggests a typical village economy. Children's jar burials have been found, sometimes in large ceramic jars apparently used just for that purpose. Near those burial sites, Chinese and Korean artifacts are often discovered in notable abundance.

Yayoi-era paddy systems included engineered features like sluice gates, irrigation canals, wells, and storage infrastructure. Competition over arable land appears in the archaeological record, and some sites show bronze and iron weaponry production and signs of armed conflict. The Chinese maintained interest in Yayoi (Wa) polities across the sea.

The Chinese paid particular attention to the first historically attested ruler in Japanese history, the shaman-queen Himiko, who lived from about 170 CE to 247 or 248 CE. At that time, the Japanese had not begun recording their history, so it is only through Chinese and Korean writers or archaeological evidence that we know anything about Himiko and her kingdom, Yamatai. This kingdom was composed of many smaller polities. The exact location of Yamatai is still debated, but it is believed to have been either in northern Kyūshū or central Honshu.

The Chinese noted that Himiko's rule was unusual in that she was a woman, but there is no indication that this was strange to the Yayoi people of the time. Still, Chinese leaders recognized her, giving her special status. The Chinese texts explain that after seventy or eighty years of disturbances and warfare among the various chieftains in the land of Wa, the Yayoi selected Himiko as their ruler, possibly because she was a woman since the period of conflict had been under the rule of a man. However, some female burials from the Yayoi period suggest that women held high status and might have acted as leaders.

What makes Himiko remarkable is her apparent control over a large part of Japan. It was said she held authority over as many as thirty separate polities. Also, she is important because she was the first Japanese leader in the historical record due to her interactions with the Chinese. Himiko was recognized as a "ruler friendly to Wei" by the state of Cao Wei during the Three Kingdoms period in Chinese history. Emissaries from Yamatai traveled to Emperor Cao Rui of Wei in 238 CE, apparently bearing gifts of slaves and cloth. While the Chinese authors put special emphasis on Himiko's magical abilities, Japan's early history includes rulers, male and female, who were believed to have spiritual powers and to communicate with the gods. For instance, Emperor Jimmu is traditionally seen as a descendant of the sun goddess Amaterasu and is said to have established the Japanese imperial line in 660 BCE. Though considered a legendary figure, his story reflects the early belief that political authority was rooted in divine ancestry.

In the Wei records, called the *Wei zhi*, the Chinese chroniclers give a description of Queen Himiko's burial, which gives us a look into the religious beliefs of the early Japanese. Priests conducted divination by burning bones and studying the cracks made by the fire for clues about the future. It was a practice the Chinese had seen before. Priests in the Shang dynasty (1600-1046 BCE) had similar methods of seeing into the future. This has led some to suggest that this, like bronze and agricultural techniques, might have reached Japan through cultural transmission from East Asia.

The Yayoi buried their dead in wooden coffins as well as large jars. They observed a period of mourning for more than ten days and then purified themselves through immersion in water, something that was later adopted into Shinto practices. The Yayoi beliefs are just the beginnings of what would become the indigenous religion of Japan.

Himiko was buried under a large mound, and one hundred attendants were buried with her to assist her in the afterlife. She was replaced by a relative named Iyo, who is said in later sources to have been thirteen years old.

At the time of her death, which is believed to have been in the 3rd century CE, Japan was entering into a new historical period that was noted for increased militarization and a shift toward more male-dominated leadership. It is called the Yamato period.

This period is often split into two. First came the Kofun period (250-538 CE), and the Asuka period followed (538-710 CE). The name "Kofun" comes from the Japanese word *kofun*, which is the type of burial mound distinctive to the period. Himiko's burial might have been among the earliest of these. They were often either square or circular mounds over burial chambers. Later examples have the famous keyhole shape with a round side and a more square side, sometimes surrounded by a moat.

The beginning of the Kofun period is marked by a great struggle between chiefdoms over local dominance. This led to a large increase in fortified structures and production, as well as the improvement of weapon technology. The Japanese became so skilled at war that they might have provided soldiers to aid both the Baekje (or Paekche) and Silla Kingdoms of Korea in the late 4th and early 5th centuries.

In the latter half of the 3rd century, there is some evidence to suggest the development of a particular confederation of states and clans around a central leader. This leader or king was associated with the Yamato lineage, and their rise to power is rooted in mystery. By the time the Yamato kingship came to control much of Japan, they had developed a family history that included legendary characters who lived incredibly long lives and enjoyed relationships with the gods.

The Yamato confederation was centered around the area that is today the Nara Prefecture. At that time, the Yamato kings had to bring the various clans, which were powerful families, under their control. The clans were led by a patriarch who performed the necessary rituals to the clan's kami or spirit to ensure success. The members of these clans would become the nobility of the Yamato court, with the head of the Yamato line being the leader of them all.

The kings were called the "Great Kings of Yamato," and they were the precursors to the *tennō*, or emperors. The *Nihon Shoki* or *Chronicles of Japan*, which was written in the 700s, tried to trace the Yamato lineage back to 660 BCE. However, it leaves out rulers such as Himiko. One of the earliest **Yamato** kings with possible historical support was Yūryaku, who ruled in the 5th century CE and is believed to have been referred to as "Wakatakeru" in contemporary inscriptions. He is believed to have sent a letter to the Chinese emperor saying that he had conquered fifty-five countries of hairy men to the east and sixty-five barbarian countries to the west. Also, he and his armies crossed the sea to Korea and conquered ninety-five more countries.

It is impossible to say if this letter was in any way accurate, but the inscription of a sword from the period **states**, "When the court of the Great King Wakatakeru was in Shiki, I aided him in ruling the realm, and had this hundred-time-wrought sword made to record the history of my service."[i]

The first widely accepted Great King was Emperor Kinmei. His reign lasted from 539 to 571 CE. He gained the throne after his brother, Emperor Senka, died at seventy-three. His reign coincided with when it is believed Buddhism was first introduced to the islands and also the beginning of the Asuka period, when the center of Yamato power moved to the Asuka region, sixteen miles south of the modern-day city of Nara.

The Yamato clan's power grew greatly in this period. They ruled largely uncontested from the capital in Asuka. In 552, it is recorded that the king of Baekje sent a bronze statue of the Buddha to Emperor Kinmei, along with artisans and monks. The introduction of Buddhism into the Yamato court led to a deep rift between the Mononobe clan, who

---

[i] Walker, Brett L. *A Concise History of Japan.* Cambridge University Press, 2015.

wanted to continue to worship Japan's traditional deities (a practice now known as Shinto), and the Soga clan, who supported the adoption of Buddhism as the national religion.

Shinto had no founder or overarching doctrine. It centers around the kami, which can be gods, principles, supreme beings, or even the mind. One of the most well-known kami is Amaterasu, the goddess of the sun and the universe. According to legend, Amaterasu gave her grandson five rice grains from heaven and sent him to lead the people of Japan, becoming the first legendary emperor of the Yamato line.

The first written records of Shinto beliefs come from the *Kojiki* or *Records of Ancient Matters* from 712 CE and the previously mentioned *Nihon Shoki*. The *Kojiki* gives hundreds of classifications of kami with different functions. Today, the Shinto religion recognizes over four million kami.

At the time, Shinto was not a formal religion but rather a collection of clan-based rituals centered on the worship of kami. Each clan maintained its own rituals to honor the kami. In contrast, Buddhism arrived as a fully developed belief system with texts, ethics, and a sophisticated material culture. For the Soga clan, supporting Buddhism offered not only spiritual appeal but also a means to align with the political and cultural prestige of continental powers like China and Korea. The Mononobe clan viewed Buddhism as a foreign intrusion that threatened Japan's traditional spiritual foundations.

Summary Timeline – Early Japanese Kingdoms
- 14,000 BCE – Earliest Jōmon settlements established; people create cord-marked pottery, pit houses, and stone tools.
- 13,000–11,000 BCE – Development of pottery linked to a more settled, foraging lifestyle after the end of the Pleistocene.
- 900 BCE – Yayoi migrants arrive from the mainland, introducing rice cultivation, bronze tools, and ironworking.
- 300 BCE – 300 CE – Yayoi period flourishes; rice-paddy agriculture spreads, and population increases.
- 170 – 248 CE – Reign of Queen Himiko, first recorded ruler of Japan, who governs the kingdom of Yamatai and communicates with the Chinese Wei dynasty.
- 250 – 538 CE – Kofun period begins; large keyhole tombs built for rulers and nobles.

- 539 - 571 CE - Reign of Emperor Kinmei; introduction of Buddhism from the Korean Kingdom of Baekje starts the Asuka period and divides Japan's leading clans.

Chapter 2: The Imperial Golden Age

When the bronze Buddha statue came to Emperor Kinmei from Korea in 552, a plague struck Japan. Out of fear that this happened because of offense given to the kami, and on the advice of the Nakatomi and Mononobe clans, the statue was thrown into a canal. But then, the great hall of the imperial palace suddenly caught fire. Caught between two possibly vengeful gods, Emperor Kinmei did not take definitive action to resolve the dilemma.

Soga no Iname, the leader of the Soga clan, married his daughter, Soga no Kitashihime, to Emperor Kinmei. Together, they had eight children, including the future Emperor Yōmei and Princess Nukatabe, who became the chief wife of Emperor Bidatsu, the ruler after Kinmei. After Bidatsu and Yōmei died, there was a power struggle between the Mononobe and Soga clans. The Soga prevailed and installed Emperor Sushun, but the new ruler disliked being controlled by the head of the Soga clan, Soga no Umako, so Umako had the king assassinated in 592.

Princess Nukatabe, Umako's niece, was selected to sit on the Chrysanthemum Throne (the imperial throne), though these early rulers would not have been called emperors during their reign. However, they were posthumously given imperial titles, so these "Great Kings" are often called emperors in modern histories.

Princess Nukatabe was given the title and name of Empress Suiko. While the son of Emperor Yōmei, Prince Shōtoku, became regent and

Soga no Umako wielded considerable power, there is clear evidence that Suiko had a certain level of independence. During her reign, the Japanese government was modernized, and the Seventeen-Article Constitution was created in 604. This constitution was mainly notable for the heavy influence of Buddhist and Confucian ideology it promoted. Suiko was the first openly Buddhist monarch of Japan, and she promoted Buddhism throughout the land.

Suiko died in 628 after being on the throne for thirty-five years. She was succeeded by Emperor Jomei (593-641), grandson of Emperor Bidatsu. The head, or *ōmi*, of the Soga clan, Soga no Emishi, helped to install Jomei on the throne and held sway over the court. After Jomei's death, he was succeeded by his wife, Empress Kōgyoku. She ruled for less than four years and then abdicated to her brother, Emperor Kōtoku, who ruled until 654. Kōgyoku returned to the throne, though she was then known as Empress Saimei. She ruled until her death in 661.

She was followed by her son with Jomei, Emperor Tenji, who had been instrumental in overturning the Soga clan's control of the imperial court. The downfall of the powerful Soga clan came in 645 during an event known as the Isshi Incident. The Soga had long held dominance over court affairs, controlling key appointments and shaping imperial succession. However, their growing power alarmed Prince Naka no Ōe, the future Emperor Tenji, and his close ally, Nakatomi no Kamatari. Together, they orchestrated a dramatic coup during a court ceremony. With swords hidden beneath their robes, they launched a surprise attack on Soga no Iruka, the head of the clan, killing him in front of assembled courtiers. Shortly after, Iruka's father, Soga no Emishi, committed suicide, effectively ending the political power of the Soga. This violent turning point cleared the way for the Taika Reforms, a series of centralizing policies aimed at weakening clan autonomy and strengthening imperial rule. As a reward for his role in the coup, Kamatari was later granted the surname Fujiwara by Emperor Tenji in 669, founding one of the most influential families in Japanese history.

Tenji compiled the first legal code, the Ōmi Code, in Japanese history. This was a *ritsuryō*, which was a code based on Confucian ethics (focused on hierarchy and proper conduct) and Chinese Legalism (which emphasized strict laws and punishments). It served as both a criminal and administrative code.

Tenji died in 672 and was succeeded by his son, Emperor Kōbun, who only ruled for a few months. He was the son of an emperor, but his mother was of lower origins. In an event known as the Jinshin War, his army was defeated by his uncle's army. The war began as a struggle over succession after Emperor Tenji's death. He had favored Kōbun, though he had earlier considered naming his brother as heir. Kōbun's uncle, Prince Ōama, quietly gathered support and then led a successful military campaign against Kōbun. After his defeat, Kōbun committed suicide. His uncle became Emperor Tenmu. Tenmu was the first monarch to receive the title of *tennō*, or emperor, in his lifetime.

Then came the reigns of Empress Jitō and her grandson, Emperor Monmu. Empress Genmei came to the throne in 707. During her reign, the capital was moved to Nara, thus beginning the Nara period. The ancestry of the Yamato imperial line was officially codified in the *Kojiki* and *Nihon Shoki*, specifically that the imperial family descended from the sun goddess Amaterasu. The kingdoms under Yamato control during the Nara period were primarily in central Japan.

One critical part of the Nara period was the conquest of the Emishi people in the northeastern part of the archipelago. The Emishi were a hunter-gatherer group far removed from the Chinese influence that permeated the Nara court. They were in many ways a holdover from the Jōmon era. "Emishi" is a term used by Nara officials to describe these northern peoples. It possibly meant something like "hairy people" or "eastern barbarians."

Despite the Yamato depiction of total control over Japan, the northern regions differed greatly from the culture at the capital. The Satsumon and Okhotsk people on the island of Hokkaido and the peoples of Sakhalin and the Amur River Estuary had long remained outside the reach of Chinese, Buddhist, and Confucian influences. They were not part of the ritsuryō (penal and administrative) codes that defined life in the core provinces.

During the Nara period (710-784), the Yamato court launched repeated military campaigns against the Emishi as part of an ongoing effort to expand imperial control over the northeastern frontier. Fort Taga (near Sendai) was constructed in 724, and its commander held the title of chinjufu shogun, or commander of the defense of the north. The Emishi fighters continually destroyed Yamato forts and resisted the conquest. It was not until the Heian period (794-1185) that a general named Sakanoue no Tamuramaro (758-811) was appointed as chinjufu shogun, and the Emishi were finally and violently subjugated.

This conflict marked the culmination of the Yamato family's ascendancy to power. While they still faced rivals, it was only in political struggles within the ritsuryō framework. An elaborate court had evolved in the capital of Nara at the beginning of the Emishi wars. Buddhism became the official religion of the court, though Shinto was still practiced by the majority of the people. Imperial rituals also continued to be conducted according to Shinto traditions. In fact, after the death of a monarch, it was normal to move the capital as an act of purification. This practice ended when the capital remained at Nara through many emperors.

Genmei abdicated the Chrysanthemum Throne in preference to her daughter, Empress Genshō, who acted as regent to her nephew, Prince Obito. During Genshō's reign, the powerful courtier Fujiwara no Fuhito of the Fujiwara clan died. He had been instrumental in establishing the ritsuryō system by helping to create the Taihō Code and later the revised Yōrō Code, which organized Japan's government into a centralized bureaucracy, outlined civil and criminal laws, and defined the roles of officials, land distribution, and taxation. After he died in 720, he was given the posthumous title of Daijō-daijin, or "Chancellor of the Realm," the highest office in the imperial court.

The Fujiwara clan, which descended from the Nakatomi clan, had risen to power after helping to topple the great Soga clan. The honorary title of Fujiwara was given to Nakatomi no Kamatari by Emperor Tenji in 669, and the clan name was passed to his son, Fujiwara no Fuhito.

After Fuhito's death, Prince Nagaya (cousin to Empress Genshō) seized political control of the court. This set up a struggle between Nagaya and Fuhito's four sons: Muchimaro, Fusasaki, Maro, and Umakai. The four sons were able to bring Nagaya up on false charges, and he was sentenced to death. Prince Nagaya was forced to commit suicide, and his wife and children were killed at the same time. It is believed that Nagaya placed a curse on his enemies because the four sons of Fuhito died one after another during a smallpox outbreak in 737.

In 724, Prince Obito ascended to the throne as Emperor Shōmu, son of Emperor Monmu and grandson of Fujiwara no Fuhito. It was during Shōmu's reign that the deadly smallpox outbreak of 735-737 broke out. It killed an estimated 35 percent of Japan's population.

Shōmu was a devout Buddhist and attempted to establish official temples and nunneries in each province. He commissioned the building of a sixteen-meter-tall Buddha statue in Nara. He moved the capital temporarily to three different places over five years, but he eventually returned it to Nara. He abdicated the throne in 749 and became a Buddhist monk. His daughter, Empress Kōken, succeeded him.

The court was largely under the control of Fujiwara no Nakamaro during her reign, and she was replaced on the throne by her relative, Emperor Junnin, in 758. Nakamaro became Junnin's prime minister (*taishi*), but he was at odds with the retired Empress Kōken and her healer and advisor, the Buddhist priest Dōkyō. It was reported that Kōken and Dōkyō were also lovers. Emperor Junnin tried to remonstrate with Kōken on this account, but it only made her angry, and she ended up giving Dōkyō even more power within her court.

Nakamaro was supported by Emperor Shōmu and his consort Empress Kōmyō, but by 760, both of them had died. He also faced epidemics and economic issues connected to the cost of building a new palace and organizing a planned invasion of Korea. Kōken took the opportunity to become more involved in politics and challenged Nakamaro's supremacy. Suspecting that Kōken was planning to usurp his power in the court, Nakamaro began placing his sons in key offices. Kōken responded by promoting her own people. In 764, things took a turn when Nakamaro took the imperial seals and station bells from Emperor Junnin and left the capital for Ōmi Province.

Nakamaro's forces met those of the empress, and the Fujiwara were defeated. Nakamaro was executed. Empress Kōken came back to the throne as Empress Shōtoku. She continued to promote the priest, Dōkyō, higher in the court. It was believed the empress was going to make him emperor, but she died in 770. Dōkyō, without her support and facing the still powerful Fujiwara clan, was stripped of his titles and sent into exile.

The new monarch was Emperor Kōnin, Kōken's half-brother. It was said that the empress had left a letter naming him as her heir when she died. He reigned for eleven somewhat uneventful years and abdicated in favor of his son, Emperor Kanmu.

During Kanmu's reign, the scope of the emperor's powers reached its highest point. His reign lasted from 781 to 806, and he proved to be an active monarch. In 784, he moved the capital from Nara to Nagaoka-kyō.

The capital would move again in 794 to Heian-kyō (Kyoto), which lends its name to the Heian period that began in the same year.

Kanmu also appointed two of the earliest generals to hold the title Sei-i Taishogun, or "Barbarian-subduing General": Ōtomo no Otomaro and Sakanoue no Tamuramaro. While the title would later become synonymous with the shogunate, at this time, it referred to a military commander tasked with subduing the Emishi in northern Honshu. Tamuramaro is remembered best for subduing the Emishi and is a celebrated military figure in Japanese legend. He went on to become war minister after Kanmu died in 806.

Heian-kyō became the center of a rich court where several different Buddhist sects flourished, despite lingering suspicion after Dōkyō's fall. Courtiers exchanged poems celebrating the fragility of life, best exemplified in the waka poems. Men in the court still wrote poems in Chinese, but courtly women wrote in newly developed Japanese scripts, giving their poems a heightened significance to later audiences. The nobles of Heian enjoyed music, appreciated the scent of incense, and dressed according to the seasons. The emperor was at the center of it all, and aristocrats often commented on his shining presence, like a god amongst mortals.

Far-reaching trade networks spread out from the capital following canals, rivers, and roads. These networks reached the far corners of the empire, and trade was monitored by government officials in the great marketplaces of Heian and the western capital, Dazaifu. Coinage was typically done in copper, and the royal privilege to mint coins was a rare and lucrative gift. Traders also bartered items since coin circulation was limited. A wise buyer knew that while the markets in the capital had a wider selection, the prices were better in smaller markets in the countryside.

The average peasant worked the land and was a foreign figure to those inside the imperial court. Noble men and women often complained of having to go to temples alongside ordinary citizens who did not dress or behave in what they considered an appropriate fashion. Worst of all to a noble's senses was the presence of beggars who regularly visited Buddhist temples and Shinto shrines.

Any important activity was postponed until the proper divinations could be performed. Signs were studied to determine if a particular military campaign, wedding, or festival would be a success. The Chinese zodiac was consulted, along with interpretations of Chinese cosmology. The calendar was based on the lunar cycle, and everything required a balance between the forces of yin and yang. The substances of the universe were wood, fire, earth, metal, and water. In an increasingly patriarchal society, male children were highly valued, while a woman's inability to give birth to a male heir might be grounds for divorce.

Kanmu was succeeded first by his son, Emperor Heizei, and then by his second son, Emperor Saga. Heizei abdicated after less than three years due to illness, but when Saga fell ill, Heizei mounted an unsuccessful rebellion against his brother that was put down by Sakanoue no Tamuramaro.

The Fujiwara continued their dominance in the imperial court. Saga was not only the son of a Fujiwara princess, but his top officials were almost all from the Fujiwara clan. After Saga abdicated, the throne passed to another of Kanmu's sons, Emperor Junna. This period saw the rise of Fujiwara no Yoshifusa.

Junna abdicated in 833, and the crown passed to Emperor Ninmyō, son of Emperor Saga. Initially, Ninmyō selected Prince Tsunesada, a son of Junna, to be the heir, but Yoshifusa was opposed to the idea, favoring his nephew and the son of Ninmyō, Prince Michiyasu. The emperor was eventually convinced, and a struggle ensued, with Yoshifusa coming out victorious and Michiyasu becoming Emperor Montoku.

Yoshifusa remained in control and then became the regent (*sesshō*) under Emperor Seiwa, Montoku's son. As regent, Yoshifusa governed the country completely. He died in 872, but his example of boy-emperors with Fujiwara regents was followed for several years.

Yoshifusa's adopted son, Fujiwara no Mototsune, became regent of the next four emperors. He invented the position of kampaku regent, which was essentially a regent for an adult emperor. The Fujiwara became the de facto rulers of Japan in the 10th and 11th centuries, effectively ruling through puppet emperors. They reached their peak under a descendant of Mototsune, Fujiwara no Michinaga (966-1028), who was the father of six empresses or royal consorts and the grandfather of three emperors. He is widely believed to have inspired the Genji character in the famous Japanese novel, *The Tale of Genji*, which was written when Michinaga was in power. *The Tale of Genji* is a classic work of literature recognized throughout the world as one of the first novels and the first written by a woman.

With the **ascendancy** of Emperor Go-Sanjō (1068–1073), the Fujiwara clan's power began to decline. Many members of the Minamoto clan took their place, but the power of the military also increased at this time. A new class, the *bushi* (samurai) or warriors, grew in power.

Summary Timeline — The Imperial Golden Age

- 552 CE – King of Baekje sends a bronze Buddha statue to Emperor Kinmei, introducing Buddhism to Japan.
- 592 CE – Assassination of Emperor Sushun; Princess Nukatabe becomes Empress Suiko.
- 604 CE – Seventeen-Article Constitution created under Empress Suiko and Prince Shōtoku, blending Buddhist and Confucian ideals.
- 628 CE – Death of Empress Suiko after thirty-five years on the throne.
- 645 CE – Isshi Incident: Prince Naka no Ōe and Nakatomi no Kamatari overthrow the Soga clan; Taika Reforms begin.
- 669 CE – Emperor Tenji grants Kamatari the surname Fujiwara, founding the Fujiwara clan.
- 672 CE – Jinshin War between Emperor Kōbun and Prince Ōama; victory of Ōama, who becomes Emperor Tenmu.
- 707 CE – Empress Genmei ascends the throne; capital moved to Nara, beginning the Nara period.
- 720 CE – Death of Fujiwara no Fuhito; posthumously named Chancellor of the Realm.
- 724 CE – Emperor Shōmu begins his reign; smallpox epidemic strikes Japan in 735–737.
- 749 CE – Shōmu abdicates and becomes a monk; succeeded by Empress Kōken.
- 764 CE – Fujiwara no Nakamaro's rebellion; Empress Kōken returns to the throne as Empress Shōtoku.
- 770 CE – Death of Empress Shōtoku; Emperor Kōnin succeeds her.
- 781 CE – Emperor Kanmu begins reign; moves capital to Nagaoka-kyō (784) and then to Heian-kyō (Kyoto) in 794.

- 806 CE – Death of Emperor Kanmu; beginning of the Heian period.
- 872 CE – Death of Fujiwara no Yoshifusa, first regent (*sesshō*) to rule for a child emperor.
- 1028 CE – Death of Fujiwara no Michinaga, the peak of Fujiwara dominance.
- 1068–1073 CE – Reign of Emperor Go-Sanjō; Fujiwara power declines; rise of the warrior class.

Chapter 3: The Rise of the Samurai

The beginnings of the warrior class that would come to rule Japan can be traced back to the late 9th and early 10th centuries, especially during the campaigns against the Emishi in the north. These conflicts contributed to a slow decentralization of military authority. Men who made their living using weapons at this time were called *bushi*, a term often translated as "warrior." During the Heian period, many of the classic weapons and armor became established, such as the tachi or long sword, the naginata or glaive, and the distinctive ō-yoroi armor for cavalry and dō-maru for infantry.

Semi-independent nobles from Kyoto relied on these men-at-arms to provide protection and for peacekeeping duties in their provinces. A patron-client relationship developed between the bushi and local administrators, and it was in this way that warriors became part of the extended political network that radiated from the capital.

At the top of these military groups were often descendants of imperial or noble families, especially younger sons who had been removed from the line of succession. These descendants were given surnames to denote their clans or houses. Over time, these groups came to represent military powers that could be called on by emperors or retired emperors for support. These private armies were used throughout the Heian period to put down rebellions and challenge imperial authority.

Any high-ranking bushi who served the emperor, the imperial family, or the nobility could be referred to as a samurai, a word derived from *saburau*, meaning "to serve." An example of a Heian period **samurai** was

Taira no Masakado, who was descended from Emperor Kanmu's greatgrandson, Prince Takamochi. The prince had been demoted to commoner status and sent to the Kantō region, where he became a powerful landholder. Masakado is best remembered for leading a rebellion and declaring himself the "new emperor." His uprising failed, and he was killed, but his legend persisted. He eventually gained status as a vengeful spirit and even as a protective deity in some local cults.

Many members of the warrior class began to harbor political ambitions, which would lead to the eventual rise of the Heishi (members of the Taira clan) and Genji (members of the Minamoto clan). The Heishi were divided into several major lines named after the emperors from whom they were descended: Kanmu Heishi, Ninmyō Heishi, Montoku Heishi, and Kōkō Heishi. Taira no Kiyomori (1118–1181) was from the Kanmu Heishi line and took control of the Taira clan after his father's death in 1153. By that time, the two major rival samurai clans were the Taira and the Minamoto.

Minamoto no Yoshihira (with antlers on his helmet) in oroyoi armor during the Heiji rebellion.[1]

The rivalry between them erupted into open conflict during the Heiji rebellion of 1159–1160. Before the rebellion, power struggles at court had seen both clans acting in shifting alliances. Minamoto no Yoshitomo and Fujiwara no Nobuyori attempted to seize control of the government, briefly taking Emperor Nijō and the retired Emperor Go-Shirakawa into custody. However, Taira no Kiyomori swiftly countered their coup, defeating the Minamoto forces and executing their leaders. With this victory, Kiyomori rose to a dominant position in court politics, setting the stage for the Taira clan's brief supremacy in the late Heian period.

The leader of the Genji was Minamoto no Yoshitomo, and his chief ally was Fujiwara no Nobuyori, who was close to Emperor Go-Shirakawa. Some opposed the high rank of Nobuyori within the court, especially the influential Fujiwara no Michinori (also known as Shinzei). Shinzei was a chief advisor to Emperor Nijō and an ally of Taira no Kiyomori. Yoshitomo and Kiyomori had worked together to defeat the rebels in the Hōgen rebellion in 1156, which was a violent conflict among court factions over imperial succession and influence. These short but brutal court wars, known as disturbances (*ran* in Japanese), were driven by rivalries between noble houses and warrior clans seeking to control the throne through the use of military force. Yoshitomo and Kiyomori's paths had diverged after the Hōgen rebellion, and they now found themselves on opposite sides of the struggle between Nobuyori and Shinzei.

In 1159, Kiyomori left Kyoto for a time. Seeing this as an opportunity, Nobuyori and Yoshitomo attacked the Sanjō Palace, abducted the former Emperor Go-Shirakawa, and set the building on fire after killing many of the staff. They then attacked Shinzei, who escaped capture, only to be found and decapitated later.

Nijō was forced to name Nobuyori as imperial chancellor; however, his victory was short-lived. Kiyomori heard of the rebellion and returned to the capital in haste. Nobuyori and his Minamoto allies were not prepared to defend the city. Kiyomori made peace offerings to Nobuyori, but these were only to buy time. The former Emperor Go-Shirakawa and Emperor Nijō were able to escape and join Kiyomori's side. With imperial authority now backing him, the Taira leader was permitted to move against Nobuyori and his ally Yoshitomo in the imperial palace.

A fierce battle between the sons of Yoshitomo and Kiyomori, Yoshihira and Shigemori, respectively, took place. The Taira force initially retreated, and the Minamoto pursued, but this was part of the ploy by Kiyomori, who then sent a force to occupy the palace. The Minamoto, cut off and disorganized, were routed, and Taira no Kiyomori was victorious.

Yoshitomo attempted to flee but was betrayed and killed shortly after his defeat. Kiyomori showed compassion and spared the lives of some of Yoshitomo's younger sons, sending them into exile. These sons— Yoritomo, Noriyori, and Yoshitsune—would go on to play a role in the history of Japan.

The result of the Heiji rebellion was that the Taira under Kiyomori were now in control of the government, and imperial power had been weakened even further. The Minamoto and Taira were even more deeply divided, with extreme animosity between them. The rebellion spawned

The Tale of Heiji, which exists in oral, visual, and written forms and is closely connected to *The Tale of Hōgen* that precedes it.

In the years that followed, Emperor Nijō remained on the throne, but his authority was hollow. The real power belonged to Kiyomori and the retired Emperor Go-Shirakawa. In 1165, Nijō abdicated in favor of his infant son and died shortly after at the age of twenty-two. His death marked another shift in power. Kiyomori continued to strengthen his position, rising to the rank of Daijō-daijin in 1167, the highest office in the imperial court. He moved the seat of government briefly to Fukuhara and arranged marriages that tied the Taira clan directly to the imperial line. Former Emperor Go-Shirakawa and others began to grow tired of the Taira's rule in the following years.

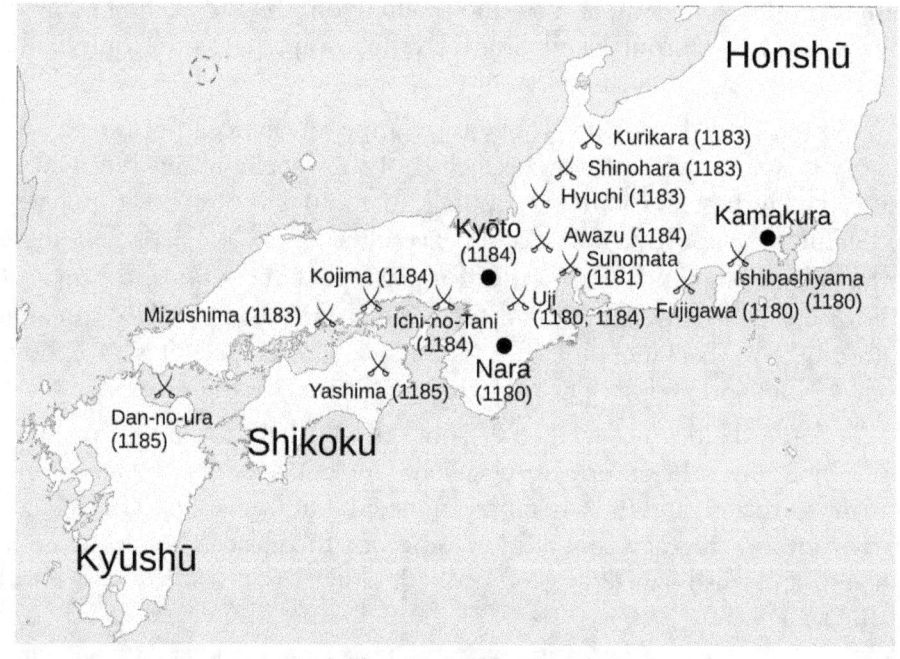

Battles of the Genpei War.³

In 1171, Taira no Kiyomori, the de facto ruler of Japan, arranged for the marriage of his daughter to Emperor Takakura. This couple had a son, Prince Tokihito, in 1178. Two years later, in 1180, Kiyomori staged a coup and forced his rivals to resign or be banished. He also imprisoned former Emperor Go-Shirakawa. Kiyomori then forced Takakura to abdicate, and Tokihito ascended the throne at just two years of age. This child emperor was later named Emperor Antoku.

Kiyomori's complete control caused many of his allies and provincial samurai to turn against him. Prince Mochihito, son of Emperor Go-Shirakawa, felt Kiyomori had gone too far and pushed his claim to the imperial throne. He called on the Minamoto to rise against the Taira and to overthrow Kiyomori. This is often cited as the beginning of what would be called the Genpei War, a civil war that once again pitted the Taira clan against the Minamoto clan in a struggle over control of Japan.

In mid-1180, Prince Mochihito sent out his call for aid. He was helped by Minamoto no Yorimasa, a poet and samurai who had once been friendly with Kiyomori but had turned against the Taira in favor of his clan. Yorimasa had become a monk upon retiring from the military, but he helped Mochihito gain support and agreed to lead the Minamoto forces.

In June of 1180, Mochihito and Yorimasa, with about 1,500 men, including Buddhist warrior monks, were chased by Taira forces across the Uji River near Byōdō-in, a Buddhist temple, and pulled up the planks of the bridge behind them. The Taira were led by an eighteen-year-old general named Tadatsuna, who became a legendary figure for his actions in the Battle of Uji. The Taira overcame the Minamoto army, and Yorimasa committed seppuku (ritual suicide) in the temple. Prince Mochihito was captured and killed shortly after the end of the battle. However, this did not end the Minamoto clan's desire for revenge against the Taira.

Minamoto no Yoritomo, the exiled son of the defeated and killed Yoshitomo, now made his move to defeat the hated Taira. He had grown up in exile and had married into the Hōjō clan. With the deaths of Mochihito and Yorimasa, Yoritomo established himself as the head of the Minamoto clan and set his capital at Kamakura in the Kantō region of Honshu. Kamakura was not only an ancient seat of the Minamoto but also a natural fortress, being surrounded on three sides by mountains and one side by the ocean.

In September 1180, Yoritomo met the Taira forces in the Battle of Ishibashiyama, where he was defeated but managed to escape. The Taira defeated other Minamoto forces later in the year but were unable to strike a definitive blow against the rebels. In the spring of 1181, Taira no Kiyomori died of a severe illness. It was said his fever was so high that those who touched him received burns on their hands.

The Taira forces now fell into the hands of Kiyomori's son, Munemori. A famine then raged through Japan, and the war was effectively put on hold for two years while the people coped with these harsh conditions. When hostilities resumed in the spring of 1183, it seemed that a great change had occurred to the fortunes of each side. The climax was perhaps the Battle of Kurikara Pass on June 2nd, 1183.

Taira no Koremori, the grandson of the late Kiyomori, organized an army to take revenge on Minamoto no Yoshinaka, who had previously invaded Taira land. Koremori divided his forces into two, with one going through the Kurikara Pass. Yoshinaka met his forces there and held an extremely formal battle with duels between samurai. This was simply a distraction to allow the other Minamoto forces to surround the Taira. They first let oxen with lit torches attached to their horns into the Taira lines and then ambushed them.

Yoshinaka wanted to defeat not only the Taira clan but also his cousin, Minamoto no Yoritomo, and gain control of the Minamoto clan. He kidnapped former Emperor Go-Shirakawa but was pursued by Yoritomo's brother, Yoshitsune, and was killed when he made a last stand at Awazu in Ōmi Province. The Minamoto, now united, turned their attention back to the Taira, who were gathering forces near the inland sea.

The Minamoto successfully defeated the Taira at Ichi-no-Tani in March of 1184. After a year of preparation, the main Taira army came under assault at the Battle of Yashima (Takamatsu). Yoshitsune tricked the Taira into thinking they were being attacked on land, so they fled in boats on the inland sea. Famously, a "pretty lady" with the Taira raised a fan and dared the Minamoto soldiers on the shore to shoot it from her hand. A soldier named Nasu no Yoichi rode into the water on horseback and did just that.

Many of the Taira were able to escape to Dan-no-ura, where a naval battle took place. This battle started in favor of the Taira, but with the changing of the tides, the Minamoto had the upper hand. This was the final defeat of the Taira clan and the end of the war.

Emperor Antoku and his grandmother, Taira no Tokiko (the widow of Kiyomori), are both said to have committed suicide by throwing themselves into the water. Many Taira commanders committed ritual suicide upon seeing that they were losing. Some of the imperial regalia were thrown into the sea but were said to have been found by divers.

The Taira dominance in the capital was over. The Minamoto took control, with Yoritomo as the clear leader. A new emperor had already been selected, the grandson of Go-Shirakawa, Emperor Go-Toba. The only person left to challenge Yoritomo's power was Emperor Go-Shirakawa and his half-brother and head general, Yoshitsune, who was made governor of Ōmi Province. Go-Shirakawa tried to give additional lands and titles to Yoshitsune, but Yoritomo nullified these appointments.

Yoshitsune was then given imperial authority to oppose Yoritomo, but Yoritomo discovered the plot. Yoshitsune was forced to flee Kyoto in 1185. He was able to find protection with the Fujiwara clan in Mutsu, but he was eventually betrayed. Yoshitsune committed seppuku when Yoritomo's forces found him. Go-Shirakawa and Yoritomo were reconciled after Yoshitsune's death.

In December of 1185, Go-Shirakawa granted Yoritomo the power to collect taxes and name constables of provinces. In 1192, Go-Shirakawa died at the age of sixty-six, and Yoritomo was granted the title Sei-i Taishogun or "commander in chief of expeditionary forces against the barbarians," typically called simply shogun. This is often considered the beginning of the shogunate period. While Go-Toba remained the emperor, his role was largely ceremonial. While Kyoto remained the official capital, the home of Yoritomo in Kamakura was where the real power resided.

As shogun, Yoritomo was ostensibly the leader of all samurai. This would mark the beginning of what is considered the feudal period in Japan. Yoritomo's shogunate did not last long, for he died in 1199. The role of shogun was considered hereditary, so Yoritomo's son, Minamoto no Yoriie, became shogun when he was only seventeen years old. He was controlled largely by his mother's father, Hōjō Tokimasa of the Hōjō clan. After a short reign, he was forced to abdicate and was succeeded by his brother, Minamoto no Sanetomo.

Sanetomo was nothing more than a puppet used by his mother, Hōjō Masako, in her power struggles with her father, Tokimasa. Sanetomo lived in constant fear of assassination and chose to pursue a career in the relatively powerless imperial court. He also focused on his poetry, becoming a well-regarded waka poet. However, he was eventually assassinated by his nephew in 1219. The assassin was executed, which ended their line of the Minamoto clan.

The shogun then became, like the emperors in previous generations, a puppet controlled by a *shikken* (regent) from the Hōjō clan. This clan, which had previously held little power and is believed to have descended from the Taira clan in Izu Province, now effectively ruled the country from Kamakura. They faced no real opposition until 1221, when former Emperor Go-Toba led a revolt against the shogunate. However, the Hōjō and their samurai soundly defeated him.

The third regent, Hōjō Yasutoki, created the Council of State, or Hyōjōshū, in 1225 and then created the Goseibai Shikimoku in 1232, which established the first true code of laws of the Kamakura shogunate. It steered the country away from the Chinese-style Confucian codes of the past and into a more militaristic legal framework. This code remained in effect in some form for the next 635 years.

At the same time, a growing menace was in the process of conquering portions of Korea. Between 1231 and 1270, the Mongol Empire conquered the Kingdom of Goryeo on the Korean Peninsula. The Mongols then set their sights on the Japanese archipelago just across the strait. In 1260, Kublai Khan was declared khagan and ruler of the vast Mongol Empire. Six years later, the Mongols and Koreans sent emissaries to Japan. They did this on six different occasions.

All of these attempts at communication were rebuffed. In 1274, it was decided that a Mongolian and Korean force would invade Japan. The invading force was about thirty thousand strong, with Japan only able to provide about six thousand warriors. These defenders were organized under the leadership of the Hōjō regency, with Hōjō Tokimune acting as the de facto commander in chief. Guided by the Zen monk Mugaku Sogen, Tokimune turned inward through meditation to confront his fear of the invasion. This spiritual resolve inspired him to promote Zen Buddhism throughout Japan.

The Mongolian forces first landed on Tsushima Island and quickly conquered it. They moved on to Iki Island, which they also took. Then, they landed at Hakata Bay on Kyūshū Island, which was the site of the Battle of Bun'ei. A large portion of the Mongolian fleet was lost due to storms, and the few who managed to land faced fierce resistance.

Still, the actual fighting was brief and uncoordinated. The Mongolian generals withdrew rather than pursue the Japanese further into unknown terrain at night. The invasion was abandoned, and the Mongolian and Korean forces that survived returned to the mainland.

To the Japanese, it seemed the invaders had disappeared overnight. But they were certain another invasion was on the horizon. The samurai trained more, and fortifications were constructed around the islands. In 1275, Kublai Khan sent another group of emissaries who refused to leave until the Japanese provided a reply. Tokimune responded by having the emissaries beheaded. Their bodies were sent back to China. The inevitable second invasion came in 1281.

This time, the Mongolian Yuan dynasty was able to provide a large force of possibly 140,000 soldiers (though this number might be exaggerated). These men were separated into two massive fleets. The first and smaller fleet advanced ahead of schedule, taking Tsushima and Iki but failing to land a sizable force at Hakata Bay due to the new Japanese fortifications, including a defensive wall. They were forced to take the islands of Shika and Noko instead. The Japanese counterattacked and were able to destroy a few ships.

The second fleet eventually arrived, and the two fleets again attacked Hakata Bay. Despite being able to land troops, the invasion reached a stalemate. Then, in August, a great typhoon, which the Japanese called the "Divine Wind" or kamikaze, struck the islands. This storm, along with the one that helped end the 1274 invasion, came to be seen as a supernatural force of protection.

A large number of ships were destroyed, and Yuan soldiers were left stranded in the sea or on some of the islands. The surviving ships abandoned the remaining soldiers and returned to China. The Japanese killed most of the Mongolian, Korean, and northern Chinese soldiers they found. However, they often spared southern Chinese conscripts, believing they had been forced into the invasion, though many were still enslaved.

While the Japanese victories were significant, Japan did not acquire any new lands, so the shogunate could not properly reward the samurai who had fought against the Yuan. This undermined the power of the Hōjō and their control of the shogunate. It also led to an increase in Japanese pirates who raided the Korean and Chinese coasts.

The loss to the Yuan was critical, as their naval power had been devastated. Korea's ability to supply ships was also crippled, having exhausted its natural resources in building the fleets. Chinese officials increasingly saw an invasion of Japan as futile, convinced that the Japanese were both brave and warlike.

Summary Timeline — The Rise of the Samurai

- 1153 CE – Death of Taira no Tadamori; his son, Taira no Kiyomori, assumes leadership of the Taira clan.
- 1156 CE – Hōgen Rebellion: conflict over imperial succession; Taira and Minamoto clans rise to prominence.
- 1159–1160 CE – Heiji Rebellion: Kiyomori defeats Minamoto no Yoshitomo and consolidates power.
- 1165 CE – Death of Emperor Nijō; Kiyomori gains further influence at court.
- 1167 CE – Kiyomori appointed Daijō-daijin (chancellor), the highest office in the imperial court.
- 1171 CE – Kiyomori's daughter marries Emperor Takakura, linking the Taira clan to the imperial line.
- 1178 CE – Birth of Prince Tokihito, later Emperor Antoku.
- 1180 CE – Kiyomori forces Emperor Takakura to abdicate; Antoku, age two, becomes emperor. Prince Mochihito and Minamoto no Yorimasa lead a rebellion, beginning the Genpei War.
- 1181 CE – Death of Taira no Kiyomori; famine strikes Japan.
- 1183 CE – Minamoto victory at Battle of Kurikara Pass, the turning point of the Genpei War.
- 1184 CE – Battle of Ichi-no-Tani; Taira forces defeated by Minamoto no Yoshitsune.
- 1185 CE – Naval Battle of Dan-no-ura; Taira clan destroyed, Emperor Antoku dies.
- 1192 CE – Minamoto no Yoritomo appointed shogun; Kamakura shogunate established.
- 1219 CE – Assassination of Shogun Minamoto no Sanetomo; end of the Minamoto line.
- 1221 CE – Emperor Go-Toba's failed rebellion; Hōjō clan solidifies power.
- 1225 CE – Hōjō Yasutoki establishes the Council of State (Hyōjōshū).

- 1232 CE – Goseibai Shikimoku code enacted; foundation of samurai law.
- 1260 CE – Kublai Khan becomes Mongol ruler.
- 1274 CE – First Mongol invasion repelled at Hakata Bay
- 1281 CE – Second Mongol invasion fails; end of Mongol threat.

Chapter 4: The Kamakura Conflict

The story of Buddhism began, perhaps, when Siddhartha Gautama found enlightenment in the yoga posture of dhyāna, which the West often translates as "meditation," though the meaning is much deeper than that word implies. Siddhartha went on to become the Buddha and the founder of Buddhism. Around a thousand years after the founding of Buddhism, a monk named Bodhidharma is said to have brought Buddhism to China in a form that would become known as Chan Buddhism. This was centered around the use of meditation to achieve self-awareness.

The character for Chan is pronounced "Zen" in Japan. Its focus was on meditation practices and finding one's own inner Buddha. Zen Buddhism does not worship any particular gods. While it emphasizes direct experience over scripture, it still draws from important sutras, such as the Heart Sutra and Diamond Sutra. Many famous Zen sayings have been passed down through the generations.

The Japanese monk Dōgen established the Sōtō Zen school in Japan in the 13th century after being taught in China. Dōgen was most likely born into the Minamoto clan around the year 1200. After his mother's death, he became a monk at a young age and became fixated on deeper philosophical questions. If humanity is born with the Buddha's nature, which many Buddhist sects teach, then why do holy people need to seek enlightenment? Dōgen was encouraged to find the answer by studying Chan Buddhism in China.

He made the journey in 1223 and eventually found a teacher, Rujing, who led him to realize the fundamentals of what would become Sōtō Zen

Buddhism, which Dōgen would teach in Japan. The answer to Dōgen's question was essentially that to reveal one's natural enlightenment was to study oneself, and in order to do that, one must forget oneself. This seemingly contradictory concept is similar to many parts of Zen Buddhism that outsiders often fail to comprehend.

Dōgen returned to Japan and began to deliver the teachings of Zen Buddhism. His followers built the Eihei-ji Temple, which remains one of the two main centers for Sōtō Zen practice and study today.

Dōgen died in 1253. He is remembered best for bringing Zen Buddhism to Japan and for his focus on dhyāna (Japanese: *zazen*), which is often translated as seated meditation. This type of meditation was connected to *hishiryō*, or "non-thinking" or "beyond thinking," a state of mind that Westerners often struggle to define.

Mugaku Sogen (also known as Bukko) came to Japan from Song China and was welcomed as a Zen monk by the regent Hōjō Tokimune. Sogen advised Tokimune during the Mongol invasions. He was awarded a temple, Engaku-ji, in 1282, where he served as chief priest. He died in 1286.

While Zen began to gain footholds in the nobility and the samurai, it was not until the appearance of Keizan that Zen started to spread among the common people. Keizan founded the other great center of Sōtō Zen, the temple of Sōji-ji. Keizan also supported the training of women in Zen Buddhism. He died in 1325.

The infusion of Shinto and Zen beliefs into the moral code of the samurai (later called bushidō) under Tokimune elevated this warrior class, giving the samurai a dose of wisdom and serenity. Tokimune is said to have formally become a Zen monk near the end of his life in April 1284. He was succeeded by his son, Sadatoki, who continued to consolidate the power of the Hōjō and resigned as regent in 1301, though many claimed he continued to rule until he died in 1311.

In 1301, a new emperor was crowned, Go-Nijō. He was the ninety-fourth emperor of Japan, according to tradition. The shogun in that year was Prince Hisaaki, a member of the Minamoto clan. After Sadatoki's apparent retirement, he was succeeded by Hōjō Morotoki, who ruled as regent from 1301 until he died in 1311. He was succeeded by Takatoki, who was just eight years old when he became shikken in 1316.

During this time, another item closely associated with Japanese culture today was beginning to spread across the country: tea. Japan had grown and used tea for centuries, but it wasn't until the mid-13th and early 14th centuries that tea began to see widespread consumption. Kyoto and Kamakura, which under the Hōjō regency had grown into a city of seventy thousand inhabitants, became centers for the tea trade. The warrior class had newfound stability and wealth, and with that, they began to enjoy the finer things in life, including tea.

Much of what is known of tea production and consumption from the late 13th and into the 14th centuries comes from the writings of Sadaaki, the head of the lesser branch of the Hōjō clan called Kanazawa. Sadaaki's correspondence shows us that the cultivation of tea was primarily done by monks. The best tea was "early tea" picked in April. Tea could be purchased as loose whole leaves, compressed into bricks for storage and trade, or finely ground into powder—what we now know as matcha. Tea fields were small, usually less than 0.3 acres. There was also "mountain tea," which was cultivated sporadically in the countryside by common folk. This tea was typically of lesser quality and, therefore, less expensive.

A critical change in tea production occurred in the mid-13th century with the introduction of stone tea grinders from China. The use of these grinders resulted in a finer and sweeter tea. It, along with the development of shade-grown tea, gave Japanese tea its distinctive green color. This brought tea out of medicinal use and into a drink for enjoyment. Along with this came the tea whisk, which helped enhance the flavor, and the first methods for preserving tea leaves. Soon, tea was a party beverage and a popular gift.

Buddhist monks performed rituals that required certain tea, and elaborate games were held at parties in which participants guessed the best quality tea. However, the famous Japanese tea ceremony had yet to be perfected. Still, during the Kamakura shogunate, tea became a much more important part of everyday Japanese life, something that has lasted to the present day.

The Kanazawa might have been an offshoot of the main Hōjō line, but they were still powerful players in Kamakura. Tea flowed from the fields of the family temple of Shōmyōji into the capitals of Japan. The temple also had a stone tea grinder, so unground tea was often sent there to be processed. Sadaaki recorded numerous gifts of varying expense given to those he maintained as political allies, friends, family, and those with whom he hoped to ingratiate himself.

At Shōmyōji, Sadaaki also had a "Pure Land garden" or Jōdō garden, which was built by the gardener priest, Shōitsu. This garden included a shrine for the Amida Buddha and a pond with an island in the center connected via a bridge. Excavations of the site have indicated that the pond also featured a pebbled beach. Japanese gardens date back to the Heian period and were usually spots to attract kami or spirits. By the time of the Kamakura shogunate, gardens had become much more elaborate, and with the rise of Zen Buddhism, the first gardens devoted to meditation were designed. These gardens could be considered the precursor to the famous Japanese Zen gardens.

While the Kamakura period ushered in many quintessential Japanese traditions, with the regency of Hōjō Takatoki in 1316, it was the beginning of the end for the dominance of Kamakura. Takatoki was born in 1304 and was the son of retired shikken (regent) Hōjō Sadatoki. He became regent at the age of eight, so the real power was held by his grandmother, Adachi Tokiaki, and a minister named Nagasaki Takasuke, who was the head of the powerful Tokusō family.

When Takatoki was twenty-three, he fell ill and retired as shikken to become a monk, though he continued to hold considerable power within the shogunate. He did not appoint a successor, and the Adachi clan, represented by Takatoki's grandmother, and the Tokusō family, represented by Nagasaki Takasuke, supported separate candidates. The Tokusō were able to push forward their candidate, Hōjō Kunitoki, the infant son of Takatoki, but they needed an interim shikken to rule until Kunitoki was an adult.

They chose none other than Hōjō Sadaaki, the head of the Kanazawa branch of the Hōjō clan and a trader in tea. Sadaaki had brought his branch of the family to new heights with cunning political savvy, but his appointment was opposed by the Adachi and because of rumors of an assassination plot. In fact, Sadaaki had requested to retire from politics and become a monk like Takatoki, but he was denied each time. In the face of this open opposition, Sadaaki resigned as regent after only ten days on the job.

He was replaced by Hōjō Moritoki, who was associated with the Akahashi line of the Hōjō clan. Moritoki was to be another interim regent, and he was nothing more than a puppet controlled by Nagasaki Takasuke and the retired regent Hōjō Takatoki. Moritoki became regent in 1326 and held the position until 1333, which was when matters took a drastic turn regarding Emperor Go-Daigo.

In 1324, Emperor Go-Daigo was discovered to be planning an overthrow of the shogunate in Kamakura to restore the imperial family as the leaders of Japan. The shogunate stopped the emperor's plans, but Go-Daigo once again was discovered to be planning to overthrow Kamakura in 1331 after he was betrayed by his close associate, Fujiwara Sadafusa. Go-Daigo was exiled to the Oki Islands. A new emperor, Go-Kōgon, was installed in his place.

However, after two years, Go-Daigo escaped with the help of Nawa Nagatoshi. The two gathered an army to face the shogunate forces, led by Sasaki Kiyotaka, at the Battle of Mount Senjō. The imperial forces were victorious, which caused leaders to switch sides and support Go-Daigo.

The Hōjō clan then dispatched two forces to suppress Go-Daigo's uprising. One, led by Hōjō Takaie, was defeated along the San'yōdō route. The other, commanded by Ashikaga Takauji, turned against the shogunate and joined the imperial side. The reason for Takauji's defection remains uncertain, but it is often attributed to his status as head of the Minamoto clan, a traditional rival of the Taira. The Hōjō had maintained a long-standing alliance with the Taira lineage, dating back to the Genpei War.

Takauji quickly took control of Kyoto. Nitta Yoshisada, head of the Nitta clan, joined the emperor's side and laid siege to Kamakura. When the city fell, Hōjō Takatoki and his entire family committed suicide. The Hōjō clan was almost entirely wiped out, ending the Kamakura shogunate in what would be known as the Genkō War.

Emperor Go-Daigo returned to Kyoto and claimed the Chrysanthemum Throne, which began a brief period known as the Kenmu Restoration. Go-Daigo hoped to return Japan to a civilian government after many generations of military rule under the Kamakura shogunate.

However, the emperor displeased the warrior class by not

Emperor Go-Daigo.[a]

rewarding them sufficiently for their support. The Hōjō lands that were seized were handed out to Ashikaga Takauji and Nitta Yoshisada for their efforts, and the rest mainly went to imperial favorites. The minor warriors who had supported the emperor were ignored, and they quickly became incensed. Important positions were given to nobles and bureaucrats. By 1335, the emperor had completely lost the support of the samurai.

In order to reestablish rule in Kamakura and the east without naming another shogun, Go-Daigo sent his young son to the east and named him governor-general of Mutsu and Dewa Provinces. Tadayoshi, the younger brother of Ashikaga Takauji, then took another son of the emperor and installed him as governor of Kōzuke Province in Kamakura. Tadayoshi's actions were not, however, ordered by the emperor. This disobedience went unchecked because the emperor did not have the resources to attack the Ashikaga clan.

In due time, the Ashikaga brothers, especially Takauji, came to represent the growing discontent of the samurai. With their support, he rebelled against Go-Daigo in 1336. Their forces met in the famous Battle of Minatogawa. Ashikaga's army was victorious, and Go-Daigo fled to Yoshino, where he established the Southern Court. Ashikaga Takauji placed Emperor Kōmyō, from the senior line of the imperial family, on the throne of the Northern Court. This divide between Northern and Southern Courts would last until 1392, a span of time known as the Nanboku-chō period. Ashikaga Takauji became shogun in the north, establishing the Ashikaga bakufu, or military government, in Kyoto.

Summary Timeline — The Kamakura Conflict
- 1200 CE (approx.) - Birth of Dōgen, later founder of the Sōtō Zen school in Japan.
- 1223 CE - Dōgen travels to China to study Chan Buddhism; trains under Rujing.
- 1253 CE - Death of Dōgen after establishing Eihei-ji Temple, a main center of Sōtō Zen practice.
- 1284 CE - Death of Hōjō Tokimune; succeeded by his son Sadatoki.
- 1301 CE - Emperor Go-Nijō ascends the throne; Hōjō Morotoki serves as regent.
- 1311 CE - Death of Morotoki

- 1316 CE – Hōjō Takatoki (age eight) becomes regent.
- 1316 CE – Beginning of Takatoki's regency; growing factionalism among Hōjō branches.
- 1324 CE – Emperor Go-Daigo's plot to overthrow the Kamakura shogunate discovered.
- 1331 CE – Go-Daigo again attempts rebellion; captured and exiled to the Oki Islands.
- 1333 CE – Go-Daigo escapes; allies with Nitta Yoshisada and Ashikaga Takauji. Kamakura falls; Hōjō Takatoki and family commit suicide. End of the Kamakura shogunate.
- 1333–1336 CE – Go-Daigo restores imperial rule during the Kenmu Restoration.
- 1336 CE – Ashikaga Takauji rebels against Go-Daigo; Battle of Minatogawa.
- 1336 CE – Takauji establishes the Northern Court in Kyoto; Go-Daigo flees to Yoshino, founding the Southern Court. Beginning of the Nanboku-chō (Northern and Southern Courts) period.

Chapter 5: The Ashikaga Era

Ashikaga Takauji.⁴

If Takauji had hoped that his time as shogun would be peaceful, he was soon proved severely mistaken. The existence of the Southern Court and the fact that Go-Daigo still held the imperial regalia would remain an issue for the rest of Takauji's life. In 1339, one year after Takauji had declared himself shogun, Go-Daigo died, and the throne went to Crown Prince Norinaga, who became Emperor Go-Murakami. For almost ten years, Go-Murakami ruled in Yoshino while Kōmyō ruled with Ashikaga support in Kyoto.

Then, in the early 1350s, a samurai general and shitsuji (shogun's deputy) named Kō no Moronao launched a campaign against the Southern Court. Emperor Go-Murakami fled his capital, but the Ashikaga forces were unable to capture Yoshino. The next year, Kō no Moronao, who was known for his violent ways and bad temper, quarreled with Ashikaga Takauji's younger brother, Tadayoshi. This led to a rift between the two brothers. Tadayoshi went as far, according to some sources, as to order Moronao's assassination, though it failed. Tadayoshi was then banished from the Northern Court despite having ruled in his brother's stead for years.

In 1351, Tadayoshi became a monk, but instead of retiring, he joined the Southern Court. Emperor Go-Murakami made him general over all the imperial troops. Tadayoshi was a skilled general, and in short order, he captured Kyoto and executed Kō no Moronao and his brother in Settsu Province.

However, Takauji gained the upper hand and defeated his younger brother at Sattayama. The brothers were briefly reconciled before hostilities broke out again, and Tadayoshi was captured in 1352. He died in prison, possibly from poisoning. The two courts remained, with Emperor Go-Kōgon in the Northern Court and Emperor Go-Murakami still on the throne of the Southern Court.

From 1352 to 1357, Takauji had to flee Kyoto multiple times due to invading forces. Each time, the Northern Court was able to recapture Kyoto. Kamakura was also captured and retaken once during this period.

Then, in 1358, Ashikaga Takauji died of illness. He was succeeded by his son, Ashikaga Yoshiakira, whose rule until 1367 saw further strife but also an attempt to consolidate power in the Ashikaga (also called Muromachi) shogunate.

This centered around noble lords known as shugo, who administered areas of Japan, though they remained in **competition** with the samurai in their districts. Yoshiakira and his deputy (*kanrei*), Hosokawa Yoriyuki, integrated the shugo into the shogun government. Hosokawa Yoriyuki held the title of Kyoto kanrei, which had supplanted the previous office of shitsuji (shogun's deputy). In an effort to balance the power of the kanrei,

Yoriyuki proposed that the three head shugo families of the time—Hosokawa, Shiba, and Hatakeyama—alternate appointments as kanrei.

In 1368, Ashikaga Yoshiakira was on his deathbed and entrusted the care of his son, Ashikaga Yoshimitsu, to Hosokawa Yoriyuki. When Yoshiakira died, ten-year-old Ashikaga Yoshimitsu became shogun.

That same year, Emperor Chōkei ascended the throne of the Southern Court. Chōkei devised a plan to attack the Ashikaga in Kyoto from both the east and south. However, in 1369, the great imperialist general and hero, Kusunoki Masanori, who had captured and been driven out of Kyoto on four separate occasions, abandoned the Southern Court and looked for a peaceful way to end the dispute between the shogun and emperor.

Kusunoki Masanori was not an ordinary general. He was renowned for his loyalty, bravery, and exceptional personality. It was said that a samurai of the Akamatsu family planned to kill Masanori but committed suicide instead, not wishing to harm such a great man. His move to seek peace with Kyoto was seen as treason by many of those he had fought with, but he had grown tired of the constant quarrels of the Nanboku-chō period, and perhaps so had the people of Japan.

Masanori's apparent defection was also seen by some as the only means to save the Southern Court. If the young emperor continued with his planned attack, then the imperialist forces might have faced annihilation. There is reason to believe that the statesman Hosokawa Yoriyuki, the regent of the young shogun, also desired a peaceful conclusion to the war between the two courts, but it was not to be. In 1374, Chōkei abdicated in favor of his brother, Emperor Go-Kameyama.

The struggle continued for ten more years. Ashikaga Yoshimitsu became an adult and rejected the conservative rule of Hosokawa Yoriyuki, who returned to his home in Awa. In 1374, an actor, author, and musician named Kan'ami performed for Yoshimitsu in Kyoto. Many consider this to be the beginning of the Noh theater. "Noh" originally referred to any play that featured singing and dancing.

Two folk traditions were the roots for what would become Japan's predominant classical theater. Sarugaku was an ancient form of entertainment featuring acrobatics and farcical displays that eventually took on more dramatic features. Dengaku was the more musical of the two. Its name literally means "rice field music." To ensure a good harvest, people would dance and sing to the accompaniment of flutes and drums.

Sarugaku attracted more serious actors, while Dengaku became more focused on music, singing, and dance. Kan'ami was a Sarugaku performer originally, but he borrowed much from Dengaku performers. When he performed for the shogun, Yoshimitsu enjoyed the performance so much that he became Kan'ami's patron. He also showed special favor toward Kan'ami's son, Zeami, supporting his education and bringing him into court circles. Some later scholars suggest this relationship might have had an erotic dimension, though the evidence remains ambiguous.

The patronage of the shogun elevated their theater troupe and the actors themselves, who were originally from the lowest class of people, to a much higher status in society. Zeami wrote many of the treatises that would go on to define Noh theater. They were mainly based on his father's teachings and ideas about the art form.

In 1378, Yoshimitsu established the Flower Palace, which was known as Muromachi-dono or Muromachi Palace because of its location in the Muromachi district in Kyoto. Because of this, the Ashikaga period is often called the Muromachi period. Though this period was often violent and unstable, this era provided artists with the freedom to experiment and borrow from various other genres and art forms to create new and interesting experiences.

Yoshimitsu desired to bring more peace and stability to the nation, so he reorganized the "Five Mountain System" or Gozan Zen temples in Kyoto and Kamakura, as well as a network of lower temples throughout the country that acted as a kind of bureaucracy for the shogunate. This did not allow Yoshimitsu to regain control of the country, but it did establish a central philosophy of education since the temples often acted as the premier schools of the time.

The Nanboku-chō period, when the country was essentially split between the Northern and Southern Courts, finally came to an end in 1392. Yoshimitsu had been working tirelessly to promote the shogun's cultural influence through patronizing the arts and education and by strengthening his connection to both the imperial court and the shugo.

Part of this included persuading the western and central shugo lords to take up residence in Kyoto so they could be directly under his influence. The lords would then need permission to leave the capital, which was rarely granted, thus ensuring they could not spark revolts. Likewise, the shugo of the Kantō region were required to build mansions in Kamakura. While some lords were required to live in Kyoto or Kamakura, it became fashionable to do so, and lords who were not required to live there did so anyway. All the same, any lord who did not live in one of the capitals risked the chance of being branded a traitor.

Yoshimitsu also formed his own army of three thousand well-trained warriors, which could be supplemented by levying troops from the shugo. If a single lord was seen as becoming too powerful, the shogun was quick to put him in check with these forces at his command. They were incredibly effective at putting down a series of revolts in the late 14th century, namely the Toki Yasuyuki Rebellion (1389), the Meitoku Rebellion (1391), and the Ōei Rebellion (1397).

Yoshimitsu's preferred tactic was to pit a powerful shugo against a family member, which he did when he ordered Toki Yasuyuki to give up one of his provinces to a relative. Yasuyuki refused, and Yoshimitsu ordered the relative, Toki Yorimasu, to attack the traitorous lord. The resulting conflict saw the defeat of **Yasuyuki**, who gave up his province.

Yet, the real prize for Yoshimitsu was the merging of the separate imperial courts. Emperor Go-Kameyama became emperor of the Southern Court in 1383. After so many years of warfare and strife, the peace faction in the **Southern** Court, first begun by General Kusunoki Masanori, had grown more powerful. Yoshimitsu had also become interested in reaching an agreement between the two courts. Masanori, who died in 1390, never saw the peace he wished for, yet just two years after the hero's death, Emperor Go-Kameyama entered into peace talks with Ashikaga Yoshimitsu, thanks in large part to the shugo and clan leader Ōuchi Yoshihiro. He convinced the Southern Court to surrender. For this, Yoshihiro was awarded two provinces.

The Sacred Treasures, or regalia of the imperial court, were handed over to the Northern Court. Emperor Go-Kameyama abdicated in 1392 on the understanding that the throne would alternate between the Northern and Southern imperial lines every ten years going forward. The Northern emperor, Emperor Go-Komatsu, became the one hundredth legitimate emperor of Japan, according to the traditional line of succession. The two courts were now unified.

Yoshimitsu had accomplished much as shogun, and perhaps as a way to celebrate his success, he purchased the estate of the nobleman and poet, Saionji Kintsune, in 1397. There, Yoshimitsu built a grand palace covered in gold leaf. It would eventually become a Zen temple called Kinkaku-ji (Temple of the Golden Pavilion). Despite having been destroyed several times, it was rebuilt and remains a popular tourist attraction in Kyoto.

The year 1394 marked the beginning of the Ōei historic period. Japanese history is broken up into brief periods, usually only a few years long, that are typically marked by significant events. The Ōei period began with Yoshimitsu officially ceding his position to his son, Ashikaga Yoshimochi. However, Yoshimitsu did not actually retire. He remained very much in control of the bakufu (military government).

During this period, tensions between Yoshimitsu and one of his most powerful retainers, Ōuchi Yoshihiro, came to a head. Yoshihiro, lord of Suō and Nagato, resisted Yoshimitsu's demand that he contribute to the construction of a new palace. His refusal was taken as defiance of the shogun's authority. In 1399, Yoshihiro raised an army and fortified himself in the port city of Sakai, hoping to rally support against the bakufu. Yoshimitsu responded with overwhelming force, personally leading a massive army against him. The conflict, remembered as the Ōei Disturbance (or Ōei Rebellion), ended quickly. Yoshihiro was defeated and killed, and his rebellion was crushed by the shogun's superior numbers. The failed rising confirmed Yoshimitsu's dominance and further demonstrated the reach of the bakufu under his rule.

In 1401, Yoshimitsu sent an envoy to Ming China to reopen communication and trade between the two nations. The diplomats also brought a tribute of one thousand ounces of gold and precious objects. The Ming emperor, Yongle, replied the following year, granting Yoshimitsu the title "King of Japan," the only medieval shogun to receive this title.

In 1408, Yoshimitsu died suddenly at the age of forty-nine. His most long-lived legacy is perhaps his golden palace, which became the Zen Buddhist temple known as Kinkaku-ji, where a statue of Yoshimitsu can still be found. Upon Yoshimitsu's death, his son, Yoshimochi, took over as shogun.

The following year, Ashikaga Mochiuji became Kantō kubō, the title given to the shogun's representative in Kamakura, making it the equivalent of shogun in eastern Japan. The post had first been created in 1349, when Ashikaga Motouji, a son of Takauji, was appointed to govern the Kantō region. Kamakura remained the capital of the east, while Kyoto controlled the west. Though the Kantō kubō was in theory subservient to the shogun in Kyoto, the arrangement divided Japan into two overlapping centers of power. Eventually, the real power in Kamakura came to be held by the Uesugi clan, who served as Kantō kanrei, the deputies of the shogun in the east. Although Motouji was officially appointed to govern the region, he was often called the Kantō shogun or simply Motouji kubō. Since the shogun in Kyoto was also commonly referred to as kubō, Motouji came to be known as the Kantō kubō, a title that distinguished him as the shogunal representative in Kamakura.

Motouji died in 1367, and the title of Kantō kubō fell to his son, Ashikaga Ujimitsu. Even using the title Kantō kubō was potentially treasonous because it implied equal status with the shogun, but Ujimitsu openly desired to become shogun and clashed with the actual ruling shogun, Yoshimitsu. However, Ujimitsu could only aspire to this because he did not have the backing to challenge Yoshimitsu for the shogunate. Ujimitsu supported Yoshimitsu in 1391 against the Yamana clan, which won him more provinces. He never fully abandoned the idea of overthrowing Yoshimitsu, but he died at just forty-one in 1398.

The title of Kantō kubō then fell to his eldest son, Ashikaga Mitsukane. Mitsukane also openly aspired to the shogunate. In 1399, he planned to join Ōuchi Yoshihiro in his rebellion, the Ōei War, but he was unable to provide support before the rebellion was crushed. Since he had not actually participated in the rebellion, he was able to feign innocence when questioned by Yoshimitsu. He swore to support the shogunate in Kyoto, and peace existed between the capital and Kamakura until Mitsukane died in 1409. Then, his son, Ashikaga Mochiuji, became Kantō kubō.

Mochiuji was just a child when his father died, so the work of governing from Kamakura went to his kanrei (deputy), Uesugi Zenshū. Shogun Yoshimochi knew to keep a wary eye on the Kantō kubō and wait for any sign of rebellion.

In 1411, Yoshimochi abruptly ended his father's policy of engagement with Ming China, cutting off all diplomatic and trade relations. Yoshimitsu's acceptance of the title "King of Japan" had been controversial, as many in Kyoto saw it as submission to the Chinese emperor. Seeking to assert Japan's independence and restore domestic authority, Yoshimochi rejected the tributary relationship altogether.

Two years later, Emperor Go-Komatsu of the Northern Court, who had ruled for twenty years instead of the ten years originally agreed upon, reneged on the compromise between the Northern and Southern Courts. He handed the throne to his son, Emperor Shōko. Supporters of the

Southern Court were incensed by this disregard for the compromise, and hostilities resumed between them and the court in Kyoto.

By 1415, Mochiuji was showing a violent and abrasive personality. Uesugi Zenshū organized a revolt against his lord with the support of several shugo. By this time, the role of the shugo as military governors had grown. They dispensed justice, supported the shogun, and levied taxes on landholding nobles in their province. They also owned land; as landowning warriors, they were called daimyo. The power of these "shugo daimyo" increased as the Ashikaga shogunate declined.

While Yoshimochi might have understood Zenshū's rebellion and might have liked the idea of getting Mochiuji out of the way, he had to send troops to put down the revolt. Zenshū had no right to defy his lord. The shogun could not let that crime go unpunished. His army finally surrounded Zenshū in 1417, and the kanrei committed seppuku instead of facing capture.

Mochiuji did not feel the death of Zenshū was enough, though. He attacked Zenshū's allies, the Takeda and Oda clans, as well as a few of the nobles of Musashi Province. He continued this punishment for several years, even though the rest of the Ashikaga clan felt as if he was going too far.

In the middle of this tension, in June 1419, the Joseon or Yi dynasty of Korea launched an invasion of the Japanese island of Tsushima. The *wokou*, Japanese pirates, had established themselves on Tsushima, and from there, they conducted repeated raids, not just on the Korean coast but also far into the mainland. The Ashikaga shogunate had been unable or unwilling to suppress this activity.

Korean armies had invaded the island and suppressed the pirates on two earlier occasions, but this had failed to solve the problem. The de facto ruler of Tsushima, Sō Sadashige, had managed to keep the island's pirates under control and maintain stable relations with Korea. When he died in 1418, however, authority on the island weakened. A pirate leader named Sōda Saemontarō seized power and led a massive *wokou* raid into Ming China. On their way, the pirates attacked the Korean coast and captured Cape Dodu on Jeju Island. Outraged, the Korean court declared war on Tsushima, and in 1419, King Sejong launched a full-scale invasion of the island.

The Korean invasion was led by General Yi Jongmu, who commanded around 230 ships with around 17,000 soldiers. After they landed in Asō

Bay, Jongmu sent out emissaries to ask for surrender. When he received no reply, he ordered his men to raid and plunder the island's settlements. The sources offer mixed stories. The Korean records indicate they killed several pirates, freed Chinese captives, burned down houses, and captured several ships. The Japanese sources indicate that the Koreans faced significant resistance, mainly from the samurai of the Sō clan. Regardless, the Koreans left after a week and decided not to return. Tsushima and the Joseon dynasty entered into peace negotiations that eventually resulted in a treaty that allowed the Sō clan to monopolize trade with Korea.

In 1423, Shogun Yoshimochi resigned in favor of his son, Ashikaga Yoshikazu, who was eighteen years old. However, Yoshikazu died only two years later, so Yoshimochi returned as shogun. He stayed in power until his death in 1428 and was succeeded by his brother, Ashikaga Yoshinori. Yoshinori had been a Buddhist monk since he was ten years old, but he had been selected by the kanrei when Yoshimochi had failed to name a successor.

Not long after Yoshinori's succession, revolts broke out in several parts of the empire, including the Ōtomo Rebellion and the revolt of the monks of Mount Hiei in 1433. Yoshinori finally had the opportunity to strike out against the Kantō kubō, Ashikaga Mochiuji, who had been continuing his punishment of his perceived enemies. Mochiuji had grown too violent and too powerful to continue, and Yoshinori knew he needed to end Mochiuji's reign. Mochiuji's resistance would be known as the Eikyō Rebellion. The rebellion lasted several years, but in 1439, Mochiuji was finally defeated. He committed seppuku at the temple of Yōan-ji, west of Kamakura.

Despite not having been raised to be shogun, Yoshinori helped consolidate Ashikaga power and reestablished the trade relationship with Ming China, though his methods were often harsh and erratic. In one seemingly inconsequential decision, he made an enemy of Akamatsu Mitsusuke, who desired to be the head of the Akamatsu clan but had been overlooked by the shogun. Mitsusuke assassinated Yoshinori in 1441 and, in turn, was hunted down and forced to commit seppuku. The assassination of a shogun was almost unheard of and perhaps undermined the idea that Yoshinori reigned over a period of relative peace.

After Yoshinori's assassination, it was decided that his eight-year-old son, Yoshikatsu, would succeed him as shogun. However, the young shogun died in a horse-riding accident after reigning for only two years.

He was succeeded by his younger brother, Ashikaga Yoshinari. Years later, the shogun changed his name to Yoshimasa, by which he is better known.

As Yoshimasa matured, a powerful rivalry developed within the shogunate. On one side was the daimyo Yamana Sōzen, who had become an ordained monk. However, due to his regular angry outbursts, he was known as the "Red Monk." Sōzen was jealous of his son-in-law, Kanrei Hosokawa Katsumoto, who, as one of the shogun's deputies, held immense power. The two waged a silent war, strategically trying to outmaneuver the other by interfering in the affairs of other families, most notably in the succession disputes of the Hatakeyama and Shiba clans.

In 1464, Yoshimasa expressed an interest in retiring as shogun. Since he had no legitimate heir, he adopted his younger brother, Ashikaga Yoshimi. However, the unexpected birth of a son to Yoshimasa a year later put the succession into question. Yamana Sōzen threw his support behind Yoshimasa's infant son, while Hosokawa Katsumoto pledged loyalty to Yoshimi.

It was at this moment that the war between the rivals turned from a silent battle of wits to an actual battle of swords in the streets of Kyoto itself. This was the beginning of the Ōnin War. The first battle took place around the Goryo Shrine. The battle was followed by looting, and a whole section of the capital was set ablaze. The younger members of the imperial family, along with most of the citizens, had been evacuated.

It was soon apparent that the nature of this war was one of destruction and ruin. After a month of fighting, most of northern Kyoto was decimated. Eventually, a stalemate existed in Kyoto, but the fighting spread into the rest of the country. Yoshimasa virtually ignored the war, instead being content with poetry readings and tea ceremonies.

In the rest of the country, the war that had initially been about the succession of the shogun devolved into battles between daimyo over land—power struggles that resembled the looting of burned-out Kyoto. The Red Monk and his son-in-law were both killed in 1473, but the civil war still raged on. Inter-clan fighting in Yamashiro Province, for example, led to a standstill between two factions of the Hatakeyama clan. The peasants and lesser samurai of the region revolted, expelled the Hatakeyama from the province, and set up a provincial government of their own.

The precarious order of the Ashikaga shogunate had toppled. While the Hosokawa clan held power over the Ashikaga shoguns, there was effectively no central power in Japan by the end of the Ōnin War. The daimyo ruled their respective provinces like kings over their own kingdoms, without answering to the shogun or the emperor. Japan had entered a new phase of history, the era of the Warring States, also known as the Sengoku period.

While the central government of Japan was crumbling, Japanese culture was reaching a new pinnacle. Under Shogun Yoshimasa and immediately following his death, many of the most quintessential Japanese art forms were formalized. The tea ceremony, a detailed and meditative ritual involving the preparation and serving of tea, became increasingly popular. Every aspect of the ceremony was prescribed and deliberate, from the utensils and movements to the setting in which the ceremony took place.

Along with the tea ceremony came the art of flower arranging, which was connected to the serving of tea. As was the creation of gardens with gravel raked into interesting patterns—what today is called a "Zen garden." Zen Buddhism, in fact, flourished at the end of the Ashikaga shogunate. Ink paintings also became a hobby of the elite, and Noh theater continued to dominate the entertainment of the wealthy and powerful.

This is just another example of the juxtaposition that seemed to be a significant element of Japanese history. While Japanese culture became more refined and ordered, the nation delved into chaos and violence. Yoshimasa was succeeded by his son, Yoshihisa, but he only remained in power for a few years before dying while trying to restore order in Ōmi Province in 1489.

Summary Timeline — The Ashikaga Era

- 1339 CE - Emperor Go-Daigo dies; Crown Prince Norinaga becomes Emperor Go-Murakami of the Southern Court.
- Early 1350s - Ashikaga deputy Kō no Moronao campaigns against the Southern Court, sparking conflict with Tadayoshi.
- 1351 CE - Tadayoshi joins the Southern Court, captures Kyoto, and executes Moronao and his brother.
- 1352 CE - Tadayoshi is defeated and dies in prison; the rival Northern and Southern Courts continue.
- 1352-1357 CE - Takauji repeatedly flees and retakes Kyoto; Kamakura changes hands as fighting spreads.

- 1358 CE – Death of Ashikaga Takauji; his son Yoshiakira becomes shogun and organizes the new Muromachi bakufu.

- 1368 CE – Yoshiakira dies; ten-year-old Ashikaga Yoshimitsu becomes shogun; Emperor Chōkei ascends in the Southern Court.

- 1369 CE – Kusunoki Masanori abandons the Southern Court, weakening its cause.

- 1378 CE – Yoshimitsu establishes the Muromachi (Flower) Palace in Kyoto.

- 1389–1391–1397 CE – Yoshimitsu crushes the Toki Yasuyuki, Meitoku, and Ōei rebellions, solidifying Ashikaga rule.

- 1392 CE – Reunification of the Northern and Southern Courts: Emperor Go-Kameyama abdicates and surrenders the regalia; Emperor Go-Komatsu recognized as the sole ruler.

- 1394 CE – Start of the Ōei era; Yoshimitsu cedes the shogunate to Yoshimochi but keeps real power.

- 1397 CE – Construction of Kinkaku-ji (Golden Pavilion), symbolizing the height of Muromachi culture.

Chapter 6: The Sengoku Period

A Sengoku period battle.

Shogun Ashikaga Yoshihisa did not leave an heir, so he was succeeded by Ashikaga Yoshitane, his cousin. However, Yoshitane faced opposition from the powerful Kanrei Hosokawa Masamoto. Yoshitane was defeated by Masamoto and sent into exile. Ashikaga Yoshizumi was then made shogun, and in 1500, Emperor Go-Kashiwabara ascended to the Chrysanthemum Throne.

Yet, the powers of Kyoto mattered little to the rest of the nation. It became a time when people talked of *gekokujō*, or "the low dominating the high." Not only did the daimyo ignore the orders of the shoguns, but commoners began to oppose their lords. Farmers, monks, and lesser warriors would band together and revolt against their superiors. They established ikkō-ikki, or "leagues of one mind," which usually followed a religious leader whose followers were guided by a single-minded faith.

They were typically backed by the "True Pure Land" sect of Buddhism, known as Jōdo Shinshū. A priest named Rennyo, descended from the founder of True Pure Land Buddhism (Shinran), had the greatest influence over the ikkō-ikki. He challenged the power of the daimyo and other powerful Buddhist temples, such as Enryaku-ji on Mount Hiei near Kyoto. The monks of Mount Hiei led their own army, and during the Sengoku period, the government was unable to restrain them.

The Mount Hiei monks destroyed Rennyo's temple of Hongan-ji in 1465, though Rennyo was able to flee before the attack. He went to Echizen Province and established the temple of Yoshizaki-gobō. From there, Rennyo wrote and published works clarifying the True Pure Land teachings, which became known as Ikkō-shū, or the "single-minded school."

In his writings, he explained that Jōdo Shinshū was primarily focused on Amida Buddha and achieving rebirth in the Pure Land. In this primordial Pure Land, located outside the current reality, it is easier to reach Buddhahood and become completely enlightened because it exists beyond the corruption of the present age.

In 15th-century Japan, these ideas challenged the feudal structure of society and encouraged rebellions among the lower classes. Through the True Pure Land sect, these disparate groups could be united and organized in a way that allowed them to overthrow their local authorities—the provincial governor (**daimyo**) and the established Buddhist order (Tendai Buddhist monasteries).

Rennyo was a pacifist and taught pacifism, but he also recognized the tumultuous times he lived in. Because of that, any temples or monasteries he built were extremely well fortified. His followers, though, were not content to remain passive. They overthrew the governor of Kaga Province, creating the Kaga ikki, also called the "Peasants' Kingdom." They restored the shugo governor at Rennyo's request, but they soon overthrew him again in 1488 during what became known as the Kaga Rebellion.

The nature of the ikkō-ikki posed a serious threat to the economic and political supremacy of the daimyo. True Pure Land Buddhism would face near extinction by the mid-16th century. The idea that farmers, low-level priests, and provincial samurai (*jizamurai*) could challenge the authority of governors and established religious sects was intolerable to the high-ranking samurai and powerful monks. These men saw themselves as the true authorities of the Sengoku period.

By the mid-1500s, the power of these leagues had become impossible for ambitious warlords to ignore. Oda Nobunaga, seeking to unify the country, viewed the ikkō-ikki as a direct obstacle to his rule. He launched a series of brutal campaigns against their strongholds at Nagashima, Kaga, and Ishiyama Hongan-ji, destroying their fortresses and massacring thousands of adherents. These defeats shattered the military and political strength of the True Pure Land sect. Though its temples lay in ruins, the faith itself survived among the common people. It had been stripped of its armies but endured as a popular form of Buddhism.

Oda Nobunaga was one of three individuals who would rise at this time and become legendary figures in Japanese history. These three were, at times, allies and enemies, and their characters seemed naturally opposed. They were the three unifiers of Japan, and there is a set of similar stories about them that seek to explain their personalities and differences. The stories are all different, but they all make the same point.

In one story, the three men come upon a cuckoo bird that will not sing. Oda Nobunaga says to kill the bird, showing that he is a man of rash and violent tendencies. Then came Toyotomi Hideyoshi, who advised trying to placate the bird to sing. Then came Tokugawa Ieyasu. He explained that all they needed to do was to wait. Another story goes that Nobunaga gathered the ingredients, Hideyoshi cooked the meal, and Ieyasu ate it.

In the early 16th century, Oda Nobuhide was the head of the Oda clan and the deputy shugo of Owari Province. He had gained the nickname "Tiger of Owari" for his ferocity and ruthlessness in war. Like other samurai lords in the Sengoku period, his life was governed by continual warfare with the other warlords around him. His chief enemies were Saitō Dōsan, daimyo of Mino Province, and Imagawa Yoshimoto, lord of

Mikawa, Suruga, and Tōtōmi Provinces. The Oda were technically vassals of the Shiba clan, which formally ruled Owari; however, the Oda clan's power had come to surpass that of their shugo.

On June 23rd, 1534, a son and heir was born to Nobuhide. He was named Oda Nobunaga. This son of an embattled deputy governor of a small province in southern Honshu would go on to become one of the greatest figures in Japanese history. He is often called the first of the "Three Great Unifiers" of Japan.

In 1548, Nobuhide attacked Okazaki Castle in Mikawa Province. When the lord of the castle called upon assistance from Imagawa Yoshimoto, Nobuhide captured the lord's son, Matsudaira Motoyasu, who was just five years old. Nobuhide threatened to kill the boy, but even though he was defeated by Imagawa, he kept Motoyasu as a hostage.

In order to secure an alliance with his enemy, Saitō Dōsan, Nobuhide arranged for Dōsan's daughter, Nōhime, to be married to Nobunaga. This alliance held even when Nobuhide died unexpectedly in 1551. Even though Oda Nobunaga was Nobuhide's legitimate heir, his behavior at his father's funeral scandalized the clan. He arrived late, dressed in casual clothes, and threw incense at the altar instead of offering it properly. His lack of decorum shocked his retainers, who saw it as proof of his unfitness to lead. Many withdrew their support and turned to his younger brother, Oda Nobuyuki.

In response, Nobunaga gathered an army to put down any unrest and intimidate his enemies. Imagawa Yoshimoto, sensing weakness, laid siege to Anjō Castle, where Nobunaga's illegitimate half-brother lived. In order to save his brother's life, Nobunaga agreed to an exchange. He handed over his father's hostage, nine-year-old Matsudaira Motoyasu. Motoyasu would serve the Imagawa clan into adulthood.

Nobunaga then faced another challenge when his uncle, Oda Nobutomo, attacked part of Nobunaga's domain with support from the Owari shugo, Shiba Yoshimune. Nobunaga defeated his uncle and burned part of his castle at Kiyosu, but he left his uncle alive. In 1554, Yoshimune tipped off Nobunaga that Nobutomo was planning to have him assassinated. Nobutomo had Yoshimune executed, officially ending the Shiba shugo of Owari.

Just a few years earlier, Nobunaga had become one of the first lords of Japan to adopt a new type of weapon. In 1543, a Portuguese ship was blown off course by a typhoon and shipwrecked on Tanegashima Island.

It was the first recorded European contact with Japan. If the Europeans found the Japanese fascinating, the Japanese found the Europeans very strange indeed. They called them *nanban*, or "southern barbarians," and while they thought their looks and dress were strange, they marveled at the items they brought with them, perhaps none as much as the matchlock firearms they carried. The Japanese called them *tanegashima*.

The Portuguese soon established trade routes to Japan, and commerce on the southern islands brought not just firearms but also wealth. And with that wealth came power. The new technology, particularly the matchlock musket, was quickly copied by the Japanese. Blacksmiths began to reproduce guns, with places like Sakai, Yokkaichi, and Kunitomo becoming famous centers of gun manufacturing. The Portuguese also traded in saltpeter, which was needed to make gunpowder, as well as silks, gold, and slaves.

They also brought Christianity in the form of Catholic missionaries, the first being Saint Francis Xavier, who arrived in 1549. Xavier was a co-founder of the Society of Jesus, known as the Jesuits. He had met a Japanese man named Anjirō, who had fled his country after being accused of murder. Anjirō led Xavier to Japan and acted as a translator and guide.

The Japanese were not easily converted. They questioned how a god that created everything, including evil, could be good in nature. They were also uncomfortable with the idea that their ancestors were eternally damned to hell.

The Jesuits found success by converting southern daimyo who desired to trade with Portugal. Those daimyo then commanded their subjects to convert as well. At first, the Catholic missionaries were tolerated, but their presence represented a threat to the power structure of the nation, which was closely tied to Buddhism and Shinto beliefs.

By the early 1550s, Nobunaga had become one of the first lords in Japan to recognize the potential of firearms in warfare. Matchlock muskets became an essential part of his growing arsenal. Nobunaga quickly learned how to deploy these weapons effectively, organizing his infantry to fire in coordinated volleys so that their line of gunfire remained constant even while others reloaded.

He used this tactic in 1554 when he faced the Imagawa clan at the Battle of Muraki Castle. Nobunaga called on the assistance of his father-in-law, Saitō Dōsan, who sent one thousand samurai, which Nobunaga used to protect his domain from attacks by his rivals within the Oda clan. He then led an army of eight hundred infantrymen armed with spears and five hundred with muskets. They sailed south and then marched north to attack Imagawa forces at Muraki Castle. This Imagawa stronghold had been taken in Owari Province in clear defiance of the Oda clan's dominance.

Nobunaga knew that if he was going to secure Owari for himself, he had to evict the Imagawa. The steady gunfire frightened the defenders so much that they surrendered almost immediately, proving not just the effectiveness of the guns but also the skill of Nobunaga's military leadership. This bolstered Nobunaga's reputation, and with this victory, he stormed Kiyosu Castle, forcing his uncle to commit seppuku.

Less than two years later, Saitō Yoshitatsu raised an army and overthrew his father—Nobunaga's father-in-law and ally—Saitō Dōsan, who was killed in battle. Yoshitatsu made himself daimyo of Mino Province and ended the alliance with the Oda clan. This loss of support led to the defection of several of Nobunaga's retainers. They rose against him and supported his brother instead, Oda Nobuyuki.

Nobunaga defeated them at the Battle of Ino but pardoned the rebels and his brother, partly due to his own mother's pleas. The next year, however, Nobuyuki once again conspired to rebel against his brother. Nobunaga was told of the plot and feigned illness. When his brother and his entourage came to visit the supposedly ailing daimyo, Nobunaga had them all killed.

It was 1559, and Nobunaga had finally established himself as the uncontested ruler of Owari Province. However, he was still far from fulfilling his destiny as the unifier of Japan.

The long-time Oda enemy, Imagawa Yoshimoto, secured an alliance with the powerful Takeda and Hōjō clans in 1560. He gathered an army of somewhere between twenty-five thousand and forty thousand troops and marched toward Kyoto to take control of the

Oda Nobunaga.[6]

capital. In order to do this, he had to cross Owari. Oda Nobunaga chose to stand in his way.

Yoshimoto placed his retainer and one-time Oda hostage, Matsudaira Motoyasu, in the vanguard of his army. The Matsudaira clan joined Yoshimoto's forces, and they quickly took Marune Fortress. Nobunaga's scouts reported that Yoshimoto's army had encamped in Okehazama, just outside the city of Nagoya. Nobunaga could only field an army of about two thousand to three thousand men, and he told his advisors that only a strong offensive could make up for their inferior numbers.

The land where Yoshimoto had camped was well known to Nobunaga and his men because they had played war games there in the guise of falcon-hunting parties. Nobunaga's forces attacked the camp during a thunderstorm in the afternoon. Yoshimoto's forces were caught completely by surprise. They panicked, and many attempted to flee. Yoshimoto was roused from his tent only to discover much of his army in flight or dying. He joined the fight but was killed, and his head was taken by an Oda samurai.

At the Battle of Okehazama, Nobunaga noticed the talents of his sandal-bearer, a samurai of humble origins named Kinoshita Tōkichirō, who is known to history as Toyotomi Hideyoshi—the second great unifier of Japan.

After Yoshimoto's defeat, the Imagawa clan was greatly reduced and would soon be destroyed by its rivals. Many lords loyal to the Imagawa abandoned the clan and followed Nobunaga, including Matsudaira Motoyasu, who had once been a hostage of Nobunaga's father. Motoyasu would be known to history as Tokugawa Ieyasu—the third great unifier of Japan. Nobunaga also forged an alliance with the powerful Takeda clan.

In 1561, Saitō Yoshitatsu, Nobunaga's brother-in-law who had killed his father to become daimyo of Mino Province, died. His son, Saitō Tatsuoki, inherited the province, but he proved to be a much weaker leader than his father or grandfather. Nobunaga saw the opportunity and began a campaign to conquer Mino Province.

Nobunaga relied heavily on his retainer, Toyotomi Hideyoshi, to encourage retainers of the Saitō clan to abandon their weak leader and pledge allegiance to the Oda clan. He accomplished this primarily through diplomacy and bribery. In 1566, Hideyoshi was instructed to build Sunomata Castle on the edge of Saitō territory. It was largely prefabricated and appeared to spring up overnight. It was intimidating and surprising to the enemy.

In 1567, Nobunaga was ready to attack Inabayama Castle, the headquarters of the Saitō clan. The so-called "Mino Triumvirate"—three Saitō generals who were expected to meet Nobunaga in battle—defected and pledged loyalty to the Oda clan instead. However, Daimyo Saitō Tatsuoki was still inside the castle, which was believed to be impregnable. A plan was devised for a small band of troops to climb the rocky slope of Mount Inaba, on which the castle was built, and gain entry. Then, they would open the gates from the inside. Toyotomi Hideyoshi was selected to lead this group.

Hideyoshi succeeded. After setting fire to the castle's gunpowder stores, he opened the gates to allow Nobunaga's army to enter. Saitō Tatsuoki either escaped and went into exile or was captured and spared. Regardless, the Saitō clan and its retainers were now under Nobunaga's control.

Nobunaga revealed his wish to conquer and unify all of Japan. He renamed the castle and the nearby town Gifu in honor of the mountain where the legendary Chinese ruler Wu Wang (King Wu of Zhou) launched his campaign to unify China. In 1567 and 1568, Nobunaga sent his general Takigawa Kazumasu to pacify Ise Province. He especially wanted the head of the Kitabatake clan, Kitabatake Tomonori, who had adopted one of Nobunaga's sons, under his control. Nobunaga also consolidated his power through a marriage alliance with the Azai clan of Ōmi Province.

Then, in 1568, Nobunaga was approached by Ashikaga Yoshiaki and his retainer, Akechi Mitsuhide, to intervene in the Ashikaga shogunate in Kyoto. At the time, the Miyoshi clan effectively controlled the shogunate and had forced Yoshiaki's brother, the thirteenth shogun Ashikaga Yoshiteru, to commit suicide in 1565. Ashikaga Yoshihide was then installed as the fourteenth shogun. However, they were unable to gain control of the capital, and Yoshihide never entered Kyoto.

Nobunaga agreed to help install Yoshiaki as shogun and began his campaign to march on Kyoto. First, he faced the Rokkaku clan of southern Ōmi Province, led by Rokkaku Yoshikata. Nobunaga's forces quickly drove the Rokkaku from their castles and defeated them in battle. Nobunaga then entered Kyoto, drove out the Miyoshi who remained there, and installed Yoshiaki as the fifteenth shogun.

Nobunaga refused to take the title of kanrei or any other appointment from Yoshiaki. He asked the new shogun to call all daimyo to the capital for a banquet. The shogun's regent, Asakura Yoshikage, refused, so Nobunaga labeled him a rebel. This caused a rift between the shogun and Nobunaga. Yoshiaki began to secretly form an alliance with the Asakura clan and Azai Nagamasa, who broke his alliance with the Oda. They also enlisted help from the Rokkaku clan, the Miyoshi, and even the ikkō-ikki (armed military leagues).

The alliance drove the Oda forces back and led to the decisive Battle of Anegawa in 1570. Nobunaga joined his forces with those of Tokugawa Ieyasu and faced the Asakura-Azai alliance across the shallow Ane River. Toyotomi Hideyoshi led troops in battle for the first time. The fighting was fierce, but Nobunaga's forces prevailed and sent the enemy into retreat. Both leaders of the Azai and Asakura clans later committed seppuku, ending this brief anti-Nobunaga alliance.

Nobunaga then faced the ikkō-ikki alliances, which challenged his dream of unification. His first attempt was a failure, but he then focused on a siege of the warrior monks of Enryaku-ji on Mount Hiei. Much has been made of the burning of temples and shrines on Mount Hiei, as well as the deaths of up to four thousand monks, women, and children, whom Nobunaga was said to have ordered killed. Careful examination of the source material, along with archaeological work done at the end of the 20th century, suggests this was an exaggeration. Nobunaga's forces defeated the monks and certainly set fire to two of the largest buildings, but many of the residents of Mount Hiei had already evacuated down the mountain by the time the assault began. The death toll recorded by Jesuit priest Luís Frόis—about 1,500—is probably more accurate.

More devastating was Nobunaga's siege of Nagashima and the ikkō-ikki who controlled it. He tried to besiege the fortress on three separate occasions but was only successful on the final attempt in 1574, when his forces surrounded the stronghold and set it on fire. This resulted in the deaths of possibly tens of thousands.

The ikkō-ikki's main headquarters was the temple-fortress of Ishiyama Hongan-ji, which Nobunaga besieged from 1570 to 1580. In 1573, Nobunaga had ousted Shogun Ashikaga Yoshiaki from power. Yoshiaki, now in exile, helped supply the ikkō-ikki in Ishiyama and even raised troops to fight Nobunaga's forces near the fortress. He also requested aid from the powerful western Mōri clan.

Nobunaga changed tactics. He attacked fortresses near Ishiyama and succeeded in cutting the Mōri supply lines. By 1580, the siege had turned in Nobunaga's favor. The abbot Kōsa (Kennyo) and his sons finally surrendered the fortress, and the fighting ended. Nobunaga spared many of the defenders but burned the complex to the ground. The site would later be chosen by Toyotomi Hideyoshi for the construction of Osaka Castle.

While Nobunaga battled the ikkō-ikki, he was also contending with daimyo across Japan, wrestling for control of various provinces. His greatest foes were the Uesugi, Takeda, and Mōri clans. He gained dominance over these clans and took Iga Province in 1581. He was now at the height of his power and had become the de facto leader of Japan. He defeated the Takeda at the Battle of Tenmokuzan in 1582, which led to the death of their leader, Takeda Katsuyori.

Akechi Mitsuhide, the former bodyguard to Shogun Ashikaga Yoshiaki, had become a trusted general of Nobunaga. In 1582, he marched to Kyoto, ostensibly under Nobunaga's orders, when he decided to assassinate the warlord for reasons that remain uncertain. Nobunaga was staying at the temple of Honnō-ji in Kyoto with a few guards. Mitsuhide and his forces surrounded the temple. Seeing no other option, Oda Nobunaga, the first great unifier of Japan, committed seppuku.

Mitsuhide attempted to take power, but he was met by the Oda clan's forces under Toyotomi Hideyoshi at the Battle of Yamazaki. The night before the battle, Hideyoshi's generals, Nakamura Kazuuji and Horio Yoshiharu, sent a group of shinobi or "ninja" into Mitsuhide's camp to cause confusion and fear, robbing the enemy of sleep.

Ninjas, or shinobi, were covert agents used during the Sengoku period to gather intelligence, carry out sabotage, and spread fear among enemy troops. They came from regions like Iga and Kōga, where local warriors developed skills in stealth and irregular warfare. Unlike samurai, they operated outside the codes of battlefield honor, using disguise, infiltration, and psychological tactics. The group of shinobi sent into Mitsuhide's camp before the Battle of Yamazaki likely aimed to unsettle the soldiers, creating confusion during the night to weaken their readiness for combat.

Hideyoshi's forces defeated Mitsuhide's men, who fled the battle. Mitsuhide was killed by bandits while attempting to escape. Hideyoshi then summoned the daimyo to Kiyosu Castle to determine Nobunaga's successor. Hideyoshi was able to handpick the heir, choosing Nobunaga's infant grandson, Oda Hidenobu. A council of four generals was appointed to assist in governing.

Hideyoshi gained more power, receiving the title kampaku (chief imperial advisor) in 1585. He was at odds with Tokugawa Ieyasu, who attempted to check his growing influence. Rather than oppose him openly, Ieyasu submitted to Hideyoshi the following year, but on terms that allowed him to keep control of his eastern provinces. While other daimyo joined Hideyoshi's campaigns across Japan, Ieyasu stayed in his own domain, quietly strengthening his position.

Like Nobunaga, Hideyoshi never assumed the title of shogun. He continued his predecessor's work of unifying Japan, waging the Negoro-ji, Shikoku, Etchū (Toyama), and Kyūshū campaigns between 1585 and 1587.

Hideyoshi **banned** peasants from owning swords and began a nationwide sword hunt (*katanagatari*) in 1588. The confiscated swords were melted down to create a statue of Buddha. This effectively ended the peasant revolts.

Hideyoshi and Nobunaga's master of the tea ceremony was Sen no Rikyū, a Buddhist monk who helped develop wabi-cha, the most refined form of the tea ceremony. This practice emphasized locally made wares in place of ostentatious utensils and a focus on rustic simplicity. Rikyū became one of Hideyoshi's closest confidants. However, during one of Hideyoshi's angry outbursts, he was ordered to commit ritual suicide in 1591, possibly for political reasons.

Hideyoshi organized and launched a campaign against Korea in 1592. The invasion was initially successful, but it stalled with the arrival of Ming Chinese reinforcements. A second invasion in 1597 met with even less success.

On **September** 18th, 1598, Toyotomi Hideyoshi died, and the forces in Korea were recalled to Japan. His heir was his young son, Hideyori, but a new and decisive power would rise to finish the unification of Japan—the one-time hostage and seasoned general, Tokugawa Ieyasu.

Summary Timeline — The Sengoku Period

- 1408 CE - Death of Yoshimitsu; his son Yoshimochi becomes shogun.
- 1428 CE - Death of Yoshimochi; Ashikaga Yoshinori chosen as shogun.
- 1441 CE - Yoshinori assassinated; Ashikaga Yoshikatsu (age eight) succeeds.
- 1443 CE - The Ōnin War begins over succession disputes of the shogunate.
- 1449 CE - Yoshikatsu dies; Ashikaga Yoshimasa becomes shogun.
- 1467–1477 CE - Ōnin War devastates Kyoto and ends centralized authority; start of the Sengoku ("Warring States") period.
- 1489 CE - Death of Yoshimasa; Ashikaga power wanes as regional daimyo rise.
- 1534 CE - Birth of Oda Nobunaga, future unifier of Japan.
- 1560 CE - Battle of Okehazama: Nobunaga defeats Imagawa Yoshimoto.
- 1568 CE - Nobunaga enters Kyoto and installs Ashikaga Yoshiaki as shogun, effectively controlling the capital.
- 1573 CE - Nobunaga expels Yoshiaki; end of the Ashikaga shogunate.
- 1582 CE - Nobunaga dies at Honnō-ji; Toyotomi Hideyoshi avenges him and consolidates power.
- 1587 CE - Hideyoshi bans Christian missionaries and asserts control over Kyūshū.
- 1592–1598 CE - Hideyoshi's Korean campaigns drain resources and weaken his regime.
- 1598 CE - Death of Hideyoshi; Tokugawa Ieyasu begins consolidating power.

Chapter 7: The Peaceful Edo Period

Tokugawa Ieyasu.'

He was born Matsudaira Takechiyo, later known as Matsudaira Motoyasu. Around 1566, he changed his name to Matsudaira Ieyasu. After he had gained control of Mikawa Province, he petitioned the imperial court to recognize a new family name, "Tokugawa," after the area from which his ancestors originated. He provided proof of descent from the ancient Minamoto clan. Thus, he came to be known as Tokugawa Ieyasu. He remained an ally of Oda Nobunaga, even after the warlord accused Ieyasu's wife and eldest son of treason and had them executed in 1579.

After Nobunaga's death and the rise of Toyotomi Hideyoshi, Ieyasu was assigned lands in the Kantō region, far from Kyoto. He established his base in the small fishing village of Edo (the site of modern Tokyo). When Hideyoshi died in 1598, Ieyasu became one of the appointed guardians of Hideyoshi's young son, Toyotomi Hideyori.

Unsurprisingly, a civil war soon broke out after Hideyoshi's death. Ieyasu was the most powerful warlord in Japan and was, therefore, in an excellent position to seize power. However, he faced strong opposition from Ishida Mitsunari, a former vassal of Hideyoshi.

Mitsunari's support came from daimyo in parts of northern and southern Japan but predominantly from the west, so his army came to be called the Western Army. Ieyasu's influence was widespread, especially in central and eastern Japan, and his coalition became known as the Eastern Army.

This led to the Battle of Sekigahara on October 21st, 1600, one of the largest and most decisive battles in Japanese history. Ieyasu's forces numbered about 75,000, while Mitsunari's numbered roughly 120,000. Ieyasu gained the upper hand—once again, a decisive factor was the effective use of firearms. Mitsunari escaped the battlefield, but he was captured by villagers near Mount Ibuki and later executed in Kyoto.

This victory paved the way for a massive shift in the power structure of Japan and resulted in Tokugawa Ieyasu being named shogun in 1603 by Emperor Go-Yōzei. The Tokugawa shogunate was mutually beneficial to both the imperial court and Ieyasu. It gave Tokugawa Ieyasu the official sanction that Nobunaga and Hideyoshi had lacked, and in return, Ieyasu replenished the depleted imperial treasury.

Ieyasu was sixty years old, having outlived the other great men of his age. He used his time as shogun to consolidate and solidify his bakufu. This began the Edo period of Japanese history, which is referred to as such because Ieyasu was based in the city of Edo.

Ieyasu retired as shogun in 1605, but he remained the effective ruler of Japan until his death in 1616. His son, Tokugawa Hidetada, succeeded him as shogun, demonstrating that the new Tokugawa shogunate would be hereditary. Ieyasu focused on the construction and expansion of Edo Castle, which became the largest fortress in Japan. Edo became the de facto capital of the country, while the de jure capital remained with the imperial court in Kyoto.

Edo entered a period of rapid growth from the beginning of the 17th century to the beginning of the 18th century, rising from about 100,000 townspeople to more than 500,000 within that time. Including roughly 500,000 samurai and their households, the population likely exceeded one million, making it one of the largest cities in the world.

However, Edo was not the commercial center of Japan during the Edo period—that distinction belonged to Osaka. Kyoto remained the cultural and artistic center. The daimyo were required to live in Edo every other year under the alternate attendance system (*sankin-kōtai*), and a large number of ronin, or masterless samurai, came to live in Edo seeking employment. After the Tokugawa destroyed the Toyotomi clan in the Siege of Osaka (1614-1615), nearly 400,000 samurai across Japan found themselves without masters. The long peace that followed only increased their number, as daimyo reduced their retainers and dismissed extra warriors. Many of these ronin drifted to the cities, where they became a restless and sometimes troublesome element of urban society.

Edo was a heavily segregated city, with distinct areas for the daimyo, samurai, and the shogun's household. These were separated from areas for the merchants, who supplied them with the goods they required. There were districts for dye merchants, mat makers, cloth traders, horse-post makers, and so on. Many groups, such as ronin, homeless wanderers, theater troupes, and itinerant workers, moved through the city.

In later years, the Edo period would be viewed as a time when Japan closed itself off from the rest of the world. The term "sakoku" is often used, which means "closing the country." However, this term was not coined until the late Edo period and does not clearly represent the nuances of the more than two centuries of Tokugawa rule.

The Tokugawa were openly opposed to the spread of Christianity within the country and expelled missionaries or put them to death. Many Christian daimyo were forced to commit suicide under Tokugawa Hidetada and Tokugawa Iemitsu. Eventually, Japan shut down trade with all but one European power—the Dutch East India Company. Nagasaki became the sole port at which the Dutch and Chinese were permitted to trade with Japan. However, the Dutch and Chinese were not the only foreign powers in contact with Japan.

Japan also had extensive dealings with Korea during the Edo period. The ruler of the Joseon (Yi) dynasty was regarded as an equal to the shogun, so an amicable relationship was maintained between the two countries throughout those centuries. This was a particularly surprising reversal from the invasions of Toyotomi Hideyoshi (1592-1598), which upended much of the civil order in Korea and had ramifications on mainland China, as the invasions contributed to the fall of the Ming dynasty and the rise of the Qing.

However, Tokugawa Ieyasu and his successors took many precautions to smooth relations with Korea. In fact, one of the Tokugawa bakufu's main aims was to restore peace to a country that had been ravaged by civil war for hundreds of years. With this in mind, they limited contact with what they saw as the most disruptive powers in East Asia: the Europeans and, to a lesser extent, the Chinese.

They also developed policies limiting overseas travel and trade, called *kaikin*, or "maritime prohibitions." This was not only to secure peace within Japan but also to preserve the dominance and control of the Tokugawa shogunate. Japan was very aware of the Spanish conquest of the Philippines, which began in 1565, and sought to prevent the rise of any daimyo who might establish independent trade with a foreign power.

The Ryukyu Kingdom, a chain of islands south of Japan, had long been a tributary state of the Ming dynasty, but during the Tokugawa shogunate, the daimyo of Satsuma Domain fought a war against Ryukyu in 1609, making it a vassal state of Satsuma. This unique dual relationship allowed the Shimazu clan, who ruled Satsuma, to maintain indirect trade with China via the Ryukyu Islands. The actual economic benefits of this arrangement are debated, but the Shimazu used their control of the island kingdom to strengthen their position within the shogunate.

By avoiding direct relations with China and by severely limiting access for the Dutch, the Tokugawa bakufu ensured that Japan did not occupy an inferior position in any diplomatic relationship. This was crucial to a power structure that needed to assert itself as the final authority and avoid showing any weakness so an enemy could sow chaos.

In fact, Korea, though considered a partner of equal standing, did not interact directly with Edo but through the Sō clan of Tsushima Island, the closest Japanese territory to Korea. Unlike China and the Dutch, Japan had its own enclave in Korea, the *waegwan*, where trading took place. Likewise, Japanese merchants traveled to Ryukyu to conduct trade. The Chinese and Dutch merchants, however, were permitted to trade only at Nagasaki, though the Chinese were allowed to live in a small enclave within the city.

As a result, the expulsion of the Portuguese and the limitation of trade under the sakoku system did not lead to a shortage of imported goods. In fact, immediately following the expulsion of the Portuguese in 1639, the bakufu requested items from Ryukyu, Korea, and the Dutch in such quantities that an overabundance of imports caused a severe drop in prices, damaging merchants' profits.

One might wonder how Japan was able to purchase the imports it required, living on an island that lacked certain resources. The answer was silver. During the 16th and early 17th centuries, Japan was one of the world's leading producers of silver, with major mines at Iwami Ginzan, Ikuno, and Sado. Much of this silver entered China through trade. The Ming Chinese economy relied heavily on silver currency.

Eventually, the supply of silver declined, and in the late 17th century, Japan placed an embargo on silver exports from Nagasaki. Instead of silver, Japan increasingly traded in copper, which was of exceptionally high quality and soon made Japan one of the world's largest copper exporters. However, silver continued to be a major export from Japan through Tsushima into Korea long after the embargo was enacted. The Koreans would exchange the silver for Chinese silk, which, in turn, found its way into the wardrobes of Osaka, Edo, and Kyoto.

The traders of Tsushima used Japanese silver coins called chōgin for commerce because their purity—around 80 percent silver—was guaranteed by the bakufu. However, by 1695, due to a shortage of silver, the Tokugawa debased their coinage to 64 percent silver, which caused a significant decline in trade with Korea.

While the rest of the country suffered from inflation, the silver merchants of Tsushima faced the additional problem of a decrease in goods to sell. As a consequence, the entire domain of Tsushima, which relied almost solely on its trade with Korea for income, suffered greatly. The Sō leaders were eventually able to convince the bakufu to mint 80 percent silver coins exclusively for their use in foreign trade, not for domestic circulation, while ordinary coins continued to be debased.

Many of the restrictions on trade were passed by Ieyasu's grandson, Tokugawa Iemitsu, who became shogun at the age of twenty-one in 1623. He only truly came into power when his father, Hidetada, died in 1632. Iemitsu was known to practice the *shūdō* tradition of forming homosexual relationships with other men, a custom that was not unusual among the samurai elite. A later story claims that Iemitsu murdered one of his lovers in a bathtub, but the tale appears only in much later sources and is considered apocryphal by historians.

At this time, the imperial throne was held by Empress Meishō, who was the niece of Iemitsu. She reigned from 1629 to 1643.

In 1640, a Portuguese ship arrived in Nagasaki carrying sixty-one envoys from Macau. They had been sent to negotiate the reopening of trade. Iemitsu ordered that all 61 be executed by decapitation, and their heads displayed, as a warning against foreign encroachment.

Empress Meishō later abdicated in favor of her half-brother, Emperor Go-Kōmyō, who reigned from 1643 to 1654. Iemitsu died in 1651.

For the next two hundred years, Japan remained largely unchanged. The shogunate passed through the Tokugawa male line, sometimes from father to son or from elder to younger brother. Violence decreased, and rebellions became rare and swiftly suppressed. The shogun ruled as the ultimate authority in the country.

The Japanese government remained isolationist and conservative. Shoguns sometimes ruled by whim. The fifth Tokugawa shogun, Tsunayoshi (1680–1709), became known as the "Dog Shogun" because of his Edicts on Compassion for Living Beings (Shōrui Awaremi no Rei), which protected dogs and other animals in Edo. Yet, the role of the shogun hardly changed, and much of the governing of Japan was done through the bureaucracy of the bakufu. It was a time of peace and stability, but it was also a time of stagnation.

For nearly two hundred years, the quality of life for the average citizen remained almost completely unchanged. While turmoil rocked much of the rest of the world, it also brought progress through reforms and new types of government. Empires rose and fell, and trade routes spiderwebbed across the globe. Yet, Japan was, in many respects, untouched.

Still, it is difficult to argue that Japan remained completely unchanged. During the Edo period, the ukiyo-e art of woodblock printing and painting flourished. The dramatic arts, particularly kabuki, became immensely popular. Originally rooted in street performance, kabuki evolved into a sophisticated theatrical form that combined elaborate costumes, stylized gestures, and music to portray historical dramas and contemporary tales. Although women were banned from performing by the mid-17th century, *onnagata*—male actors playing female roles—became iconic figures in Edo's entertainment culture.

Poetry also flourished. The haiku, a highly condensed poetic form consisting of seventeen syllables, was refined under masters such as Matsuo Bashō, who elevated the form through his philosophical depth and focus on nature, travel, and transience. In the cities, playful and witty *senryū*—the satirical cousin of the haiku — circulated widely, offering commentary on daily life and human folly.

The military government of the shogunate took on more civil administrative features, especially after a series of bad harvests in the 18th century. Yet, taxes on commoners were fixed amounts and did not adjust for inflation. As a result, the financial resources of the daimyo dwindled over time.

While the shogunate tried to enact reforms to stop the migration of rural people into the cities, Japanese urban centers became among the largest in the world. During the Tokugawa shogunate, Edo was likely the most populous city in the world, with well over one million inhabitants by the early 18th century. Osaka, Kyoto, and Edo each had more than 300,000 residents at a time when only about 20 cities worldwide could make such a claim.

During the Edo period, a new nation had been formed and prospered. It was looking to expand its trade. **This** nation was the United States of America, and it was particularly interested in opening trade with the "closed country" of Japan. A whaling ship called *Manhattan* sailed out of Sag Harbor, New York, in 1843. Two years later, it rescued twenty-two shipwrecked Japanese sailors near the Bonin (Ogasawara) Islands. The ship was allowed to enter Uraga Bay, near Edo (Tokyo Bay), to return the survivors. It was the first time in more than 220 years that so many foreigners were permitted to approach Edo, yet the Americans were not allowed to land.

The Americans returned in 1846 when Commodore James Biddle entered Edo Bay with two warships, but his attempt at diplomacy was unsuccessful. Then, in 1853, US Navy Commodore Matthew Perry arrived with four warships. The Japanese called them the *kurofune*, or "Black Ships." After demonstrating the power of his cannons, Perry demanded that Japan open its ports to trade with the United States.

This marked the beginning of a new period called the Bakumatsu, which encompassed the final years of the Tokugawa shogunate. The country was split between those who desired to open Japan's borders and those who wished to remain a closed nation. At the same time, many factions sought to exploit the turmoil for their own advantage.

Despite the isolationist policies of the Tokugawa regime, Japanese scholars were able to study and apply advances in science and medicine through *rangaku*, or "Dutch learning." Through contact with Dutch traders in Dejima, Nagasaki, the Japanese learned of the Scientific and Industrial Revolutions taking place in Europe. They obtained and translated important books on a wide range of subjects. Japanese scholars kept abreast of developments in medicine, astronomy, and technology. So, while Japan was a "closed country," it was far from an ignorant one.

In 1854, the Americans returned, and under threat of force, the Tokugawa shogunate signed the Convention of Kanagawa. The shogun at the time was Tokugawa Iesada, the thirteenth Tokugawa shogun. Because the shogun was young and in poor health, the administration of government fell largely to Abe Masahiro, head of the Rōjū (Council of Elders). Abe was forced to confront the crisis of the "Black Ships."

In an effort to legitimize his decision, Abe polled the daimyo on how to respond to the Americans. The results were divided, which weakened the shogunate's authority. Yet the opinions of the Japanese mattered little in the face of Perry's overwhelming naval power. Japan simply could not match the strength of the American military at the time.

The resulting treaty, the Convention of Kanagawa, required Japan to grant peace and friendship to the United States, provide assistance to shipwrecked American sailors, and open the ports of Shimoda and Hakodate for resupply and trade.

Abe then sought to strengthen the shogunate by commissioning warships and artillery from the Netherlands. In 1855, Japan launched its first steam warship, the *Kankō Maru*. From 1854 to 1855, a series of devastating earthquakes struck Japan, including one that damaged

Shimoda, one of the newly opened ports. Many regarded these disasters as signs of divine displeasure.

In 1858, the Americans imposed a far more unequal treaty on Japan, the Harris Treaty (Treaty of Amity and Commerce), negotiated by US Consul Townsend Harris. It opened additional ports, granted extraterritorial rights to Americans, and fixed low import tariffs. Similar treaties soon followed with Britain, the Netherlands, Russia, and France.

Uncontrolled trade caused a devaluation of the Japanese currency and destabilized the economy. A political crisis followed over the succession of the shogun, resulting in twelve-year-old Tokugawa Iemochi becoming the fourteenth Tokugawa shogun in 1858. As foreigners flooded into treaty ports, violence between samurai and outsiders escalated. Efforts to revise the treaties proved unsuccessful.

Japan was once again in disarray, and a new movement of reform began, not in the palace of the shogun or the mansions of the daimyo but in the imperial court. Emperor Kōmei had ascended the throne in 1846, and during the turmoil following the arrival of the Black Ships, he began to assert a moral and political authority that had not been seen since the Kenmu Restoration of the 14th century.

The fall of the Tokugawa shogunate would lead to the restoration of imperial power through Kōmei's son, Emperor Meiji. During this transformation, Japan would move from its feudal roots to a rapidly modernizing global power. It was the dawn of a new era in the "Land of the Rising Sun."

Summary Timeline — The Edo Period

- 1600 CE - Battle of Sekigahara: Ieyasu defeats western daimyo rivals.
- 1603 CE - Tokugawa Ieyasu named shogun; foundation of the Edo (Tokugawa) shogunate.
- 1614-1615 CE - Siege of Osaka: Ieyasu crushes Toyotomi resistance, securing Tokugawa power.
- 1616 CE - Death of Tokugawa Ieyasu; Hidetada succeeds him.
- 1632 CE - Tokugawa Iemitsu assumes power and strengthens national isolation.
- 1640 CE - Spanish envoys executed at Nagasaki; foreign contact further restricted.

- 1651 CE – Death of Iemitsu; succession continues within the Tokugawa line.
- 1700s CE – Peace and prosperity foster urban growth and cultural development in Edo.
- 1843 CE – American whaling ship *Manhattan* arrives; first direct foreign contact in centuries.
- 1853 CE – Commodore Perry's "Black Ships" arrive at Edo Bay.
- 1854 CE – Treaty of Kanagawa signed with the United States, ending national isolation.
- 1867–1868 CE – Tokugawa Yoshinobu resigns; Meiji Restoration returns power to the emperor.

Chapter 8: The Meiji Transformation

The Tokugawa bakufu had proved unable to handle the pressure of the wave of foreign powers entering Japanese waters and ports in the mid-19th century. Each treaty technically required approval by the emperor, who remained the head of state, if not the leader of the government. Yet, many treaties were signed without imperial sanction or even knowledge. As the shogunate's power began to decline, imperial influence grew, though it remained limited to an advisory role.

Emperor Meiji.'

In 1862, Charles Lennox Richardson, a British merchant traveling with friends, was murdered on the Tōkaidō Road near Kawasaki when he failed to dismount upon encountering the procession of Shimazu Hisamitsu, father of the daimyo of Satsuma Domain. The attack caused an international incident that led to the Anglo-Satsuma War of 1863, during which the British navy bombarded Kagoshima. The battle ended indecisively, but the Satsuma leadership agreed to pay reparations for Richardson's death and later developed friendly ties with Britain.

In the face of such incidents, the shogunate looked increasingly to the imperial court for advice on how to weather the political, economic, and cultural crisis. The country was in dire need of strong leadership and a clear vision. Emperor Kōmei saw the crisis as an opportunity, and a flurry of communication passed between Edo and Kyoto. Eventually, Kōmei summoned Tokugawa Iemochi in 1863. The shogun led a grand procession to the capital. It was the first time in 230 years that a shogun had visited a reigning emperor.

Kōmei also issued the "order to expel the barbarians" (*jōi chokume*) in 1863. Though the bakufu had no intention of enforcing it, the edict further undermined the shogun's authority and emboldened anti-foreign samurai, leading to a series of violent attacks on foreigners and shogunate officials. The British retaliated by bombarding Shimonoseki, which was held by the Chōshū Domain, in 1864.

The Tokugawa shogunate responded by sending an army to suppress Chōshū that same year. The matter was resolved when Chōshū leaders executed or expelled the samurai responsible for the uprising. The Satsuma Domain helped mediate the peace, and no major battle took place.

In 1865, Shogun Iemochi sought military assistance and technical expertise from Napoleon III of France, leading to the dispatch of a French military mission to Japan in 1867. The mission, composed of seventeen officers and instructors from various branches of the French Army, arrived shortly before Iemochi's death in 1866 and met his successor, Tokugawa Yoshinobu. Meanwhile, Satsuma had strengthened its relationship with Britain despite their earlier conflict.

The French, therefore, looked to support and modernize the shogunate, while the British and Americans increasingly aligned themselves with the imperial cause. The stage was set for a civil war. Both sides modernized their armies and adopted Western military tactics. A coup in Chōshū brought anti-shogunate reformers to power, prompting the bakufu to launch another punitive expedition.

This time, Satsuma entered into a secret alliance with Chōshū. Although both sides had modernized their forces, the Chōshū army was better equipped and organized. The ensuing battles resulted in a decisive defeat for the shogunate. Yoshinobu managed to negotiate a ceasefire, but the Tokugawa regime had been fatally weakened. It was unable to maintain peace or assert authority.

Emperor Kōmei died in 1867, and the crown passed to his son, Emperor Meiji. Meiji, first known as Prince Mutsuhito, was born in 1852, the year before Commodore Perry sailed into Edo Bay. His mother was Nakayama Yoshiko, the daughter of Nakayama Tadayasu. Tadayasu was from the Fujiwara clan and held the title of Minister of the Left (Sadaijin), which by that time was largely ceremonial. He was a close advisor to Emperor Kōmei and became Meiji's guardian upon his birth.

Tadayasu was among the growing number of nobles who had spoken openly against the "unequal treaties" with European powers, and he passed this belief on to his grandson. The slogan of the imperialist movement was *sonnō jōi*, or "Revere the Emperor, Expel the Barbarians," a reference to Emperor Kōmei's previously ignored order. In 1867, perhaps seeing his survival at stake, Shogun Tokugawa Yoshinobu resigned from his post and handed his governing authority back to the emperor (an event known as *Taisei Hōkan*).

This was the end of the Tokugawa shogunate, but the leaders of Chōshū and Satsuma were fearful that Yoshinobu would continue to exert authority over the daimyo. So, they claimed to have obtained an imperial order to move against him. Their armies entered Kyoto, where Yoshinobu had withdrawn. Tokugawa forces soon arrived, but they were denied entry into the city.

This confrontation turned into the Battle of Toba-Fushimi in January 1868, the first battle of the Boshin War (named after the era in which it occurred, 1868–1869). This war pitted the shogunate's remaining forces, which wanted to preserve the old government, against imperial forces seeking to restore the emperor's rule and expel the foreign influences that many blamed for Japan's troubles.

Yoshinobu abandoned his army once the imperial troops raised the emperor's banner. He retreated to Edo. His adopted heir, Tokugawa Iesato, later became head of the Tokugawa family, and Yoshinobu retired to Shizuoka Prefecture, just as Tokugawa Ieyasu had done two centuries earlier.

Emperor Meiji entered Kyoto and declared his restoration and the return of imperial power. He was just fifteen years old. His rise was orchestrated by Saigō Takamori, Ōkubo Toshimichi, and Kido

Takayoshi, three samurai known as the "Three Great Nobles of the Restoration" (*Ishin no Sanketsu*) and considered the founders of modern Japan.

Saigō Takamori led the imperial forces, which were victorious in several battles and eventually surrounded Edo in 1868. The city and Edo Castle were handed over peacefully to the imperial army after negotiations between Saigō and the Tokugawa official, Katsu Kaishū. Despite small outbreaks of violence from Tokugawa loyalists, the imperialists were unquestionably victorious in the south, though resistance in the north, centered around the Aizu and Sendai Domains, continued for months.

Foreign powers remained largely neutral during the conflict. The imperial side promised to maintain foreign trade and protect foreigners in Japan, though some isolated attacks still occurred. Later in 1868, the remaining rebel forces in the north were defeated.

On October 26th, 1868, Edo was renamed Tokyo, combining the words "east" (*tō*) and "capital" (*kyō*). Tokyo became the new imperial capital. The Meiji Restoration had officially begun.

The new power in Japan was not so different from the old power. The emperor did not exercise much direct authority; instead, political power rested in an oligarchy composed of men from Satsuma, such as Saigō Takamori and Ōkubo Toshimichi, and Chōshū, including Kido Takayoshi, Itō Hirobumi, and others.

The oligarchy sought to modernize Japan through a series of sweeping reforms. Among the first was the abolition of the "four occupations" system (*Shi-nō-kō-shō*), which had divided citizens into samurai, farmers, artisans, and merchants. They also replaced the hereditary daimyo domains with non-hereditary prefectures, appointing governors (*chiji*) loyal to the central government.

A crucial element of the Meiji Restoration was the gradual abolition of the samurai class. The samurai were a massive financial burden on the new government, as many still received stipends from state revenues. These payments were a legacy of the feudal system, when warriors were supported by their lords in return for hereditary service. The Meiji government initially maintained the stipends to prevent unrest, but the cost quickly became unsustainable. To create a modern national army, the Meiji leadership introduced universal male conscription in 1873, ending the samurai's exclusive right to bear arms. Samurai were also prohibited from wearing swords in public after the Haitōrei Edict of 1876, which symbolically ended their privileged status.

While many samurai adapted to the new order, serving as bureaucrats, officers, or educators, others were discontented. A large number of these disgruntled samurai lived in Satsuma Prefecture. Although Saigō Takamori had been loyal to the Meiji government, he reluctantly became the figurehead of a major revolt against it. The imperial army defeated the Satsuma Rebellion, and Saigō committed suicide following the final battle at Shiroyama. However, he was later pardoned posthumously and remains revered as a national hero.

The Meiji **Constitution** was perhaps the greatest achievement of the Meiji Restoration. Promulgated in 1889, it established a constitutional monarchy that blended imperial authority with Western-style government institutions. The emperor was officially the head of state and the supreme commander of the armed forces, but real power lay with the Cabinet, led by a prime minister appointed by the emperor.

Japan thus became the first Asian nation with a parliamentary system, the Imperial Diet (Teikoku Gikai), which was modeled largely on the constitutional structure of the German Empire. Yet, Japan did not see itself as subservient to Western powers; rather, it viewed modernization as a means to stand equal with—and eventually surpass—the West.

A clear demonstration of Japan's new status as a world power came with the First Sino-Japanese War, which broke out in 1894. The Qing dynasty of China had also been attempting to modernize its military, but it was put to the test when Japan realized that Korea, which was still underdeveloped and unstable, posed a threat to its national security. Japan feared that Korea's weakness could invite domination by foreign powers, such as China or Russia, either of which could threaten Japanese independence.

After the Imo Incident (a mutiny of Korean soldiers protesting corruption and foreign interference) in 1882, **Chinese** troops entered Korea to restore order. This allowed China to exert greater influence in Korean political affairs. In response, Japan supported a pro-Japanese coup in 1884, known as the Gapsin Coup, which failed due to Chinese intervention. Tensions between the two nations remained high until they erupted into war in 1894, following the Donghak Peasant Rebellion in Korea, fueled by resentment toward corrupt officials and foreign encroachment. The Korean court requested Chinese military aid, which prompted Japan to send troops of its own. Although the rebellion was quickly suppressed, neither side withdrew its forces. Their standoff in Korea soon erupted into the First Sino-Japanese War.

At the outset of the war, most foreign observers expected a Chinese victory. The Qing possessed greater numbers and resources, and their Beiyang Fleet was one of the largest in Asia. However, the Imperial Japanese Navy, modeled on the British Royal Navy, and the Imperial Japanese Army, organized on the Royal Prussian Army, were far better trained, equipped, and coordinated. Japan also had a universal conscription system for men aged seventeen to forty. China was dealing with internal unrest, including rebellions in the north, which limited its ability to deploy troops effectively.

The first major engagement, the Battle of Pyongyang (September 1894), saw the Japanese surround and defeat a Chinese garrison. When China attempted to send reinforcements by sea, its fleet was decisively defeated by the Japanese at the Battle of the Yalu River. Japan then advanced into Manchuria and captured Port Arthur (Lüshun) and the Pescadores Islands, forcing China to sue for peace.

The resulting Treaty of Shimonoseki (1895) compelled China to recognize Korea as an independent nation, cede Taiwan and the Pescadores Islands to Japan, and pay a large indemnity. The victory marked a fundamental shift in the balance of power in East Asia. Japan had replaced China as the dominant regional power. China's defeat led to deep internal unrest and helped pave the way for later uprisings, including the Boxer Rebellion.

In the early 20th century, Japan engaged in another major conflict, this time with the other great imperial power in East Asia: Russia. The Russo-Japanese War (1904–1905) was fought primarily over influence in Manchuria and Korea. Japan again prevailed, though Tsar Nicholas II initially refused to surrender, fearing the humiliation of defeat. The war was finally settled by the Treaty of Portsmouth, which was mediated by US President Theodore Roosevelt, who later received the Nobel Peace Prize for his efforts.

Japan's victory solidified its position as the preeminent power in Asia and showed the world that a modern Asian nation could defeat a major European empire. Japan formally annexed Korea in 1910, further expanding its own empire. For Russia, the loss exposed deep weaknesses in the Romanov regime, sparking domestic unrest that led to the 1905

Revolution and, in the longer term, contributed to the Russian Revolution of 1917.

Japan's triumph over Russia inspired nationalist movements throughout Asia. Even in China, intellectuals saw Japan as proof that modernization could resist Western imperialism. The British were deeply impressed by Japan's naval victory at the Battle of Tsushima (1905). They often compared it to Admiral Horatio Nelson's victory at Trafalgar. They even sent a symbolic gift of a lock of Nelson's hair to Japanese Admiral Tōgō Heihachirō. Japan had shown the world that it stood as an equal among the great powers of Europe. Emboldened by its success, it sought to expand its sphere of influence across Asia.

Summary Timeline — The Meiji Transformation

- 1862 CE - British merchant Charles Lennox Richardson killed; leads to British retaliation against Satsuma.
- 1863 CE - Emperor Kōmei summons Shogun Iemochi to Kyoto for the first time in centuries; issues an order to expel foreigners; British bombard Kagoshima.
- 1864 CE - Chōshū Expedition: Tokugawa forces punish Chōshū Domain; peace brokered by Satsuma.
- 1865 CE - Shogun Iemochi seeks French military assistance.
- 1866 CE - Iemochi dies; Tokugawa Yoshinobu becomes shogun.
- 1867 CE - Emperor Kōmei dies; Yoshinobu resigns the shogunate and returns power to the emperor; Prince Mutsuhito (Emperor Meiji) ascends the throne at age fifteen.
- 1868 CE - Boshin War: Saigō's forces surround Edo; Edo Castle surrenders peacefully; northern rebels defeated. Edo renamed Tokyo and made the imperial capital. Beginning of the Meiji Restoration.
- Post-1868 reforms - Domains abolished and replaced by prefectures; samurai privileges ended; conscription law and social reorganization enacted.
- 1890 CE - Meiji Constitution completed and promulgated.
- 1894-1895 CE - First Sino-Japanese War; Japan defeats China and gains Taiwan.

- 1904-1905 CE - Russo-Japanese War, ends with Treaty of Portsmouth.
- 1910 CE - Japan annexes Korea.

Chapter 9: The Shōwa Era

Emperor Meiji died in 1912 and was succeeded by his son, Emperor Taishō, who had long shown signs of a neurological disorder. Emperor Taishō played a very small role in political affairs. After 1919, he performed no official duties. His son, Crown Prince Hirohito, became regent in 1921. Hirohito was born in 1901 while his grandfather, Meiji, was still emperor. He was a sickly child, and his education was focused on physical fitness and health.

Emperor Shōwa (Hirohito).

Hirohito was commissioned into both the Imperial Army and Navy at a young age and became regent when he was twenty years old. Around that time, he took a six-month tour of Europe and became fascinated with the West. He enjoyed European fashion and food, and the trip deeply influenced his outlook on Japan's place in the world.

While the emperor was involved in important decision-making and the nation officially revolved around him, the real power lay with the prime minister. However, the prime minister typically served a short term, sometimes less than a year. During the Meiji Restoration, Japan had adopted a European-style peerage system, and most prime ministers were viscounts or barons, though many came from humble beginnings.

Viscount Takahashi Korekiyo, who served as prime minister from 1921 to 1922 when Hirohito was regent, was the illegitimate son of a court painter. He traveled to California in the 1860s, where he worked as a laborer—some accounts even suggest he was briefly indentured—but he eventually returned to Japan. He showed great talent in finance, helping to secure funding for the Russo-Japanese War, and was later honored with the title of viscount for his service.

The first prime minister appointed by Emperor Hirohito after he ascended the throne in 1926 was Tanaka Giichi, president of the Rikken Seiyūkai political party. Tanaka ordered a series of arrests of suspected communists and pursued an aggressive military policy abroad. It was clear that nationalist elements in Japan were seeking to expand their territories. Tanaka also pushed a strategy to separate Manchuria from China, laying the groundwork for Japan's later control over the region.

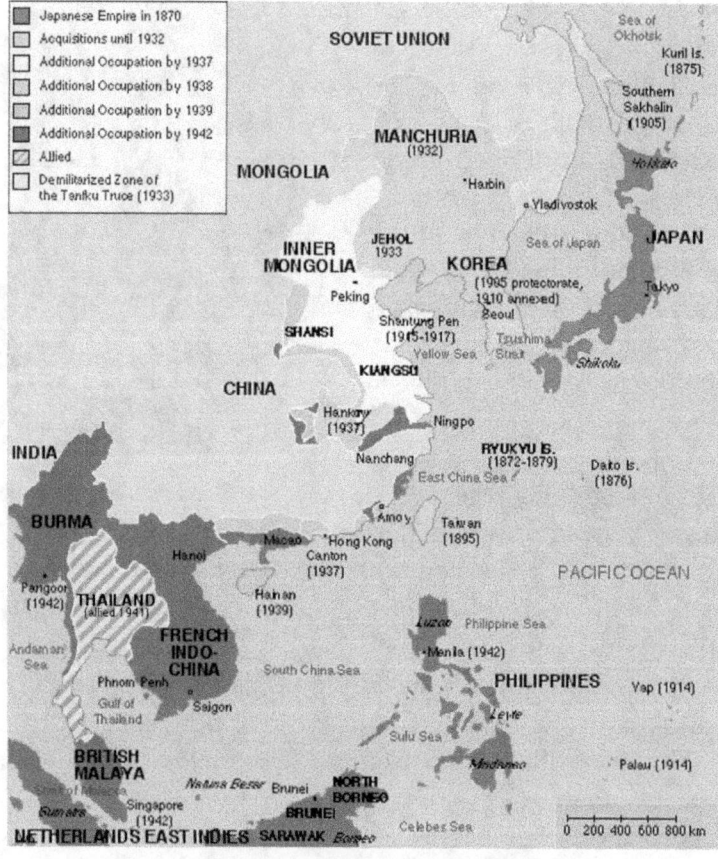

The expansion of the Japanese Empire.[10]

The Manchurian warlord Zhang Zuolin was assassinated in 1928 by junior officers in the Kwantung Army, a Japanese military force stationed in Manchuria. Although Zhang had once cooperated with Japan, he had begun to assert his independence, moving his regime southward and showing signs of reconciliation with Chiang Kai-shek's Nationalist government in China. This alarmed the Kwantung Army, which feared a loss of Japanese influence in the region.

Determined to protect Japan's strategic and economic interests in Manchuria, a group of radical officers orchestrated his assassination by bombing his train near Mukden. Prime Minister Tanaka Giichi was shocked by the incident but chose to cover up Japanese involvement, fearing political fallout and discord within the military. The failure to hold the perpetrators accountable not only undermined civilian control over the military but also drew the disapproval of Emperor Hirohito. After losing the emperor's confidence, Tanaka resigned in July 1929.

Hamaguchi Osachi was then selected to be the prime minister. Hamaguchi belonged to the Constitutional Democratic Party, or Rikken Minseitō. This party focused more on domestic economic reform than on the conquest of East Asia. Japan's economy was in serious trouble following World War I. Though Japan had been allied with the United Kingdom, fought the German Navy in the Pacific, and provided support to the Allies in Europe, the war had led to rapid inflation. The nation was facing rising debt, despite having gained former German territories in the Pacific.

The Great Kantō earthquake of 1923 had also worsened Japan's economic strain. The 7.9 magnitude earthquake caused massive destruction and loss of life in Tokyo and Yokohama. In the aftermath, rumors spread that ethnic Koreans were poisoning wells and planning attacks, which led to vigilante and police violence that killed an estimated six thousand to ten thousand Koreans in what became known as the Kantō Massacre.

The situation further deteriorated when the Great Depression struck soon after Hamaguchi took office. He responded with austerity measures, including significant reductions in military spending. However, his decision to restore the yen to the gold standard in 1930 worsened the economic crisis by making Japanese exports less competitive.

In November 1930, Hamaguchi was shot by a right-wing nationalist at Tokyo Station. Though he initially survived and was reelected while recovering, his health declined. He died of his wounds in August 1931.

He was succeeded by Wakatsuki Reijirō, who served only briefly before being replaced by Inukai Tsuyoshi. Inukai supported increased military expenditure and the expansion into Manchuria. He took Japan off the gold standard, which helped exports but further empowered the military. Despite Emperor Hirohito's requests to avoid escalation with China, Inukai reluctantly approved Japanese military operations in Manchuria following the Mukden Incident of 1931, though his control over the military was limited.

The Mukden Incident was orchestrated by officers in the Kwantung Army and involved the staged explosion of a section of the South Manchurian Railway near Mukden (modern-day Shenyang) on September 18th, 1931. Though the damage was minimal and train service quickly resumed, the army used it as a pretext to launch a full-scale invasion of Manchuria without prior approval from the civilian government in Tokyo. This marked a turning point in Japanese militarism, as the **military** increasingly operated beyond the control of elected officials.

Tensions between the **civilian** government and the armed forces rose sharply. In May 1932, Inukai was assassinated by a group of young naval officers in what became known as the May 15 Incident. His death effectively ended Japan's era of civilian leadership. Real power shifted increasingly to the military, and the prime ministers who followed were moderates who tried—but failed—to restrain Japan's growing militarism.

The culmination of the internal tensions in Japan was the February 26 Incident of 1936. A group of lower-ranking young officers from the Imperial Japanese Army conducted a coup d'état against the military and government, hoping to remove what they called the "evil" advisors around the emperor and the privileged classes they believed were ruining the nation's economy.

This group, numbering about 1,400 soldiers and roughly 100 officers, called itself the Kokutai Genri-ha, or "National Principle Faction." They were all heavily influenced by ultranationalist and **anti**-corruption ideals, and they believed they represented the working and lower classes against the entrenched elites.

Previous outbursts of political violence in which the perpetrators received light or no punishment **convinced** the Kokutai Genri-ha that, with proper organization and willpower, they could achieve the political change they desired with only a small number of men. In 1935, Lieutenant

Colonel Saburō Aizawa murdered Major General Tetsuzan Nagata, a leading member of the rival "Control Faction." Though Aizawa received the death penalty, he was hailed as a hero by many in the Imperial Way faction, which only emboldened the Kokutai Genri-ha.

During the uprising, the conspirators assassinated former Prime Minister Saitō Makoto, Finance Minister (and former Prime Minister) Takahashi Korekiyo, and Army Inspector General Watanabe Jōtarō. Prime Minister Keisuke Okada narrowly escaped death when the rebels mistakenly killed his brother-in-law. The young officers were inspired by, and in some cases aided by, senior officers aligned with the Imperial Way Faction (Kōdōha), a radical group within the army that sought to restore imperial rule by purging corrupt politicians, bureaucrats, and senior officers.

At first, it seemed that the coup might succeed, as the rebels occupied key government buildings in Tokyo. However, Emperor Hirohito was furious and personally demanded that the rebellion be crushed immediately. This gave the rival Control Faction (Tōseiha) the authority to suppress the uprising. Within a few days, the rebellion was crushed, and the conspirators were arrested. The punishments were severe. Seventeen officers and two civilian ringleaders were tried in secret and executed by firing squad. With this, the Tōseiha Faction solidified its dominance within the army. More broadly, the incident further increased the military's influence in government affairs, as civilian leaders grew even more reluctant to challenge them.

Outside Japan, the military continued its policy of expansion, despite the disapproval of most Western powers. The Japanese Empire had already clashed with China in 1932, establishing a puppet government in Manchuria called Manchukuo, and had begun a campaign to suppress any armed resistance there. Following the Mukden Incident, Japanese forces quickly overran the region, encountering only scattered Chinese opposition. In 1932, they declared the creation of Manchukuo under the nominal leadership of Puyi, the last emperor of the Qing dynasty, though real authority rested with the Japanese military and civilian administrators.

The League of Nations condemned the invasion and refused to recognize Manchukuo's legitimacy, prompting Japan to withdraw from the League in 1933. Despite international criticism, Japan expanded its occupation, waging brutal counterinsurgency operations against Chinese guerrilla fighters and local resistance movements.

In 1933, the Japanese defeated Chinese forces and gained control of Rehe (Jehol) Province in Inner Mongolia. These actions were not the result of direct orders from Tokyo but rather the independent operations of the Kwantung Army, whose ambitions often exceeded official policy. This unchecked military activity led directly to the outbreak of the Second Sino-Japanese War, known in China as the War of Resistance Against Japan.

At the same time that Japan was entering into war with the rest of China, it was also mobilizing the emigration of Japanese farmers from the homeland to Manchuria. The original goal was to settle one million emigrants, but ultimately only about 300,000 made the move. The idea of others leaving for a new land was more appealing than doing so oneself, and many emigrants were encouraged or pressured to leave Japan.

The political climate in Japan was dominated by the increasing power of the military. The prime minister in 1936, Kōki Hirota, attempted to placate the armed forces by reinstating the rule that the Army and Navy ministers had to be active-duty officers. This policy, first introduced in 1900, effectively gave the military veto power over any civilian Cabinet. Hirota condemned some of the military's actions, but he did little to restrain them.

Hirota served for less than a year and was replaced by Senjūrō Hayashi, who had previously commanded forces in Korea and played a role in the Manchurian invasion following the 1931 Mukden Incident. Hayashi failed to form a stable Cabinet and served only four months before being replaced by Prince Fumimaro Konoe. It was during Konoe's first term that the full-scale invasion of China began.

On July 7th, 1937, a skirmish broke out between Chinese and Japanese troops near the Marco Polo Bridge (also known as the Lugou Bridge) outside of Beijing. The clash began during night maneuvers between local units but quickly escalated when both sides called for reinforcements. Neither the Chinese nor the Japanese government initially intended to start a war, but the confrontation spiraled out of control. Within weeks, Japan had launched a general offensive in northern China. This incident is often considered the true beginning of World War II in Asia.

Later in July, the Battle of Beiping-Tianjin saw the National Revolutionary Army of the Republic of China face the Imperial Japanese Army. The Japanese were victorious and took Beijing soon after. Japan justified its actions by claiming it sought to form a "unified front" against

Soviet expansion and to resist Western imperialism, particularly from Britain and the United States.

Imperial Japan was openly opposed to communism, especially the growing power of the Soviet Union, and because of this, relations between Germany and Japan improved. In November 1936, they signed the Anti-Comintern Pact, an agreement directed against the Communist International (Comintern). By this time, Germany had been under Nazi control for three years. That same year, Prince Chichibu, Emperor Hirohito's younger brother, attended the 1937 Nuremberg Rally, where the Nazis declared the Japanese to be "honorary Aryans." Italy joined the pact soon after, marking the beginning of what became known as the Axis Powers.

With the outbreak of the Second Sino-Japanese War, Adolf Hitler abandoned his earlier cooperation with Chiang Kai-shek's China and declared support for Japan's campaign in East Asia, even though it meant conceding territories that had once been under German control before World War I.

In August 1937, the Battle of Shanghai began, pitting Chinese and Japanese forces in one of the bloodiest early battles of the war. The Chinese fielded around 700,000 troops, while the Japanese had about 300,000. The battle lasted until November 1937 and ended in a Japanese victory and the occupation of Shanghai. The success led to the decision to march on Nanjing (also known as Nanking), the capital of the Republic of China, which Japanese forces reached by December 1937.

What followed was the Nanjing Massacre, also called the Rape of Nanjing, in which the victorious Japanese forces committed mass rape, arson, murder, and looting over the course of six weeks. It is unclear who sanctioned the massacre—some sources refer to a "kill-all-captives order"—but the Japanese commander, Prince Asaka Yasuhiko, certainly made no attempt to stop it. Captured Chinese soldiers, as well as male civilians, were killed indiscriminately. The total number of those killed is impossible to determine, but estimates range from 40,000 to over 300,000, while cases of rape are estimated to be between 20,000 and 80,000.

The cruelty exhibited in Nanjing was not an isolated occurrence. Japanese soldiers committed numerous war crimes during the invasion of northern and central China. The exact reasons for these atrocities remain debated. Some historians point to the adoption of fascist ideology within the military, others to the dehumanization of the enemy, and still others to the brutal militarism of Japanese culture at the time. Undoubtedly, these actions were also fueled by racist attitudes toward other Asian peoples, whom Japanese propaganda depicted as inferior.

Prime Minister Fumimaro Konoe defended the campaign by claiming it was retaliation for Chinese aggression by the Republic of China and the Kuomintang Party. The Kuomintang's leader, Chiang Kai-shek, had actually proposed peace talks before the Battle of Nanjing, but Konoe rejected the offer. In later years, the Japanese government destroyed many documents related to the massacre and sought to downplay or deny the atrocities inflicted on the people of Nanjing.

The war in China continued until the Japanese army realized it could extend itself no further. In 1939, a stalemate had been reached. By that time, war had broken out in Europe, and World War II was underway. Despite Japan's alliance with Germany and its shared hostility toward communism, Germany signed a non-aggression pact with the Soviet Union in 1939—the Molotov-Ribbentrop Pact—leaving Japan diplomatically isolated.

In 1941, Japan and the Soviet Union signed a neutrality pact, while Germany prepared for its invasion of Russia. Meanwhile, Japan sought to resolve growing tensions with the United States. The US demanded that Japan withdraw from China, and in response to Japan's continued expansion, it imposed embargoes on key materials, most importantly oil.

Japanese leaders refused to abandon their conquests in China and recognized that their only access to essential raw materials—particularly oil and rubber—lay in Southeast Asia, especially the Dutch East Indies. Knowing that such an expansion would provoke war with the United States, Japan decided to launch a preemptive strike against the US Pacific Fleet.

Prime Minister Konoe resigned and was replaced by Hideki Tōjō. Konoe had attempted to negotiate a settlement with the United States, but talks stalled over Japan's continued occupation of China and Southeast Asia. Increasingly isolated within his own Cabinet and unable to restrain the military's influence, he stepped down, recognizing that he no longer had the authority to shape policy. His resignation cleared the way for the Minister of the Army, Tōjō, to assume the premiership and direct Japan more decisively toward war. Emperor Hirohito agreed to the plans for the attack, and on December 7th, 1941, the Japanese carried out a surprise assault on the naval base at Pearl Harbor in Hawaii. They simultaneously attacked Guam, the Philippines, Wake Island, and Hong Kong.

The Japanese hoped to cripple the US fleet long enough to establish their Southeast Asian empire and create defensive buffer zones. However, while the attack at Pearl Harbor was devastating, its long-term impact was limited since many of the primary targets, including three aircraft carriers, were at sea when the attack occurred. The attack on Pearl Harbor outraged the American public, who had previously been opposed to entering the war but now felt compelled to retaliate.

Japan captured Hong Kong by Christmas of 1941. In 1942, Japanese forces advanced down the Malay Peninsula and drove the British out of East Asian waters. They then attacked the Philippines and forced American forces to surrender, leaving around seventy-eight thousand American and Filipino **prisoners** of war. By February of that year, Japan had taken Singapore. They seized Burma, Java, Sumatra, and other islands that had once been part of the Dutch East Indies.

These victories, though rapid, came at the cost of overextension. By mid-1942, Japan's momentum stalled. The Battle of the Coral Sea in May halted its push toward Australia, and the Battle of Midway in June inflicted serious losses on the Imperial Japanese Navy, including four aircraft carriers. At **Milne** Bay in the fall, Australian forces repelled a Japanese landing, marking Japan's first major defeat on land. From then on, the Allies slowly pushed back against Japanese forces, island by island. The US retook the Philippines in 1944, and bombing raids on Japan itself soon followed.

Japanese forces fought with a doctrine that emphasized honor, discipline, and sacrifice. Surrender was considered shameful, both for soldiers and civilians. This mindset contributed to the ferocity of Japanese resistance, especially in the later stages of the war. Suicide attacks, including the use of **kamikaze** pilots who deliberately crashed aircraft into Allied ships, became increasingly common as defeat loomed. Civilians were often caught in the middle or mobilized for defense. By 1945, Japan was preparing for a final homeland battle.

The **government** remained divided between those seeking a negotiated peace and those insisting on continuing the war. One key obstacle was the fate of Emperor Hirohito, whom many leaders wanted to preserve as a condition for surrender.

In late July 1945, the United States and its allies issued the Potsdam Declaration, calling for Japan's unconditional surrender. It warned of "prompt and utter destruction," but it did not mention atomic weapons directly. Leaflets were dropped over Japanese cities in the following days, but there is no evidence that Hiroshima was specifically warned before the bombing.

On August 6th, the United States dropped the first atomic bomb on Hiroshima, killing tens of thousands. No surrender came. On August 8th, the Soviet Union declared war on Japan and invaded Manchuria. The very next day, the US dropped a second atomic bomb on Nagasaki. The government still hesitated, but internal divisions and the fear of total collapse pushed Emperor Hirohito to act.

On August 15th, Hirohito addressed the nation by radio. It was the first time the Japanese people had ever heard the emperor's voice. He told them the war must end, stating that continuing to fight would only bring further suffering. For many listeners, the speech was difficult to understand, both because of its formal language and the shock of hearing it at all. Still, the message was clear: Japan would surrender.

The decision to drop the atomic bombs has remained controversial. Some American officials argued it was necessary to force Japan's surrender without a costly invasion of the home islands. Others believed Japan was already on the verge of collapse and that alternatives, such as a demonstration of the bomb's power or modifying surrender terms to preserve the emperor, were not seriously explored. Critics also point to the speed with which the second bomb was used, leaving little time for Japan to respond to Hiroshima.

On the ground, the effects were catastrophic. The blasts in Hiroshima and Nagasaki killed tens of thousands instantly and left many more to suffer from burns, radiation sickness, and long-term illnesses, including cancer and genetic damage. Entire neighborhoods were flattened, and survivors—known as *hibakusha*—faced discrimination for years due to fears of contamination. Environmental effects included contaminated water, soil, and increased rates of birth defects.

After Japan surrendered, it adopted a new constitution, which was largely written under the supervision of American officials. The country was occupied by US forces led by General Douglas MacArthur. Japan was accused of committing war crimes that had resulted in the deaths of as many as fourteen million people across Asia.

One of the darkest aspects of Japan's wartime conduct was Unit 731, a covert military program based in Manchuria that conducted human experimentation under the guise of medical research. Prisoners, many of them Chinese civilians but also Koreans, Soviets, and others, were subjected to vivisection, biological weapons testing, and forced exposure to extreme conditions without anesthesia. Estimates of those killed range into the thousands.

After the war, the US quietly granted immunity to many of Unit 731's leaders in exchange for access to their research, which was seen as valuable for biological warfare. As a result, few were prosecuted, and public discussion of the unit was suppressed in both Japan and the United States for decades.

Although those involved in Unit 731 largely did not face repercussions, several high-ranking officials were convicted and executed, including Prime Minister Hideki Tōjō, former Prime Minister Kōki Hirota, General Kenji Doihara, General Heitarō Kimura, and General Akira Mutō. Emperor Hirohito was spared. Many believe this was because his symbolic role as emperor was crucial to MacArthur's plan for stabilizing Japan. Hirohito played an important part in transforming Japan from a militarist empire into a peaceful nation focused on reconstruction and economic growth.

Hirohito was compelled to publicly declare that he was not a divine being but rather a constitutional monarch representing his people, like other modern monarchs. He continued to perform ceremonial duties and appeared to accept his new role as a figurehead of peace. His personal transformation reflected that of his nation, as Japan redirected its energy from conquest to rebuilding, modernization, and prosperity.

Hirohito reigned until his death in 1989, providing stability during Japan's long postwar recovery. He met with world leaders, including US President Gerald Ford in 1975. His presence offered a sense of continuity through decades of change. By the end of his life, Japan had become a democratic and prosperous nation. It was far different from the empire he once ruled.

Summary Timeline — The Shōwa Era

- 1901 CE - Birth of Crown Prince Hirohito.
- 1912 CE - Emperor Meiji dies; Emperor Taishō succeeds.
- 1919 CE - Emperor Taishō withdraws from public duties because of illness.

- 1921 CE – Hirohito becomes regent for his ailing father.
- 1923 CE – Great Kantō earthquake and the subsequent Kantō Massacre of ethnic Koreans.
- 1928 CE – Warlord Zhang Zuolin assassinated by Kwantung Army officers in Manchuria.
- 1929 CE – Prime Minister Tanaka Giichi resigns after covering up the assassination.
- 1931 CE – Prime Minister Hamaguchi Osachi dies from wounds from an assassination attempt.
- 1932 CE – Prime Minister Inukai Tsuyoshi assassinated by young naval officers; civilian leadership collapses.
- 1932 CE – Manchukuo established as a puppet state in Manchuria.
- 1935 CE – Lieutenant Colonel Aizawa kills Major General Nagata; extremists hail him as a hero.
- 1936 CE – The February 26 Incident: attempted coup by young army officers; revolt suppressed.
- 1937 CE – Japan launches a full-scale invasion of China, beginning the Second Sino-Japanese War.
- 1940 CE – Japan joins Germany and Italy in the Tripartite Pact; Japan enters World War II.
- 1941 CE – Attack on Pearl Harbor.
- 1942 CE – Early victories across the Pacific; Japanese control extends to Southeast Asia.
- 1944 CE – US forces recapture the Philippines; Japan begins to lose the war.
- 1945 CE – Atomic bombings of Hiroshima and Nagasaki; Emperor Hirohito announces Japan's surrender; end of the war and of the empire's expansion.
- 1975 CE – Emperor Hirohito visits US President Gerald Ford, symbolizing postwar reconciliation.
- 1989 CE – Emperor Hirohito dies; end of the Shōwa era.

Chapter 10: Modern Japan

After the close of World War II, Japan seemed to be a devastated country without a future. However, by the 1960s, it had become the third-largest economy in the world after the United States and the Soviet Union. This period, from the 1950s to the mid-1970s, is often referred to as the "Japanese Miracle." It was a period of rapid change and extreme economic growth that allowed Japan to rise from the ashes of war to become an economic powerhouse.

Japan benefited from the economic boom caused by the Cold War, during which the United States funneled money into Japan to support the Korean War and to maintain a strategic buffer against Soviet influence in Asia. Because of Japan's location, it became an obvious choice to supply the US Armed Forces with the materials and equipment needed to fight in Korea.

The US occupation of Japan ended in 1952, and by then—thanks partly to government reforms and American economic stimulus—the nation was once again a global trading power. Japan's government, **specifically** the Ministry of International Trade and Industry (MITI), adopted the "Inclined Production Mode," which focused on producing key raw materials such as steel, coal, and cotton. The government also encouraged women to join the workforce, something that had previously been uncommon.

After the US withdrawal, Japan concentrated on heavy industrialization. A system known as "over-loaning," in which companies borrowed beyond their means from city banks that in turn borrowed from the Bank of

Japan, allowed the central bank to maintain control over much of the nation's economic growth. The result was the rise of large corporate conglomerates, or *keiretsu*, which thrived under relaxed anti-monopoly laws. Examples of keiretsu include Toyota, Mitsubishi, Kawasaki, Hitotsubashi Group (a major publishing house), and Sega Sammy Holdings.

During this period, Japan saw a dramatic increase in its standard of living as it completed its industrialization process. This era is often called the "Golden Sixties." The decade began with Prime Minister Hayato Ikeda announcing a plan to double Japan's economy within ten years. Ikeda strengthened the US-Japanese alliance and sought to calm the anti-US sentiment that had erupted during the 1960 **Anpo** protests, which opposed the US right to maintain military bases in Japan.

Ikeda, unlike his predecessor, adopted a stance of tolerance and patience. He held a summit with President John F. Kennedy to assure the United States that Japan would support its Cold War policies, including support for **Taiwan's** independence and non-recognition of mainland China. Kennedy had even planned to visit Tokyo, but he was assassinated before he could make the trip.

Ikeda's administration expanded Japan's social safety net and established a national pension plan. Tokyo hosted the 1964 Summer Olympics, making up for its earlier selection in 1940, which had been canceled due to Japan's invasion of China and the outbreak of World War II. These were the first Olympics held in Asia and also the debut of the Paralympic Games. They were the first Olympic Games to be telecast via satellite to other parts of the world.

Japan showcased its technological achievements during the Olympics. Toshiba's new color broadcasting system was used to record events such as judo and sumo demonstrations in color, though these broadcasts were limited to domestic audiences. These Olympic Games marked the debut of judo. Japan finished third in the medal count, behind the United States and the Soviet Union. Among the highlights was the undefeated performance of Osamu Watanabe in freestyle wrestling, who retired after winning gold and remains the only wrestler in history to finish his career without a single loss.

Ikeda's administration championed a mixed economic model featuring low interest rates and heavy investment in infrastructure and communications. It also encouraged liberal trade policies, promoting free trade with minimal restrictions on imports and exports. However, many Japanese companies resisted this approach. The media dubbed the liberalization of trade as the "second coming of the Black Ships," referencing Commodore Perry's infamous arrival in Tokyo Bay.

Ikeda served two terms. By the end of his second term, Japan's economy was growing at a remarkable rate of around 13 percent annually. His successor, Eisaku Satō, served the longest consecutive term of that era, from 1964 to 1972. Under his leadership, Japan continued its phenomenal growth. Satō supported the United States during the Vietnam War, which sparked protests at home, but overall, he was a well-liked prime minister, thanks largely to the prosperity Japan enjoyed during his time in office.

Satō, a member of the Liberal Democratic Party (LDP), was openly opposed to the communist government of the People's Republic of China and even opposed US President Nixon's visit to China in 1972. The prime minister was convinced that Japan needed nuclear weapons to safeguard against China, but the United States opposed such measures. Satō ultimately signed the Nuclear Non-Proliferation Treaty in 1970 and was awarded the Nobel Peace Prize in 1974, largely for his role in promoting Japan's "Three Non-Nuclear Principles." These principles stated that Japan would not possess nuclear weapons, not produce them, and not permit their introduction into Japanese territory.

Okinawa (the largest of the Ryukyu Islands) had been in US hands since the end of World War II. However, Satō was **able** to work out an agreement with President Nixon in which Okinawa would be returned to Japan while allowing the US to maintain military bases on the islands. The official reversion took place in 1972, the same year Satō retired as prime minister.

He was succeeded by Kakuei Tanaka, who had previously worked under Ikeda and Satō in various roles. Tanaka normalized relations with China and met with Chairman Mao Zedong in 1972. His administration expanded welfare programs and invested heavily in infrastructure. However, the country faced an economic downturn during the 1973 oil crisis. Confronted by that crisis and a scandal involving his business dealings, particularly the Lockheed bribery scandal, Tanaka resigned in 1974.

The case involved payments from the Lockheed Corporation to secure the sale of its aircraft to All Nippon Airways. The revelation came from hearings in the United States and quickly drew public outrage in Japan. Tanaka denied the accusations but was later arrested in 1976 and found guilty in 1983. However, even after stepping down, he continued to wield influence within the Liberal Democratic Party.

He was followed by Takeo Miki, who was selected by leaders of the Liberal Democratic Party for his integrity and lack of strong ties to any particular power base. Miki attempted to reform the LDP while in office, especially by trying to stamp out corruption, but he was not entirely successful. This made him unpopular within his own party, and he was forced to resign in 1976.

The Japanese economic miracle was over by this point. A series of prime ministers oversaw a period of slowed growth. What endured from this period was not just infrastructure and social welfare but also Japan's enormous influence on global popular culture. This era saw the birth of kaiju monster films—most famously *Godzilla*—as well as the rise of anime, a style of animation that began in the 1960s and continues to this day.

Nintendo, a company founded in 1889, first became publicly traded in the 1960s and entered the video game market with its Color TV-Game console in 1977. Japanese arcade games became smash hits worldwide, replacing more expensive physical toys after the oil crisis. Nintendo went on to release Donkey Kong in 1981 and Super Mario Bros. in 1985, becoming an industry giant.

Japanese writers like Yasunari Kawabata and Yukio Mishima were active during this period. Kawabata won the 1968 Nobel Prize in Literature. American troops stationed in Japan brought home artifacts, stories, and cultural influences that inspired generations of Americans to study Zen Buddhism, create Zen gardens, practice karate, and drink green tea.

In 1989, Emperor Hirohito died at the age of eighty-eight. He was posthumously given the name Emperor Shōwa. His reign lasted sixty-two years, making him one of the longest-reigning monarchs in history. He was succeeded by his son, Akihito, who was fifty-five at the time. Akihito worked tirelessly to express sorrow and apologize for the atrocities committed by Japan during World War II. He also sought to connect more directly with the Japanese people by personally visiting every prefecture. Akihito's reign, from 1989 to 2019, is called the Heisei era.

In 1989, Japan's economy had recovered from the oil crisis of the 1970s and entered a period of significant growth. The Tokyo Stock

Exchange reached record highs that year, but this was fueled by inflated real estate and stock values, creating what came to be known as the "bubble economy." In 1990, the stock market fell to half its value, and by 1992, the bubble had burst. This began the so-called "Lost Decade," which refers primarily to the 1990s, though economic stagnation continued well into the early 21st century.

In the 1990s, the Japanese economy grew by only about 1 percent annually—an alarming drop from the height of the Japanese economic miracle. This slowdown was partly caused by Japanese banks continuing to over-lend to companies that were unprofitable and financially insecure, often referred to as "zombie firms." As these firms collapsed, they dragged many banks down with them, leading to a wave of consolidation that resulted in four major national banks in Japan.

Japanese companies that had once dominated global markets were now facing serious competition from other Asian economies, especially South Korea and China. Wages stagnated, and many jobs became temporary or part-time positions without benefits.

The Liberal Democratic Party lost support after the 1988 Recruit Scandal, which involved insider trading and political corruption. Shares in Recruit Cosmos, a real estate subsidiary, had been offered to politicians, bureaucrats, and business leaders before the company went public, allowing them to profit illegally. The scandal implicated members of both major parties and eroded confidence in Japan's political system. The LDP briefly lost power in 1993 but returned the following year by helping elect Tomiichi Murayama of the Japan Socialist Party as prime minister through a coalition government.

Public trust was tested again in 1995. In January, the Great Hanshin earthquake struck the city of Kobe and surrounding areas, killing more than six thousand people and leaving hundreds of thousands homeless. The government's slow and disorganized response drew widespread criticism, as many felt the central authorities were unprepared and indifferent to the suffering of victims. Only two months later, Japan was shaken again by the Aum Shinrikyō sarin gas attacks on the Tokyo subway. Members of the religious cult Aum Shinrikyō released nerve gas during the morning rush hour, killing thirteen people and injuring thousands. The attacks exposed serious weaknesses in Japan's emergency response system and raised concerns about the growing alienation and extremism within parts of Japanese society. As a result of these events, non-governmental organizations were established to provide relief and continue to play key roles in disaster response.

It was also during the 1990s that Japan began to take cautious steps toward becoming a more active **military** power. It sent financial aid for the Gulf War in 1991, even though direct participation was restricted by Article 9 of the Japanese Constitution, which prohibits offensive military actions. Later, in 2003, Japan sent about one thousand members of the Japan Self-Defense Forces to Iraq to assist with reconstruction efforts following the Iraq War.

By 2008, Greater Tokyo had become the largest metropolitan economy in the world and the most populous metropolitan area. In 2010, Japan's population peaked at around 128 million, but it has been in **decline** since due to a persistently low birth rate. In 2011, Japan was struck by the strongest earthquake ever recorded in the country—a magnitude 9.0 quake known as the Great East Japan earthquake or the Tōhoku earthquake. This disaster triggered the Fukushima Daiichi Nuclear Disaster, the worst nuclear accident since Chernobyl in 1986.

Japan's economy did not begin to see substantial recovery until around 2018, due in large part to the **policies** of Prime Minister Shinzō Abe, a member of the LDP. His economic program, often called "Abenomics," sought to revive growth after two decades of stagnation through a combination of aggressive monetary easing, increased government spending, and structural reforms. Abe worked closely with the Bank of Japan to combat deflation by expanding the money supply and keeping interest rates near zero. His government also encouraged corporate investment, greater participation of women in the workforce, and limited immigration to address labor shortages.

Emperor Akihito abdicated in 2019, citing declining health. He was succeeded by his son, Emperor Naruhito, marking the beginning of the Reiwa era. In 2020, Shinzō Abe became the longest-serving prime minister in Japanese history. As of this writing, every prime minister has been a member of the LDP since then.

In 2021, due to the pandemic, the postponed Summer Olympics were finally held in Tokyo. In 2022, after resigning as prime minister, Shinzō Abe was assassinated while giving a campaign speech in Nara. The killer, who used an improvised firearm, claimed to have acted out of resentment toward the Unification Church (often called the "Moonies"). He said he targeted Abe because of the former prime minister's connection to the organization.

The Unification Church was founded in South Korea in 1954 by Sun Myung Moon, a self-proclaimed messiah who taught a unique interpretation of Christianity focused on spiritual "purification" and global unity. The church spread rapidly during the Cold War and established strong ties with conservative political movements in Japan, South Korea, and the United States. In Japan, it gained influence through its staunch anti-communist stance and close association with right-leaning groups within the Liberal Democratic Party.

However, the church also became notorious for its aggressive fundraising and recruitment practices. Many followers were persuaded to make enormous financial donations, often leading to bankruptcy or family hardship. Over the decades, thousands of Japanese families filed complaints claiming they had been exploited. The church was accused of using guilt-based persuasion, telling followers their ancestors' souls could only be saved by giving large monetary offerings.

After Abe's assassination, the revelation that numerous LDP politicians, including Abe himself, had accepted support or appeared at church-related events sparked outrage. It was not illegal to associate with the church, but many Japanese saw these connections as ethically troubling, given the group's history of exploiting vulnerable people. For the public, the scandal symbolized the blurred line between religion and politics in Japan and raised uncomfortable questions about how fringe organizations could influence national leaders.

Summary Timeline — Modern Japan

- 1988 CE – The Liberal Democratic Party loses support after the Recruit Scandal involving insider trading and corruption.
- 1994 CE – The LDP helps elect Socialist Prime Minister Tomiichi Murayama through a coalition government.
- 1995 CE – The Great Hanshin earthquake and Aum Shinrikyō sarin-gas attacks shake public confidence in the government.
- 2003 CE – About one thousand Self-Defense Force personnel are sent to Iraq for reconstruction assistance.
- 2008 CE – Greater Tokyo becomes the world's largest city economy.
- 2010 CE – Japan's population peaks at roughly 128 million.
- 2011 CE – The Great East Japan earthquake and Fukushima nuclear disaster devastate northeastern Japan.

- 2018 CE – Economic recovery begins under the policies of Prime Minister Shinzō Abe.
- 2019 CE – Emperor Akihito abdicates; Emperor Naruhito ascends, beginning the Reiwa era.
- 2020 CE – Shinzō Abe becomes Japan's longest-serving prime minister.
- 2021 CE – Tokyo hosts the Summer Olympics amid the pandemic.
- 2022 CE – Former Prime Minister Shinzō Abe is assassinated while campaigning.

Conclusion

Japan continues to be a place of extremes. As a nation, it has struggled with a past that is at times glorious and at others unsettling. Yet, it stands at the edge of the future, ready to embrace and create new technologies that improve and expand human understanding. Scientists from Japan regularly win international awards and contribute to global research, while archaeologists and historians continue to uncover new insights into Japan's ancient past.

Japan still holds an air of mystery for much of the Western world, even as its cultural influence is impossible to ignore. Two of the most successful intellectual properties of all time—Pokémon and Hello Kitty—are Japanese. Japan's art, design, cuisine, and technology shape global trends. Its film, literature, and animation have inspired generations.

Politically, Japan today is a stable democracy with one of the highest standards of living in the world. The country continues to grapple with a declining population and a rapidly aging society—challenges that have reshaped its economy, workforce, and family life. Despite these difficulties, Japan is the world's third-largest economy and a leader in robotics, renewable energy, and high-speed transportation. Tokyo stands as one of the most advanced cities on Earth, blending ancient shrines with neon skylines and cutting-edge technology.

Yet, this economic strength faces an unexpected challenge from its overwhelming success. Japan welcomed a record 36.9 million foreign visitors in 2024, shattering the previous high of 31.9 million set before the pandemic. The surge has continued into 2025, with visitor numbers climbing steadily month after month. What was once seen as a triumph has become a double-edged sword. Tourism spending now ranks as Japan's second-largest export industry after automobiles, pumping billions into the economy, yet the sheer weight of these numbers is transforming beloved neighborhoods and sacred sites in ways no one anticipated.

Walk through Kyoto's ancient Gion district today, and you'll find something has changed. Local residents speak of feeling like strangers in their own city, pushed to the margins by selfie-seeking crowds. The harassment of geisha and maiko (apprentice geisha) became so severe that authorities banned tourists entirely from certain backstreets. In Fujikawaguchiko, a convenience store gained such viral fame for its view of Mount Fuji that the town erected a large black screen to block the sight. They saw it as the only way to restore peace to a neighborhood overrun by photographers. These aren't isolated incidents. They're symptoms of what the Japanese call *kankō kōgai*—tourism pollution.

The Japanese government finds itself in a delicate position, celebrating record numbers while scrambling to address their consequences. Officials have allocated billions of yen to combat overtourism, funding everything from crowd-monitoring systems to initiatives that steer visitors toward less-traveled regions. Some attractions have introduced tiered pricing, with international visitors paying more than locals. Another issue is that 73 percent of overnight stays are in just five prefectures, leaving much of Japan's beauty largely undiscovered.

Japanese people view this tourism boom differently. The weak yen has made Japan remarkably affordable for foreign visitors, yet this same currency weakness makes it harder for Japanese citizens to travel abroad themselves. The money flowing in helps businesses and creates jobs, but residents in Kyoto, Tokyo, and Osaka increasingly find themselves priced out of their own neighborhoods, stuck in traffic jams of tour buses, and unable to get seats on trains they've ridden their entire lives.

The government has set an ambitious target of sixty million visitors by 2030. Whether Japan can achieve this goal while preserving what makes it special remains one of the country's most pressing questions. The very qualities that draw people to Japan—the tranquility of its temples, the orderliness of its streets, and the careful preservation of tradition—are the same qualities most threatened by their arrival.

Another threat Japan faces today is not foreign conflict but the changing climate itself. Its geographical position makes it particularly vulnerable to rising temperatures, heavier rainfall, and more frequent typhoons. These changes have affected harvests, coral reefs, and coastal communities. Japan has taken a leading role in addressing climate change and developing sustainable technologies.

The Japanese Self-Defense Forces remain among the most capable in the world, though it is constitutionally bound to act only in defense. In recent years, there have been debates about revising Article 9 of the Constitution to allow for a more active military role as global tensions rise. Yet, Japan continues to advocate for diplomacy and peace, often leading humanitarian and disaster relief efforts across Asia.

If Japanese history teaches us anything, it is never to underestimate the Japanese people. They are guided as much by intellect and innovation as by an enduring and indomitable spirit. From rebuilding after wars to thriving amidst adversity, Japan has shown the world that resilience, discipline, and imagination can turn even the harshest trials into opportunities for renewal.

In many ways, Japan embodies both the memory of its past and the promise of the future. It is a nation forever looking forward while never forgetting where it has come from.

Part 2: Japanese Folktales and Legends

An Enthralling Collection of Stories, Mythical Creatures, Heroes, and Timeless Tales

Introduction

In every corner of the world, folktales and legends have been an essential part of cultures, passed down through generations as sources of wisdom, caution, and inspiration. The history of these stories is as old as humanity itself, originating from the earliest times when people sought to explain the mysteries of the natural world, teach moral lessons, and preserve their cultural heritage.

The journey through the history of folktales and legends reveals how societies have understood and interacted with their world. From tales of the mythological gods of Greece to the trickster spirits of African folklore, these stories have shaped human history and culture, serving as mirrors that reflect the hopes, fears, and aspirations of their storytellers.

In Japan, folktales and legends hold a special place in the nation's cultural heritage. These stories are not merely entertainment; they offer insights into the Japanese way of life, values, and deep connection with nature. Two of the most significant historical texts that capture these ancient stories are the *Nihon Shoki* and the *Kojiki*.

The *Nihon Shoki*, also known as *The Chronicles of Japan*, is one of the oldest histories of Japan, completed in 720 AD. It was commissioned by the imperial court and offers a comprehensive account of Japan's early history, from the creation of the world to the eighth century. The *Nihon Shoki* is written in classical Chinese and is considered a fundamental text for understanding Japan's early myths, including the tales of the kami, or gods, and the legendary emperors.

The *Kojiki*, or *Records of Ancient Matters*, predates the *Nihon Shoki* and was completed in 712 AD. Unlike the *Nihon Shoki*, the *Kojiki* is written in a mixture of classical Chinese and phonetic Japanese. It provides a more intimate and poetic account of Japan's creation myths, the genealogy of the gods, and the deeds of early emperors. The *Kojiki* is treasured for its vivid storytelling and its preservation of the earliest forms of Japanese language and myth.

These two texts are not just historical records; they are the foundation of Japan's mythological heritage. They offer a window into the ancient world of the Japanese people, where gods walked the earth and the natural world was imbued with divine presence. Through these chronicles, the creation of the Japanese islands by the divine couple Izanagi and Izanami, the exploits of the sun goddess Amaterasu, and the heroic deeds of legendary warriors are revealed.

Apart from these ancient texts focusing on myths, many written records detail stories and folktales that carry the wisdom of the elders. These stories have been passed down through generations, capturing the essence of Japanese culture and the collective wisdom of its people. Tales of cunning animals, wise elders, and brave heroes provide moral lessons and reflect the values and beliefs that have shaped Japanese society.

As our exploration into the folktales and legends of Japan begins, we enter a realm where the lines between the natural and the supernatural blur. These stories are populated with powerful deities, brave samurai, cunning tricksters, and fearsome yokai (supernatural creatures). However, the myths and legends explored in this book are more than just stories; they are living traditions that continue to influence contemporary Japanese culture.

Chapter 1: Tales from Ancient Times

In ancient Japan, nestled between lush forests and sparkling rivers, there lay a small village. The thatched-roof houses, built from wood and straw, clustered together. Smoke curled lazily from the chimneys, mingling with the morning mist that hung low over the fields. The scent of fresh rice, harvested from the terraced paddies that hugged the hillsides, filled the air, mixing with the earthy aroma of the surrounding woods.

Children ran barefoot through the narrow dirt paths, their laughter echoing. The villagers went about their daily tasks with a sense of purpose. Farmers tended to their crops, fishermen cast their nets into the crystal-clear streams, and artisans crafted tools and pottery with practiced hands. Life here moved in rhythm with the seasons.

Beyond this serene village, the land of Japan stretched out in all directions, a mosaic of mountains, rivers, and forests. Majestic volcanoes pierced the horizon, their peaks shrouded in swirling mists, standing like silent sentinels watching over the archipelago. It was a land where the very ground seemed alive, where mountains whispered secrets to the wind and rivers sang ancient songs as they wound their way to the sea. Ancient forests, dense and teeming with life, cloaked the landscape, their leaves rustling like the soft murmur of a thousand voices. The air was thick with the scent of blooming flowers and fertile soil.

Mount Yōtei, an active stratovolcano in Hokkaido. [11]

This, however, was not always the case: scientists believe that the Japanese islands were under the sea before the Miocene. From a scientific perspective, this enchanting archipelago was born from the clashing of tectonic plates. For millions of years, the relentless forces of the Earth's crust had been at work beneath the ocean, pushing and pulling, creating massive earthquakes and volcanic eruptions. The Pacific Plate and the Philippine Sea Plate collided and subducted, forcing the seafloor to buckle and fold, giving birth to underwater mountains that eventually breached the surface. These geological processes sculpted the islands, resulting in towering peaks and expansive valleys.

However, there was another explanation for the creation of this land. The people of ancient Japan saw their world as not just the result of natural forces but as a place imbued with spirit and magic. To them, the mountains, rivers, and forests were not mere geographical features but living entities, each with its own soul and story. The volcanoes were the abodes of fiery deities, and the forests were sanctuaries for countless spirits.

The Legend of Izanagi and Izanami, the Two Creators of Japan

One such legend that talks about the birth of the Japanese islands begins with two divine figures: Izanagi and Izanami. It all started when these celestial beings stood on the stairway of heaven known as Ama-no-hashidate. Here, they gazed upon the chaotic expanse below, seeing nothing but a vast, dark, and lifeless ocean. In their hands they held a jeweled spear. They dipped the spear into the primordial waters, stirring the chaos. When they lifted the spear back out, droplets of water fell into the ocean, solidifying into land. The very first island, Onogoro-shima, had been created.

It was on this sacred island that Izanagi and Izanami decided to make their new home. They built a palace and prepared for their wedding ceremony. Central to their new abode was a majestic pillar (or another spear, according to other sources). Around this pillar, the two gods performed a ritual to consecrate their union. Izanagi and Izanami circled the pillar in opposite directions. However, as they passed each other, Izanami spoke first, breaking the sacred order.

Izanagi and Izanami, stirring the ocean with the legendary spear to create Japan. [13]

The consequences of this mistake were immediate and profound, yet they did not directly affect the two gods. Instead, the consequences fell onto their first child. Known as Hiruko, the child was born without bones.

Disheartened, they placed Hiruko in a basket and set him adrift on the sea, hoping the waters might show him mercy. Despite his tragic beginning, Hiruko would later become known as Ebisu, the patron of fishermen and one of the seven gods of good luck. He was revered for his resilience.

Undeterred, Izanagi and Izanami continued their efforts, giving birth next to the island of Awa. Yet, they were not satisfied with the result. Confused, they turned to the seven invisible gods, their parents, who revealed the reason behind their misfortunes. The gods explained that their improper performance of the marriage ritual had caused their misfortune. Determined to set things right, Izanagi and Izanami repeated the ceremony, this time ensuring that Izanagi spoke first.

With the ritual properly completed, their union flourished. Together, they created the eight principal islands of Japan: Awaji, Shikoku, Oki, Tsukushi (Kyushu), Iki, Tsushima, Sado, and Oyamato. These islands became the heart of the Japanese archipelago. But the islands were not their only progeny. Izanagi and Izanami also gave birth to a multitude of divine beings, known as kami.

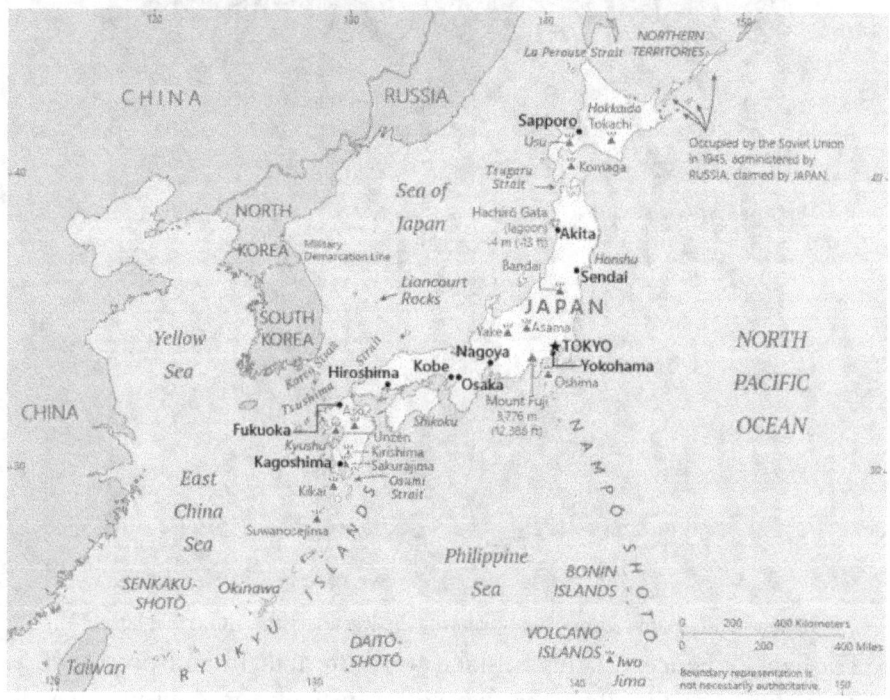

A map showing Japan's major cities and islands. [18]

The concept of kami is deeply rooted in the essence of Japanese spirituality. Kami are not just gods but also spirits that inhabit all things, both animate and inanimate. They can be the spirits of nature, ancestors, or even ideas and forces. Among the notable children of Izanagi and Izanami were Oho-wata-tsu-mi, the god of the sea; Kuku-no-shi, the god of trees; and Oho-yama-tsu-mi, the god of mountains.

These kami embodied the natural elements and forces that shaped the world. They were revered and worshiped, and their presence was felt in every corner of the land. But luck was not meant to linger around the divine couple for long. Izanami was destined to face her demise the moment she gave birth to another kami known as Kagutsuchi, the god of fire.

The birth of Kagutsuchi was a scene of both wonder and tragedy. As Izanami labored, the very air seemed to crackle with intensity. The process was excruciatingly painful, and Izanami's screams and cries filled the heavens. Her tears transformed into many more kami. Despite Izanami's agony, Kagutsuchi was successfully brought into the world, blazing with the fierce energy of a newborn god of fire. But Izanami's injuries were grievous, and she succumbed to the fatal burns inflicted during the birth.

Izanagi's reaction to his celestial wife's death was one of overwhelming rage and despair. Enraged, he unsheathed his sword and, with swift vengeance, sliced Kagutsuchi into pieces. From each fragment of the god of fire, more kami sprang forth, their forms emerging from the smoldering remains. However, Izanagi's fury quickly turned into great sadness. Unable to bear the loss of his beloved Izanami, he resolved to follow her into the underworld, known in the Japanese tongue as Yomi.

In the gloomy and foreboding realm of Yomi, Izanagi sought out Izanami, determined to bring her back. But he was too late; Izanami had already consumed food in the underworld, binding her to that desolate place. Forbidden from returning to the realm of the living, Izanami listened to Izanagi's desperate pleas and agreed to negotiate with the gods of the underworld. However, before he left, she made him promise one thing: Izanagi must be patient and not attempt to see her while she sought a way to return to the land of the living.

Time passed, but to Izanagi, it passed at an excruciatingly slow pace. His heart undoubtedly ached with longing. Unable to wait any longer, he broke his promise and lit a torch to see his beloved wife, perhaps hoping a glance at her could cure his sadness. However, what he saw filled him with horror and sorrow. Izanami's once beautiful form was now a decomposing corpse, ravaged by death. The sight of her decayed body shattered Izanagi's heart.

Enraged by his betrayal, Izanami called upon the hags of hell to pursue the fleeing Izanagi. These demons, grotesque and relentless, chased after him with fervor. As Izanagi fled, he threw seeds behind him, which grew into grapevines and other plants, entangling the hags and slowing their pursuit. Desperate to escape, Izanagi also tossed peaches, known in ancient Japan for their mystical powers, to distract and fend off his pursuers.

Finally reaching the outside world, Izanagi quickly grasped a colossal boulder and hauled it to block the entrance to Yomi, sealing it before Izanami could reach him. This, however, did not stop Izanami from cursing her husband one last time. Through the barrier, their voices echoed in the dark, final confrontation. Enraged and heartbroken, Izanami not only cursed her once beloved husband, but also vowed to claim a thousand lives each day as retribution. In response, Izanagi, with a heavy heart, declared that he would ensure 1,500 new lives were born each day. This exchange symbolized the perpetual cycle of life and death.

Yomotsu Hirasaka, believed to be a border between Yomi and the world of the living. [14]

Having sealed the entrance to the underworld, Izanagi was determined to rid himself of the impurities he had accumulated during his journey through Yomi. He traveled to the river Woto, where he prepared to perform a cleansing ritual to purify his body and soul. Standing in the clear, flowing waters, Izanagi began to wash away the taint of the underworld.

As he washed his left eye, the brilliant sun goddess Amaterasu emerged, her radiance lighting up the heavens. Next, Izanagi cleansed his right eye, and from it came Tsuki-yomi, the god of the moon, whose serene light complemented his sister's brilliance. When Izanagi washed his nose, the storm god Susanoo was born, embodying the fierce and untamed power of nature. Additionally, the god of wind, Shina-tsu-hiko, emerged from Izanagi's breath. These deities would soon become the principal gods of Shinto, central to both spiritual and cultural aspects of Japan to this day.

But the birth of gods did not end there. As Izanagi cast off his clothes, twelve more deities sprang into existence, each piece of clothing giving life to a new divine being.

Shinto

Shinto is deeply rooted in the country's history, nature, and culture. Unlike many organized religions, Shinto does not have a founder, a sacred scripture, or a fixed set of doctrines. Instead, it revolves around the worship of kami, emphasizing the relationship between humans and nature.

Shinto, which means "the way of the gods," is an animistic belief system where every element of the natural world is considered sacred. The kami are seen as manifestations of the divine essence in all things, from towering mountains and ancient trees to rivers and stones. This belief fosters a profound respect for nature and an understanding of the interconnectedness of all life.

However, Shinto beliefs extend beyond the kami. They encompass many spirits and supernatural beings that inhabit the natural world, each with its own unique traits and stories.

One such tale is of the spirit known as Yuki-onna, who is both beautiful and deadly, embodying the dual nature of winter. Believed to dwell in the remote, snow-covered mountains of Japan, Yuki-onna is often described as a tall, ethereal figure with long, flowing hair as black as a winter's night and skin as pale as freshly fallen snow. Her eyes, cold and piercing, can enchant or terrify those who meet her gaze. She drifts silently through the blizzards, her white kimono blending seamlessly with the snowy landscape, making her appear almost ghostly.

Yuki-onna's story varies across different regions of Japan, but a common theme is her dual nature—capable of both kindness and cruelty. In some tales, she is a protective spirit who watches over travelers lost in the snow, guiding them to safety or providing a peaceful death for those who are beyond saving. In others, she is a vengeful spirit who preys on those who dare to invade her frozen domain, freezing them with her icy breath or leading them astray until they succumb to the cold.

A depiction of Yuki-onna, c. 1700. [15]

One of the most well-known versions of Yuki-onna's tale involves a young woodcutter named Minokichi and his mentor, Mosaku. One bitterly cold night, as a blizzard raged outside, Minokichi and Mosaku sought shelter in a small, abandoned hut. Exhausted, they fell into a deep sleep. In the middle of the night, Minokichi awoke to see a stunningly beautiful woman, dressed in white, standing over Mosaku. Her breath froze him to death.

Terrified, Minokichi lay still, watching the woman as she turned her gaze upon him. She approached, her cold breath chilling him to the bone. Just as she was about to freeze him, she paused, captivated by his youth and beauty. She told him that she would spare his life on the condition that he never speak of what he had seen. If he broke this promise, she would return and take his life.

Years passed, and Minokichi kept his promise, never speaking of that fateful night. He eventually met and married a beautiful woman named

Oyuki, who appeared mysteriously one winter day. They lived happily together and had children, but somehow, Minokichi always felt a chill in Oyuki's presence. One night, unable to contain his secret any longer, he told Oyuki about his encounter with Yuki-onna.

As he finished his story, Oyuki's expression changed, and the warmth drained from her face. She revealed herself to be Yuki-onna, the very spirit who had spared his life years before. Angry, she shouted at Minokichi, reminding him of her promise to take his life should he ever tell the story of that fateful night. However, despite her sorrow and anger, she could not bring herself to kill him in front of their children. With tears of ice, she disappeared into the night, but not before warning Minokichi one last time, "Take care of our children or I will come after you. Without hesitation next time."

From then on, Minokichi never saw his wife again.

This tale of Yuki-onna shows the delicate balance between humans and nature in Shinto belief. It highlights the respect and reverence that must be shown to the spirits inhabiting the natural world, as well as the consequences of failing to honor these ancient bonds.

Shinto rituals and festivals, or matsuri, are vital aspects of Japanese culture, serving to honor the kami and maintain harmony with nature. Worship in Shinto is different from many other religions, focusing on rituals and offerings rather than prayer. The practice of purification, for one, is central to Shinto. Known as harae, this cleansing ritual was first performed by Izanagi upon his return from Yomi.

Harae is a fundamental practice in Shinto aimed at removing spiritual pollution, known as tsumi or kegare. Kegare encompasses impurities like death, disease, filth, and blood, while tsumi refers to wrongful actions such as crime, murder, or disrespecting elders.

Shinto does not preach an extensive set of ethics; neither does it promise a reward-based heaven or a punishment-based hell. Instead, it views nature as inherently good. Impurity is an anomaly that can be corrected or purified. For example, before interacting with a kami in rituals or prayer, it is essential to remove impurities to ensure harmony and respect. Almost all Shinto shrines feature water basins with wooden ladles for a purification ritual known as temizu. This practice involves washing first the left hand, then the right, and finally pouring water into the hands to rinse the mouth, symbolizing both internal and external purification.

Two Japanese women performing temizu.[16]

Another form of harae is misogi, which involves immersing oneself in natural bodies of water, such as the ocean or a waterfall, to cleanse and purify. Shubatsu, a purification practice using salt, is commonly observed at the beginning of a sumo match when salt is spread around the ring to ward off impurities. Additionally, there is a purification ritual involving a wand, known as the haraigushi, which is waved over a person, object, or plot of land. This ritual is often performed before construction work begins to purify the site and ensure it brings nothing but good fortune.

Shinto festivals, such as the New Year's celebration (Shogatsu), the Doll Festival (Hinamatsuri), and the Gion Matsuri in Kyoto, are occasions to honor the kami with offerings, dances, and prayers.

Shrines, the sacred spaces of Shinto, are places where the kami are enshrined and worshiped. Each shrine is dedicated to specific kami, and people visit to make offerings, participate in rituals, and seek blessings. The architecture of the shrines reflects the harmonious relationship between humans and nature, with torii gates marking the transition from the mundane to the sacred.

A torii gate.[17]

Shinto, with its deep reverence for nature and the kami, provides a unique perspective on spirituality. It emphasizes purity, respect for the natural world, and the importance of rituals in maintaining harmony. The practices and beliefs of Shinto continue to shape the cultural and spiritual landscape of Japan, reflecting a timeless connection to the divine forces that inhabit the world.

Chapter 2: Tales of the Kami

The term kami is often translated as "god" or "deity." However, these translations do not fully capture the essence of what kami truly represents. As we discussed in the previous chapter, kami in Shinto can embody a wide range of entities. Kami can be god-like figures, such as Amaterasu, the sun goddess, or Hachiman, the god of war, or natural phenomena like mountains, rain, earthquakes, and storms. Even a solitary tree can embody the spirit of a kami, symbolizing the deep connection between nature and the divine in Japanese spirituality. To put it simply, anything in this world that evokes a sense of wonder or awe can be considered a kami.

One such example of this huge reverence for nature is the sacred camphor tree in Kayashima Station. This tree has stood for over seven centuries, witnessing the long history of Japan. The train station, on the other hand, was first opened in 1910 and was originally rather small and simple. Sixty years later, the region experienced rapid population growth. Overcrowding soon became a pressing issue, and plans for an expansion were put forward in the 1970s. Of course, these plans included the removal of the ancient camphor tree.

The decision to cut down the tree was not taken lightly. It quickly sparked a large uproar among the locals in the area. Stories soon began to circulate about the anger of a certain spirit residing in the tree and the various misfortunes that befell anyone who attempted to harm it. Legend has it that a worker who cut a branch of the ancient tree almost immediately developed a high fever. Another rumor spoke of a white snake, which the Japanese often consider an omen, wrapped around the tree. Others claimed they saw smoke rising from it, as if the tree was expressing its displeasure.

Kayashima Station today, with the sacred tree in the middle. [18]

Faced with these ominous signs and growing opposition from the community, station officials reconsidered their plans. Rather than removing the tree, they decided to incorporate it into the new station's design. Construction began in 1973 and was completed in 1980. Today, the camphor tree stands proudly in the middle of Kayashima Station. It even features a small shrine at its base, allowing commuters to offer their respects as they go about their daily lives.

The Kami of Hair

In the same spirit of reverence for nature and the divine, Shinto belief extends to even the most personal aspects of human life, such as hair. The kami associated with hair, known as Kamigami, is revered for its influence over this part of the human body. Interestingly, the only shrine dedicated to this unique kami is known as Mikami Jinja and can be found in Kyoto. At this shrine, people come to pray for various hair-related issues, particularly seeking help with baldness or other hair problems. It is believed that by honoring Kamigami, they can receive blessings that improve their hair's health and vitality.

However, unlike many other kami, the background of Kamigami is not so extensive. Kamigami is rooted in the life of a man named Masayuki

Fujiwara, who lived many centuries ago. Renowned for his exceptional skills as a hairdresser, Masayuki gained fame for his ability to transform and enhance the beauty of his clients through his meticulous and artistic haircuts. His reputation spread far and wide, and he was celebrated not only for his technical skills but also for his understanding of the deeper significance of hair in Japanese culture.

After his death, Masayuki Fujiwara was venerated for his contributions to the art of hairdressing. His spirit was enshrined at Mikami Jinja, and he became the kami of hair.

The Kami of Rice

Rice has long held a place of immense importance in Japan, serving as both a staple food and a symbol of life and prosperity. From ancient times to the present day, rice cultivation has been central to Japanese society and culture. The history of rice in Japan dates back thousands of years, with evidence of its cultivation appearing around 300 BC. Rice was not just a dietary staple but also a measure of wealth and a form of currency, influencing the social and economic structures of early Japan.

The kami of rice, Inari, emerged as one of the most revered deities in Japanese folklore. Inari's significance extends beyond agriculture. In earlier Japan, Inari was also the patron of swordsmiths and merchants. The origins of Inari's worship can be traced back to the founding of the shrine at Inari Mountain in 711 AD, though some scholars suggest that the veneration of Inari began as early as the late fifth century.

One of the enduring legends associated with Inari tells of a time of great famine when Inari descended from Heaven to aid the people of Japan. Riding on a white fox, Inari brought with her sheaves of cereal grains. As she arrived, the swamps and waterlogged lands of ancient Japan began to yield a new crop, which would eventually be known as rice. This miraculous intervention alleviated the famine and cemented Inari's status as a benefactor of the Japanese people.

Inari's depictions are as diverse as the beliefs of her followers. She is often portrayed in three main forms: a young female food goddess, an old man carrying sheaves of rice, and an androgynous bodhisattva in Japanese Buddhism. This flexibility in depiction makes Inari a deeply personal and accessible deity. Inari is also closely associated with foxes, or kitsune, which are considered her messengers. These magical foxes are believed to possess shape-shifting abilities and can appear in various forms, including dragons, snakes, and even giant spiders.

One intriguing tale tells of a wicked man who was taught a lesson by Inari through her transformation into a giant spider. This form was intended to instill fear and drive home the importance of humility and respect.

The symbols associated with Inari are varied, with the fox being the most prominent. Fox statues, often adorned with red yodarekake (votive bibs), are commonly found at Inari shrines, symbolizing the foxes' role as messengers. These statues typically come in pairs, representing male and female, and hold various symbolic items in their mouths or beneath their paws, such as jewels, keys, sheaves of rice, scrolls, or fox cubs.

A statue of kitsune wearing a red yodarekake. [19]

Inari shrines are distinctive, marked by the iconic red torii gates that signify the entrance to a sacred space. These torii, along with parts of the shrine buildings, are painted a bright red, a color associated with protection against illness and misfortune in Shinto.

The head shrine of Inari, known as Fushimi Inari Taisha, is in Fushimi, Kyoto. It is the largest and most important Inari shrine in Japan, boasting approximately 10,000 torii gates that lead up to the main shrine building on Inariyama. This path of gates, known as Senbon Torii, creates a mesmerizing tunnel of red that guides worshipers on a spiritual journey up the mountain.

The thousands of torii gates at Fushimi Inari Taisha. [90]

Inari is also revered in Japanese Buddhism, where she is often depicted as female or androgynous and referred to as Dakiniten. In this form, she is represented as a bodhisattva and rides upon a flying white fox. This blending of Shinto and Buddhist traditions highlights Inari's significant role in Japanese spiritual life.

Raijin, the Kami of Thunder

Raijin is a dualistic spirit, embodying both the destructive power of storms and the life-giving rain essential for agriculture. His duality is central to his nature. While his storms can wreak havoc, they also bring the rain that nourishes crops and sustains life. This complex character makes Raijin a significant and multifaceted figure in Japanese mythology.

The story of Raijin's birth begins with Izanami, the goddess who died and descended into Yomi, the underworld. When Izanagi, her husband, ventured into Yomi to bring her back, he witnessed a horrifying scene. Izanami, now a decaying corpse, had given birth to eight thunder deities from different parts of her body. These eight thunder kami represented various types of thunder: Great-Thunder from her head, Fire-Thunder from her chest, Black-Thunder from her stomach, Blossoming-Thunder from her womb, Young-Thunder from her left hand, Earth-Thunder from her right hand, Rumbling-Thunder from her left foot, and Couchant-Thunder from her right foot. Together, these eight manifestations form Raijin, the god of thunder and storms. Izanami commanded Raijin to pursue Izanagi out of Yomi after he broke his promise not to look at her decaying form.

Raijin's appearance reflects his fearsome nature. In a country frequently beset by powerful storms, it is no wonder that Raijin is depicted as menacing. His gravity-defying and wild, spiky hair mirrors the chaos of a storm, while his fierce eyes and sharp teeth add to his intimidating presence. Often, Raijin is shown with three fingers on each hand, representing the past, present, and future. Unlike many other Japanese deities who are draped in flowing robes, Raijin is typically depicted bare-chested, emphasizing his power. His appearance is so formidable that those who are not familiar with Japanese myth have sometimes mistaken him for an oni, the fearsome ogres of Japanese folklore.

Raijin is also frequently depicted with a halo around his body, adorned with symbols from Taoism, Buddhism, and Shinto, indicating his wide-reaching influence across different spiritual traditions. This halo distinguishes him from other deities and highlights his unique role in Japanese mythology.

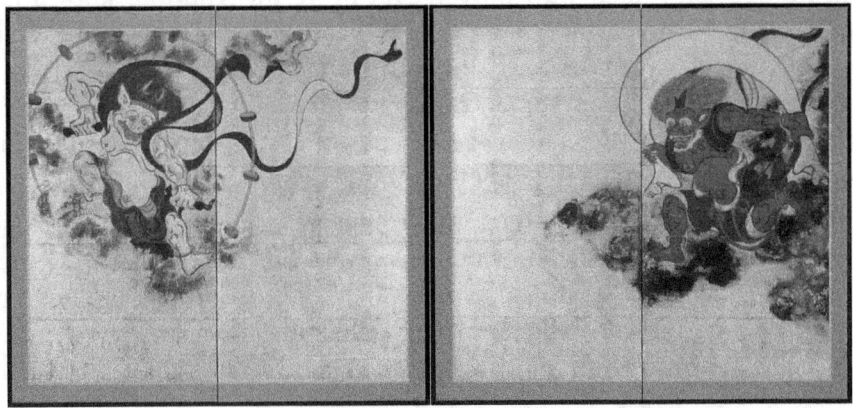

Folding screens featuring Raijin (left) and the god of wind, Fujin (right). [31]

Raijin is often shown wielding hammers and drums, instruments with which he creates thunder. His companion is usually Fujin, the wind god, who also controls the weather. Raijin is also sometimes seen with Raiju, a beast made of lightning that can take various animal forms, especially a dog or wolf. Despite his destructive potential, Raijin's ability to bring rain is crucial for agriculture. Without him, drought would devastate the land. This duality of destruction and nourishment explains why he is also considered a protector of shrines and temples. In fact, a lightning strike on a crop was historically seen as a sign of an abundant harvest, thanks to Raijin's blessings.

Raijin features prominently in numerous myths, many of which date back centuries. One particularly frightening tale warns children to cover their belly buttons during storms, lest Raijin devour them. This myth likely stems from the belief that Raijin, born from supernatural forces, envies humans born naturally and covets their belly buttons.

The most significant legend involving Raijin is his role in protecting Japan from the Mongol invasions in the thirteenth century. This story reads like a mythical fantasy. Kublai Khan, the Mongol emperor, had already conquered much of East Asia and set his sights on Japan. In November 1274, the Mongol fleet approached Japan's shores, ready to invade. However, as the fleet neared, an overnight storm suddenly struck, pushing the Mongol ships back out to sea and decimating over half of their proud forces. This unexpected storm gave the Japanese much-needed time to strengthen their defenses.

Five years later, in 1281, the Mongols attempted another invasion with an even larger fleet. But, as they approached the Japanese coast, their eyes were immediately filled with horror as a powerful typhoon, known as a kamikaze or "divine wind," swept through, destroying nearly the entire Mongol fleet. This miraculous storm was attributed to Raijin and Fujin, who were hailed as the protectors of Japan. These divine storms were seen as manifestations of the kami's intervention, saving Japan from foreign conquest and reinforcing the belief in their protective powers.

Raijin's tales are not limited to his heroic acts. In one tale, Raijin caused widespread destruction with his storms. The relentless thunder and lightning brought chaos and suffering to the land, prompting the emperor to take decisive action. The emperor called upon Sugaru, a renowned god-catcher, to imprison Raijin and restore peace.

Sugaru, known for his cunning and bravery, approached Raijin with a petition, invoking the authority of the emperor. He requested Raijin to give himself up willingly and cease the storm. Raijin, in his defiant and mischievous manner, responded with a thunderous laugh, dismissing Sugaru's plea. Undeterred by Raijin's mocking, Sugaru turned to Kannon, the bodhisattva of mercy.

Kannon, moved by the suffering caused by Raijin's storms, intervened on behalf of Sugaru. She ordered Raijin to submit to Sugaru's request. Reluctantly, Raijin obeyed Kannon's command. With Raijin now subdued, Kannon delivered him to Sugaru, who tied him up in a sack and brought him before the emperor.

Under the control of Sugaru and the emperor, Raijin was forced to cease his destructive behavior. The once chaotic storms that had plagued the land were transformed into life-giving rains. Raijin's newfound restraint brought prosperity and bounty to Japan, ensuring that his storms would nourish the crops rather than destroy them.

Raijin's tales also extend to his interactions with other deities and his influence on human affairs. For instance, in the Sanjusangendo Temple and the Taiyuin Rinnoji Temple, Raijin is honored alongside his brother Fujin. At the Kaminarimon Gate of the Sensoji Temple, Raijin and Fujin stand guard, their statues made of wood with lacquer, gold leaf, paint, and crystal inlaid eyes. These sculptures are considered national treasures and symbolize the protective power of these kami.

In the Taiyuin Rinnoji Temple, Raijin and Fujin are depicted in the Niten-mon Gate, with Raijin holding his iconic drums and Fujin his wind bag. These statues, crafted with meticulous detail, serve as reminders of the kami's presence and their role in safeguarding the temples.

Raijin's presence in Japanese mythology and religious practices highlights the complex relationship between humans and the natural world. His ability to bring both destruction and life-giving rain makes him a symbol of nature's duality, respected and revered across Japan. Through his stories and depictions, Raijin continues to embody the powerful and unpredictable forces of nature, illustrating the delicate balance between chaos and order, destruction and creation.

Amaterasu, the Most Important Kami in Shintoism

Amaterasu, the sun goddess, is the most prominent and revered kami in Shinto. She occupies a central role in both Shinto and Japanese Buddhism, symbolizing light, purity, and order. As the goddess of the sun, Amaterasu is believed to illuminate all things, providing nourishment for life to flourish and marking the passage of time from day into night.

Amaterasu, accompanied by Izanagi and Izanami on the right. [22]

In Shintoism, the sun represents order and purity, two of the most fundamental concepts of the faith. The orderly movement of the sun across the sky, from sunrise to sunset, reflects the structured and harmonious nature of the universe. Amaterasu, as the embodiment of the sun, upholds this cosmic order, ensuring that all things in creation, from the heavens down to the denizens of Jigoku (hells), follow a divine hierarchy. This sense of order is mirrored in Japanese society, where social harmony and respect for hierarchy are deeply ingrained values.

Amaterasu's primary role as the sun goddess also makes her a provider of life. Her light dispels darkness and nurtures growth in all living creatures. In this capacity, she is venerated for her life-giving energy, which sustains the natural world and humans.

In Japanese Buddhism, Amaterasu is often incorporated into the pantheon of deities, symbolizing enlightenment and the all-seeing eye of wisdom. While she maintains her identity as a Shinto goddess, her attributes are harmoniously integrated into Buddhist practices, reflecting the syncretic nature of Japanese religion.

Amaterasu is typically depicted as a radiant and majestic figure. She is often shown with long flowing hair and wearing traditional regal garments. In some depictions, she holds a mirror, symbolizing self-reflection and truth. Her divine radiance is often illustrated with a halo or rays of light emanating from her, emphasizing her role as the source of illumination and purity.

Central to the story of Amaterasu is her tumultuous relationship with her brother, Susanoo, the storm god. Susanoo's reckless and destructive behavior often brought chaos and disorder, starkly contrasting with Amaterasu's embodiment of order and light. This sibling rivalry reached a climax in a famous tale that underscores Amaterasu's significance and the impact of her withdrawal from the world.

The popular tale begins with yet another episode of Susanoo's mischief. In a fit of rage, Susanoo rampaged through the heavens, destroying rice fields, defiling Amaterasu's sacred weaving hall, and frightening her attendants. He even went so far as to hurl a flayed horse through the roof of the weaving hall, causing one of Amaterasu's weavers to die from shock.

Heartbroken and furious, Amaterasu decided to withdraw from the world. She retreated into a cave called Ama-no-Iwato, sealing the entrance with a massive boulder. As the sun goddess hid away, the world was plunged into darkness. Without her light, crops failed, cold swept across the land, and chaos ensued. The absence of the sun caused immense suffering among both the gods and humans.

Desperate to bring light back to the world, the other gods convened a council to devise a plan to lure Amaterasu out of the cave. They gathered outside the cave and performed a series of rituals to coax her out. At the heart of their efforts was a grand celebration designed to catch Amaterasu's attention and curiosity.

First, they placed a large mirror on a tree directly outside the cave's entrance. This mirror, known as Yata-no-Kagami, was meant to reflect light and symbolize Amaterasu's brilliance. Next, they hung beautiful jewels and other treasures around the area, creating a scene of dazzling beauty. Then, the goddess of mirth, Ame-no-Uzume, took center stage. She overturned a large tub and began to dance atop it, stamping her feet rhythmically and creating a powerful beat. Her dance was wild and uninhibited, filled with joyous abandon. As she danced, Ame-no-Uzume began to disrobe, causing the other gods to roar with laughter and cheer.

Amaterasu, emerging from the cave. [38]

Hearing the commotion and laughter outside, Amaterasu's curiosity was piqued. *How could the others laugh and cheer while she was absent?* Amaterasu might have thought to herself. And so, unable to resist, she peeked out from the cave to see what was happening. When she did, she was immediately captivated by the reflection of her radiant beauty in the mirror and the joyous scene before her. The other gods seized this moment. The strong deity Ame-no-Tajikarao, who had been waiting in hiding, quickly pulled away the boulder blocking the entrance, allowing Amaterasu to step out fully.

As Amaterasu emerged, her light once again bathed the world in warmth and brilliance. The darkness receded, and life began to flourish once more. To ensure that such a crisis would never occur again, the gods devised measures to keep Susanoo in check, eventually banishing him from the heavens.

This legend of Amaterasu's retreat and return from the cave highlights her importance as the sun goddess. It underscores the balance between light and dark and the harmony that must be maintained for life to thrive. Through this tale, the reverence for Amaterasu and her central role in the cosmos is beautifully illustrated, reminding all of the delicate balance that sustains the world.

Indeed, Amaterasu's significance is not confined to mythology; her role is also woven into the very fabric of Japan's imperial tradition. According to tradition, the first emperor of Japan, Emperor Jimmu, was a direct descendant of Amaterasu. This divine ancestry established the imperial family's authority and reinforced its sacred status.

The connection between Amaterasu and the imperial family is symbolized by the Imperial Regalia of Japan, which includes three sacred treasures: the sword Kusanagi no Tsurugi, the jewel Yasakani no Magatama, and the mirror Yata no Kagami. The mirror, which played a crucial role in luring Amaterasu out of the cave, is particularly significant. It symbolizes wisdom and honesty, reflecting Amaterasu's radiant purity and the sun's illuminating power.

The Grand Shrine of Ise, or Ise Jingu, is the most important shrine dedicated to Amaterasu. Located in the Mie Prefecture, it is considered the spiritual heart of Shinto and the primary place of worship for the sun goddess. The shrine complex consists of two main shrines: the Inner Shrine (Naiku), dedicated to Amaterasu, and the Outer Shrine (Geku), dedicated to Toyouke Omikami, the goddess of agriculture and industry.

Ise Grand Shrine. [24]

Ise Jingu is renowned for its unique architectural style, known as shinmei-zukuri, characterized by simplicity and natural materials. The Inner Shrine houses the sacred mirror, Yata no Kagami, which is said to have been given to the first emperor by Amaterasu herself. This mirror is enshrined in the most sacred part of the Inner Shrine, where only the highest-ranking priests and the emperor may enter.

Interestingly, the shrine is rebuilt every twenty years in a ritual known as Shikinen Sengu, a tradition that has continued for over a millennium. This practice symbolizes renewal and the impermanence of all things, reflecting the cycles of nature that Amaterasu oversees. The old shrine is dismantled, and a new one is constructed on an adjacent site using fresh materials. This process involves transferring the sacred objects to the new shrine in a solemn and elaborate ceremony.

Celebrations and rituals dedicated to Amaterasu are an integral part of Japanese culture. One of the most significant festivals is the annual New Year's celebration, during which people pray for a prosperous and healthy year. The shrine's priests offer prayers and perform rituals to honor Amaterasu and seek her blessings for the coming year.

Another important festival is the Kannamesai, held every October, a harvest festival where the first fruits of the season are offered to Amaterasu. This festival reflects the goddess's role in providing nourishment and sustenance, emphasizing the gratitude of the people for the blessings of the harvest.

The Mikagura-uta, or sacred dances, are performed at Ise Jingu and other shrines to honor Amaterasu. These dances, accompanied by traditional music, are believed to please the goddess and ensure her continued favor. The rituals and ceremonies dedicated to Amaterasu are not only acts of worship but also expressions of cultural identity, linking the people to their divine heritage and the natural world.

Chapter 3: The Samurai Spirit

It was just another normal day in ancient Japan. On one side of the village, the farmers could be seen working hard on their crops. On the other side, a lone samurai could be seen standing in a tranquil garden, practicing his swordsmanship. The morning mist clung to the ground, and the first rays of the sun reflected off the glistening blade of his katana. The samurai's movements were deliberate and precise, each swing of the sword echoing the discipline and honor that defined his very existence.

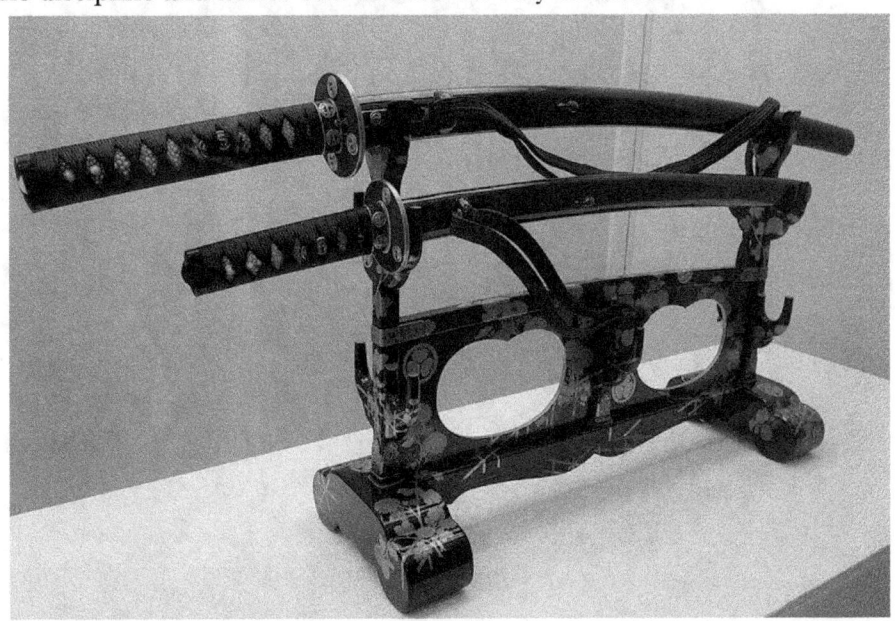

The daishō (a matching set of katana) owned by the Uesugi clan in the late Edo period. [35]

The katana, with its elegantly curved blade and razor-sharp edge, was more than just a weapon to the samurai. It was a symbol of honor, social status, and spiritual connection to the code of bushido—the way of the warrior. The samurai code was a philosophy that shaped the lives of these warriors. It required them to uphold a strict moral code, valuing loyalty to their lord and bravery in battle above all else. The samurai were expected to maintain their katana meticulously, regularly polishing and sharpening the blade to ensure it was always in perfect condition. This ritualistic care for their weapon was not just about functionality; it reflected their inner discipline and reverence for their role as warriors. The katana, often referred to as the soul of the samurai, embodied the spirit of bushido. Its gleaming surface symbolized purity and precision, while its lethal edge reminded the samurai of their duty to protect their honor and that of their master.

The origins of the samurai date back to ancient Japan, where they emerged as a distinct class of warriors during the Heian period (794-1185). The term "samurai" itself means "one who serves" and was initially used to describe the armed retainers of the nobility. The first samurai are thought to have been the bushi, or warrior aristocrats, who protected their lords' estates from bandits and rival clans. Over time, they evolved from mere protectors to the elite military class that dominated Japanese society.

Samurai in armor.[26]

The samurai played an important role in the history of Japan, serving as the military backbone of the various feudal lords and shoguns who ruled the country. They were not only warriors but also administrators and bureaucrats, ensuring the smooth functioning of their domains. The samurai went to war clad in elaborate armor, wielding their katanas with deadly precision. They fought on horseback and on foot, employing various martial techniques honed over years of rigorous training.

Central to the samurai's identity was their adherence to the shogunate, the military government that ruled Japan from the late twelfth century until the mid-nineteenth century. The shogunate was led by the shogun, a powerful military leader who commanded the loyalty of the samurai. In return for their service, the samurai were granted land and status, solidifying their position in the social hierarchy.

Of course, honor was paramount in samurai culture, and the ultimate expression of this was the practice of seppuku, or harakiri. This ritual suicide was performed to restore honor to a disgraced samurai or demonstrate loyalty to his lord. Seppuku involved the samurai disemboweling himself with his own sword, often followed by decapitation by a trusted assistant.

A samurai was indeed highly respected by the Japanese—pretty much like how the Europeans held their knights in high regard. To become a samurai was not at all easy. Their journey was rather perilous and teeming with formidable enemies left and right.

Miyamoto Musashi was one of Japan's most revered samurai whose story reverberated through the ages.

The Tale of Miyamoto Musashi

Miyamoto Musashi was a master swordsman and a figure of intense intrigue. It was not uncommon for samurai to adopt different names throughout their lives, reflecting their evolving status and identity. Musashi himself was initially known as Bennosuke. However, as he matured and his reputation grew, he came to be formally known as Miyamoto Musashi Genshin. The name "Miyamoto" is believed to reference the village where he was born, adding a layer of mystery and reverence to his persona.

The early life of Musashi is debated. Various theories suggest he was born in either the provinces of Harima or Mimasaka between 1582 and 1584. The question of whether Musashi's biological father was a samurai adds another layer of mystery to his origins. Despite these uncertainties, what is clear is that Musashi was adopted and displayed exceptional talent from a young age. His adoptive father, Shinmen Munisai, was a brave warrior in his own right and took it upon himself to train young Musashi in the ways of the sword.

Musashi's relationship with Munisai was tumultuous, marked by frequent arguments and clashes of will. The intensity of their conflicts grew over the years, and eventually, Musashi was cast out. This expulsion could have broken a lesser spirit, but Musashi was resolute. Determined to prove his worth, he went on a journey that would define his legacy. Musashi's first significant test of his skills came in the form of a duel at the tender age of thirteen. He challenged Arima Kihei, a samurai of the Shinto Ryu sword school. Kihei was known for his arrogance and eagerness to battle, though he was not particularly skilled. Despite this, challenging a samurai was a bold move, especially for someone as young as Musashi.

The duel was nearly called off due to Musashi's youth, but his determination could not be swayed. On the day of the duel, Musashi charged at Kihei with a fierce resolve that belied his years. Armed with a long staff, he deftly deflected Kihei's blade, knocking him to the ground. Musashi continued his assault, pummeling Kihei's head repeatedly—fourteen to fifteen times—until the ground was stained with blood and Kihei lay lifeless.

This brutal victory was a defining moment for Musashi, showcasing not only his raw talent but also his almost-divine spirit. This was only the beginning of a journey in which he would rise to legendary status, embodying the very essence of the samurai code.

From this moment onward, Musashi embarked on musha shugyō, a samurai's pilgrimage in which the warrior wandered across the land, practicing and honing his skills without the protection of his family or school. This journey, akin to the Chinese Youxia or European knight-errantry, was not only a test of skill but a way to earn a reputation. During these early years until 1600, Musashi was said to have fought and bested numerous opponents, each duel adding to his growing legend. At the age of sixteen, Musashi reunited with his adoptive father.

There is a popular belief that Musashi participated in the Great Battle of Sekigahara, a pivotal conflict that shaped Japan's future. While this remains speculative, during this period, Musashi and Munisai served a Daimyo aligned with Tokugawa Ieyasu, the first shogun of the Tokugawa shogunate. They fought in the eastern army's campaigns on Kyushu Island, providing Musashi with his first real taste of war.

As the Sekigahara conflict ended, Musashi turned his focus back to his swordsmanship. He traveled to Kyoto, where he sought out and challenged many of Japan's most skilled swordsmen. It was during this time, at the age of twenty-one, that he engaged in his famous duels against the Yoshioka school of swordsmanship, the official sword school for the shogun.

The confrontations with the Yoshioka school were defining moments in Musashi's life. He first defeated Seijuro Yoshioka, the head of the school, in a highly anticipated duel. Not long after, he faced Seijuro's younger brother, Denshichiro, and emerged victorious once again. The Yoshioka school, humiliated and desperate for revenge, laid an ambush for Musashi. Undeterred, Musashi faced the ambush with remarkable skill and composure, defeating a significant number of attackers. This series of victories marked the downfall of the Yoshioka house and solidified Musashi's legendary status.

In 1605, Musashi established his own sword school, initially named Enmei-ryu. Around this time, he also began writing one of his earliest works on swordsmanship, the Heidokyo, which he would continue to refine throughout his twenties. This period was characterized by intense learning and teaching, during which Musashi's techniques and philosophies began to spread, leaving a lasting impact on the martial traditions of Japan.

Musashi's journey across Japan did not end there; he continued to traverse the land, engaging in numerous legendary duels that further cemented his reputation. Among his most notable opponents were the Hozoin temple warrior monks, renowned for their mastery of Sojutsu (spear technique). The monks of Hozoin were formidable adversaries, their skills honed through rigorous training and spiritual discipline. Musashi's encounters with these monks were tests of his adaptability and ingenuity.

Another significant duel was against Muso Gonnosuke, the founder of Jojutsu Shindo Muso Ryu (staff techniques). Gonnosuke, a master of the bo staff, was said to be one of the few who managed to challenge Musashi and survive. According to legend, after an initial defeat, Gonnosuke developed a shorter staff technique, allowing for greater maneuverability and versatility.

Musashi also faced Shishido Baiken, a specialist in the kusarigama, a weapon consisting of a sickle attached to a chain with a heavy iron weight at the end. This weapon required a unique blend of offensive and defensive techniques, combining the reach of the chain with the lethality of the sickle. Musashi's victory over Baiken further demonstrated his unparalleled skill as a swordsman.

Despite the diversity of his opponents and the challenges they posed, Musashi never lost a duel. Each victory added to his growing legend and solidified his status as one of the greatest swordsmen of his time.

Among Musashi's many duels, the most legendary was his confrontation with Sasaki Kojiro, which took place on Ganryū-jima, an island between Honshū and Kyūshū, sometime around 1612. Sasaki Kojiro, also known as Demon of the Western Provinces, was the founder of the Ganryu school and a samurai of immense skill and renown. Known for his use of the nodachi, an extra-long sword, Kojiro's techniques and prowess were feared and respected throughout Japan. Unlike Musashi, who developed his own style through practical experience, Kojiro followed a long and prestigious lineage. He studied under Master Toda Seigen of the Chujo Ryu school and Kenemaki Jisai—a disciple of the famous sword master Itto Itosai, the founder of the Itto Ryu school, one of the most important swordsmanship styles in history. To put it simply, Kojiro was a challenging rival.

The duel between Musashi and Kojiro is undeniably one of the most famous in Japanese history. First, Musashi deliberately arrived late to unsettle his opponent. He kept Kojiro waiting on the beach for two hours past the appointed time. When Musashi finally arrived, he appeared calm and confident, carrying a wooden bokken he had fashioned from an oar during his boat ride to the island. This bokken was longer than a typical wooden sword, designed specifically to counter Kojiro's nodachi.

The duel began immediately upon Musashi's arrival. With intense focus, Musashi moved to strike in a single, decisive motion. He was well aware of Kojiro's preference for using the long reach of his sword to his advantage. Musashi's longer bokken allowed him to maintain distance while delivering a powerful blow. As Kojiro swung his nodachi, Musashi deflected the attack and struck Kojiro with precision, stunning him. Kojiro also landed a glancing blow on Musashi's forehead, but unfortunately for Kojiro, the strike was not fatal.

A depiction of the duel between Musashi (left) and Kojiro (right). [27]

The fight was quick and intense. After the initial exchange, Kojiro attempted a final, desperate strike from the ground, aiming at Musashi's legs. Musashi, anticipating the move, leaped to avoid the attack and delivered a fatal blow to Kojiro's hips, ending the duel. Kojiro's death marked the conclusion of one of the most storied encounters in samurai history, further immortalizing Musashi's legend.

The duel against Kojiro deeply affected Musashi. As he reflected on his victories, he was troubled by questions. Why had he won so many duels? Was it his physical strength? The weakness of his opponents? Or was it the will of the gods? These thoughts haunted him, driving him to spend the rest of his life searching for answers. This quest led him to refine his techniques into a style he called Niten Ichi Ryu, dedicating himself to passing on his knowledge to future generations.

Musashi's journey did not stop with swordsmanship; he explored the arts with the same dedication. He practiced Zen painting, creating minimalist and evocative artworks that mirrored his inner philosophy. He also took up sculpture, poetry, and architecture, finding solace and expression in these pursuits.

While he continued to fight in wars and accept duels, Musashi's focus shifted to teaching and developing his combat philosophy. He wrote extensively, aiming to share his insights with the world. In his later years, Musashi retreated to a cave, living as a hermit while pondering the deeper meanings of swordsmanship. It was in this solitude that he wrote his most famous work, the *Gorin no Sho* (*The Book of Five Rings*). This book, detailing his strategies and martial arts philosophy, became a cornerstone of his legacy.

Musashi never married but adopted two sons who went on to serve significant feudal lords. He died in 1645, but his legacy lived on. The *Gorin no Sho* and his life story cemented his status as a kensei, a "sword saint," a title reserved for warriors of legendary skill. Musashi's teachings and philosophy have inspired countless martial artists worldwide, making him one of history's greatest swordsmen.

The Revenge of the 47 Ronin

The Edo period, spanning from 1603 to 1868, is often heralded as a period of peace in Japan. Under the rule of the Tokugawa shogunate, Japan experienced unprecedented stability and prosperity. While many might imagine samurai during this era as constantly preparing for war, clad in armor with their katanas brandished, the reality was quite different.

With the absence of warfare, the life of a samurai shifted toward intellectual pursuits—chiefly poetry, calligraphy, and other arts. Although martial arts like Kenjutsu (swordsmanship) were still practiced, they became more ritualized, focusing less on combat and more on the preservation of tradition. Samurai transitioned into roles within administration and bureaucracy, living as civil servants dedicated to serving their feudal lords and, by extension, the shogun.

In April 1701, Edo Castle was abuzz with activity in preparation for a significant event. The rituals and protocols of the Edo period were taken very seriously, with intricate etiquette governing every aspect of ceremonial life. The event in question was a farewell ceremony for the emperor's representatives who had been staying at the castle. Kira Yoshinaka, a kōke, or master of ceremonies, was at the center of these preparations. Known for his strict adherence to protocol and his influential position, Kira's role was to ensure that all aspects of the ceremony were conducted flawlessly.

Among those involved in the ceremony was a young daimyo named Asano Naganori. Asano was tasked with receiving instructions from Kira on the necessary court etiquette. However, tensions quickly arose between them. Various accounts suggest different reasons for this animosity: some claimed Kira was displeased with the insufficient presents Asano offered, while others believed Kira's natural arrogance and corruption clashed with Asano's devoutly moral and Confucian principles. Asano, struggling to maintain his composure amidst Kira's insults, finally reached his breaking point.

Asano waited for Kira in the main corridor of the castle. When Kira appeared, Asano, unable to contain his rage any longer, slashed at him with his wakizashi (a short sword worn by samurai). Although Asano's first strike wounded Kira, his second strike missed, hitting a pillar instead. The commotion quickly attracted the castle guards, who secured Kira and restrained the enraged Asano.

A depiction of Asano's assault on Kira Yoshinaka. [38]

Attacking a shogunate official, especially within the shogun's residence, was a grave offense. Drawing a weapon inside Edo Castle was strictly forbidden, and samurai were only allowed to carry their wakizashi within the castle grounds. Additionally, shedding blood in the presence of the shogun and the emperor violated the Shinto belief in purity. Asano's actions were met with swift punishment: he was ordered to commit seppuku that very day. The shogun also stripped Asano's family of their lands and wealth, reducing his samurai retainers to ronin—masterless samurai.

To be a ronin was to live in disgrace, often viewed by society with suspicion and disdain. Unlike samurai, who had a lord to serve and a stable place in the social hierarchy, ronin wandered without purpose, often struggling to survive. This fate befell Asano retainers, but among them, forty-seven chose a path of vengeance.

Led by Oishi Yoshio, the forty-seven ronin plotted to kill Kira Yoshinaka. They knew Kira would be expecting retaliation, so they bided their time, waiting until he let his guard down. For two years, they lived as if they had abandoned their grudge. Oishi, to convince everyone of his supposed resignation, took to heavy drinking and public displays of debauchery. Their patience paid off, as Kira eventually relaxed his defenses.

In December 1702, the forty-seven ronin gathered at a secret location and finalized their plan. They vowed to avenge their master, making it clear that their mission was an act of katakiuchi (revenge). Oishi instructed his men to avoid harming women, children, and the helpless. Their goal was to kill Kira and place his severed head on Asano's tomb before surrendering themselves to face their fate.

Then, on a cold December night, the forty-six ronin (one was sent on another mission) stormed Kira's residence. One climbed onto the roof to loudly announce their intentions, ensuring that the public knew they were not robbers or murderers but masterless samurai seeking revenge. Many of those who despised Kira silently cheered and did nothing to impede the ronin.

Kira, hearing the commotion, attempted to flee and hide with his wife and female servants. His retainers fought valiantly, but the ronin were relentless. Sixteen of Kira's men were killed and another twenty-two wounded. Kira himself was nowhere to be found. Oishi, checking Kira's bed and finding it still warm, deduced that Kira was close by. The ronin eventually discovered a hidden courtyard where Kira had taken refuge.

Upon finding Kira, Oishi respectfully addressed him, offering him the chance to die honorably by seppuku. Oishi even offered to act as Kira's kaishakunin (second), the one who would decapitate him to minimize his suffering. Kira remained speechless. Seeing no other option, Oishi ordered his men to pin Kira down. He was killed with a dagger—the same one Asano had used for his seppuku.

The ronin washed Kira's severed head in a well before placing it on Asano's tomb alongside the dagger. They offered prayers and left their remaining money with the temple's abbot, asking for their bodies to be decently buried and prayers to be offered for their souls. They then turned themselves in, fully expecting the death sentence.

As anticipated, the shogun sentenced the forty-six ronin to death. However, recognizing their act of loyalty and honor, they were allowed to commit seppuku rather than face execution as common criminals. The youngest among them was only sixteen years old. The forty-seventh ronin,

Terasaka Kichiemon, returned and was later pardoned. The forty-six ronin were buried at Sengaku-ji, in front of their master's tomb.

The graves of the ronin at Sengaku-ji. [39]

The tale of the forty-seven ronin quickly became famous and remains one of Japan's most enduring stories, conveying the message of the samurai's undying loyalty and honor. The story, known as "Chūshingura" (The Treasury of Loyal Retainers), has been retold in countless plays, books, and films, each time reinforcing the ideals of bushido—the way of the warrior. The ronin's act of avenging their master and willingly facing death to uphold their honor exemplifies the deepest values of the samurai: loyalty to one's lord, the importance of honor, and the willingness to sacrifice everything for one's principles.

Even today, the graves of the forty-seven ronin at Sengaku-ji Temple are a site of pilgrimage. Visitors come to pay their respects and honor the memory of these loyal samurai. The annual festival held at Sengaku-ji on December 14, commemorating the day the ronin avenged their master, draws people from all over Japan and beyond. This festival is a celebration of the virtues that the forty-seven ronin embodied and that continue to resonate in Japanese culture.

Chapter 4: Folktales of Love and Destiny

Once upon a time, in the verdant countryside of ancient Japan, there lived an elderly bamboo cutter named Taketori no Okina. Each day, he ventured into the thick bamboo groves, his sharp axe gleaming under the sunlight as he meticulously cut and gathered the slender stalks. His humble life was filled with the rhythmic sounds of nature and the soft rustle of bamboo leaves, but there was a void in his heart, for he and his wife, Asagao, had no children.

One tranquil morning, as the golden rays of the sun pierced through the emerald canopy, Taketori no Okina noticed an extraordinary glow emanating from a bamboo stalk. Mesmerized, he approached the luminous plant and, with great care, split it open. To his astonishment, nestled inside the stalk was a tiny, radiant baby girl, no larger than his thumb. Her delicate features and ethereal glow filled Taketori no Okina's heart with joy and wonder. Believing her to be a divine gift, he gently cradled the tiny girl and brought her home to his wife.

Asagao was equally enchanted by the miraculous child. Together, they named her Kaguya-hime, meaning "radiant princess." Miraculously, within just a few days, Kaguya-hime grew from a tiny infant to a beautiful young woman, her beauty unmatched by any other. Her hair shimmered like the midnight sky, and her eyes sparkled like the brightest stars. The bamboo cutter and his wife cherished her deeply, their lives now brimming with happiness and love.

Strangely, after Kaguya-hime came into their lives, every time Taketori no Okina cut the bamboo, he found nuggets of gold within the stalks. Soon, the once humble couple became wealthy, their home filled with treasures and their hearts with gratitude for the extraordinary gift bestowed upon them.

Kaguya-hime's beauty soon became legendary, and word of the celestial maiden spread far and wide. Noblemen from distant lands traveled to the bamboo cutter's modest home, each hoping to win her hand in marriage. Five princes, each renowned for their wealth and status, were the most persistent suitors. Headstrong to marry the beautiful Kaguya-hime, these suitors met Taketori no Okina one day, hoping they could persuade his radiant daughter into accepting one of their marriage proposals. Nevertheless, Kaguya-hime remained uninterested. But, not planning on disappointing her father, Kaguya-hime agreed to marry any one of the suitors who successfully fulfilled her rather impossible condition.

The first prince was asked to retrieve the stone begging bowl of the Buddha. Determined, he set off on the long journey but soon realized the task was impossible. Desperate, he found an old bowl from a local temple and tried to pass it off as the true relic. However, Kaguya-hime saw through his deception—the bowl did not have a certain glow—and sent him away in shame.

The second prince was tasked with finding a branch from the mythical island of Horai, made of gold and adorned with jeweled fruits. He hired an exceptionally skillful craftsman to create a magnificent fake branch, hoping to deceive Kaguya-hime. The beautiful maiden was slightly surprised when he presented the branch, but the prince's deceit was revealed when Kaguya-hime received a messenger sent by the craftsman, asking for payment.

The third prince was to obtain a robe made from the fire-rat's fur, which could not be burned. He traveled to distant lands, spending a fortune, only to return with an ordinary robe. When Kaguya-hime tested the robe by setting it on fire, it burned to ashes, and the prince departed in defeat.

The fourth prince was asked to bring back a colored jewel from a dragon's neck. He went on a journey across the seas and was later forced to face the merciless storm. Afraid for his life, the prince decided to abandon the mission. As for the fifth prince, he faced a grimmer fate. Tasked to fetch a cowry shell born from swallows, the undeterred prince went and searched tirelessly for a swallow's nest. He found one, but it was high above the ground. The prince tried to reach for it but unfortunately fell to his death.

Later, the emperor, having heard of Kaguya-hime's unmatched beauty, also decided to venture to the outskirts, hoping he could catch a glimpse of the legendary maiden. Unsurprisingly, upon laying eyes on Kaguya-hime, the emperor was immediately captivated by her grace and beauty. Almost immediately, he sought her hand in marriage, offering her the luxuries and power of his court. But Kaguya-hime, with a heavy heart, refused. She explained that she was not from his country; the marriage was impossible. However, the two remained in contact. For three years, they continued to send each other letters.

Nevertheless, Kaguya-hime remained lonely and wistful. Then came summer, when she would often gaze at the moon with longing. Her eyes filled with sadness that her foster parents could not understand. As the seasons changed and summer gave way to autumn, Kaguya-hime's melancholy deepened. One evening, under the soft glow of the moon, she finally revealed to Taketori no Okina and Asagao that she was not of this world but a princess from the Moon Kingdom. She had been sent to Earth as a punishment for a certain wrongdoing that she refused to explain. The gold that they receive was sent from the heavens as some form of payment for the princess's upkeep. This punishment had come to an end, and she must return to where she belonged.

Her foster parents were devastated by the revelation, unable to fathom losing their beloved daughter. They pleaded with her to stay, but Kaguya-hime's fate was sealed. She assured them that she would always cherish the love and care they had shown her. Meanwhile, the news soon reached the emperor, who vowed to keep her on Earth. When Kaguya-hime revealed that her time on Earth was nearing its end, the emperor wasted no time. He deployed his most loyal guards to surround her house on the night of her departure, determined to thwart the celestial beings who would come to take her back.

On that fateful night when the full moon bathed the land in its silvery light, celestial beings descended from the heavens in a resplendent chariot. Dressed in shimmering robes, they approached Kaguya-hime, who was now adorned in a radiant garment that enhanced her otherworldly beauty. The emperor's guards, brave and resolute, formed a barrier around the house, but they were no match for the celestial beings. The ethereal figures effortlessly bypassed the guards, their divine presence overwhelming all resistance.

Taketori no Okina and Asagao wept as they watched their beloved daughter bid them farewell, her luminous eyes filled with tears of gratitude and sorrow. Kaguya-hime wrote moving letters of farewell to her family and to the emperor, expressing her deep love and gratitude for their kindness. She also left a small bottle with the Elixir of Life for the emperor, a final gift to the one who had loved her so dearly.

As Kaguya-hime ascended to the sky, she looked back at the couple who had given her a life of love and happiness. Her celestial entourage then draped a feather robe around her, erasing all her earthly memories as she ascended to the moon, heading straight to Tsuki no Miyako (the Capital of the Moon).

Kaguya-hime ascending to the moon. [30]

The emperor, devastated by Kaguya-hime's departure, read her letter and felt an overwhelming sense of loss. Distraught, he wrote her a heartfelt letter, expressing his undying love and sorrow. He then ordered his men to climb to the top of the tallest mountain in Japan and burn the letter, hoping that the smoke would carry his words and feelings to Kaguya-hime in the heavens. The Elixir of Life was also burned as the emperor did not wish to reach immortality without the princess by his side. From that day on, it was said that the plume of smoke from the mountain symbolized the emperor's eternal love and longing for Kaguya-hime. Legend also has it that the word for immortality (fushi) became the mountain's name: Mount Fuji.

The tale of the bamboo cutter and his moon princess, Kaguya-hime, was written during the Heian period—possibly in the late ninth or early tenth century, making it one of the oldest folktales ever recorded. It immediately became a cherished story passed down through generations. The tale reminds all who heard it of the beauty of love, sacrifice, and the ethereal magic that sometimes graces the world.

This is not the only tale that speaks of love. Another popular legend that blends human emotions with mystical elements is the story of Tsuru Nyōbō (The Crane Wife).

The Tale of the Crane Wife

The story takes place in a small village, home to a certain young man. He was a kind-hearted person, living a simple life in a modest cottage at the edge of a dense forest. One crisp autumn day, as the young man walked through the forest to gather firewood, he heard a faint, sorrowful cry. Following the sound, he discovered a beautiful crane with an arrow piercing its wing. The crane's pristine white feathers were stained with blood, and its eyes pleaded for mercy.

Moved with compassion, the young man carefully removed the arrow. "You have to be careful of the hunters next time," he softly said while tending to the crane's wounds.

The grateful bird gazed at him with deep, intelligent eyes before spreading its majestic wings and soaring into the sky. The young man watched the crane disappear into the distance, his heart warmed by the knowledge that he had saved a life.

That night, as the wind rustled through the trees and leaves fell softly to the ground, there was a gentle knock on the young man's door. When he opened it, he found a stunning young woman standing on his doorstep. She introduced herself as his wife. Though confused, the young man explained that he had no wealth to support them both. The woman reassured him, saying she had brought a sack of rice large enough to feed them both.

To the young man's amazement, the rice never depleted, and they were never left hungry. As the days passed, they grew closer, and the young man found himself captivated by her gentle demeanor and mysterious beauty. One evening, under the soft glow of the hearth, the woman asked the young man to build her a weaving room. Despite his modest means, he set to work and soon had a small room ready for her.

Before she began her weaving, the young man's wife made him swear never to peek at her while she worked. She closed herself in the room, and the young man waited outside, listening to the steady clatter of the loom. Days passed. At last, after seven days, the sound ceased. His wife, now frail and thin, emerged from the room holding the most exquisite cloth he had ever seen.

The following day, the young man took the fabric to the village market, where it fetched a very high price. Their lives improved, and their once simple home became cozy and warm. Yet, the young man's curiosity kept growing. How could his wife create such remarkable fabrics?

One night, unable to resist any longer, he tiptoed to the room where his wife worked. Peering through a tiny crack in the door, he was stunned to see a large crane at the loom, pulling feathers from its own body to weave into the fabric. As he gasped in surprise, the crane transformed back into his wife, who turned to him with tears in her eyes.

"You have broken your vow," she said sorrowfully. "I am the crane you rescued, and I became your wife to repay your kindness. But now that you have seen my true form, I must leave."

Devastated, the young man pleaded with her to stay, but it was too late. She wept as she turned back into the crane, spread her wings, and with a sorrowful cry, flew off into the night. The young man watched her vanish into the darkness, his heart aching with regret and sadness. But, before she left, the crane had given the young man one last piece of fabric to remember her by. He clutched the beautiful cloth, knowing it was her final gift to him.

From that day forward, the young man often wandered through the forest, hoping to glimpse the crane he had once saved and loved. Though he never saw her again, he would sometimes hear a sorrowful cry echoing among the trees, a reminder of the love he had lost because of his broken promise.

The tale of The Crane Wife imparts important lessons. It shows that true love is generous and kind but also emphasizes the importance of keeping promises. Curiosity can lead to heartache, and sometimes it's best to trust and respect the privacy of those we care about. The young man's sorrowful experience serves as a reminder to cherish and honor the trust others place in us.

The Tale of the Star-Crossed Lovers

This next tale is a cherished legend that paints the night sky with a story of love and longing. Represented by the stars Vega and Altair, these celestial lovers are separated by the Milky Way.

In the heavens far from our world, there was once an enchanting weaver named Orihime. She was not merely an ordinary weaver; Orihime was, in fact, a princess, the daughter of the God of the Sky. Most of the time, Orihime could be seen working diligently at her loom by the banks of the Amanogawa (the River of Heaven), which is known to us today as the Milky Way. With her celestial skills, her weavings were always so exquisite that they shone like the brightest stars themselves.

Despite her skill and dedication, Orihime was always lonely. She longed for companionship and love, but her constant weaving left her no time for such pursuits. Seeing his daughter's sadness, the God of the Sky decided to help. He introduced her to Hikoboshi, a handsome young cowherd who lived on the opposite side of the Amanogawa. Hikoboshi was known for his kindness and his devotion to his herd of celestial cows.

When Orihime and Hikoboshi met, it was love at first sight. They were instantly drawn to each other, and soon they were inseparable. Their love blossomed, and for a time, both were blissfully happy. They spent every moment they could together—laughing, talking, and enjoying each other's company.

However, their newfound happiness came with a price. Orihime's weaving was neglected, Hikoboshi's cows wandered unattended, and chaos threatened the celestial order. Orihime's father, noticing the disorder, was greatly displeased. And so, he summoned Orihime and Hikoboshi and decreed that they must be separated by the Amanogawa as punishment for their neglect.

Heartbroken, Orihime and Hikoboshi were placed on opposite sides of the Milky Way, forbidden to see each other. The separation was unbearable, and both spent their days gazing longingly across the river of stars, their hearts aching with sorrow. The sadness eventually grew so strong that it attracted the attention of the God of the Sky. Seeing his daughter's misery and moved by her tears, Orihime's father decided to show mercy.

He allowed Orihime and Hikoboshi to meet once a year on the seventh day of the seventh month—this is known as Tanabata, which means "Evening of the Seventh." There was, however, a condition; they could only meet if they agreed to work hard and complete their duties throughout the rest of the year. Perhaps desperately longing for each other's company, the two lovers quickly agreed on the terms. They continued to complete their duties. Following this, chaos disappeared from the heavens.

When the day finally came, the two were elated. It was the first day that they were to be reunited after a full year. However, they soon found the river to be too difficult to cross. Orihime was immediately consumed by sorrow. But as before, her sadness soon attracted the attention of others. A flock of magpies came to help the two lovers reunite. They made a bridge for Orihime to cross the river, allowing her to embrace Hikoboshi once again. The pair cherished every moment of their reunion, perhaps holding each other close and sharing stories of their time apart. The sight of their love rekindled brought hope and happiness to all other celestial beings. However, it is said that the magpies could only assist them on their yearly journey if the day was clear. If rain came on the date, the two lovers must wait another year to be reunited.

Today, the story of Orihime and Hikoboshi is celebrated with the Tanabata festival. People write their wishes on colorful strips of paper called tanzaku and hang them on bamboo trees, creating beautiful wish trees. On the following day, these decorated trees are floated on a river or in the ocean and burned as an offering, carrying the wishes to the heavens.

A bamboo tree full of tanzaku. [81]

Throughout Japan, Tanabata is marked by various celebrations. The streets come alive with parades, food stalls, and colorful decorations. People of all ages participate in the festivities, enjoying traditional foods, music, and games. Fireworks light up the night sky, mirroring the joy of the heavenly reunion and adding to the magical atmosphere of the festival.

The Tanabata festival is a time for people to come together and celebrate love, hope, and the beauty of the stars. Families and friends gather to share the story of Orihime and Hikoboshi, teaching the next generation about the power of love and the importance of perseverance and hard work. As they gaze up at the Milky Way, they imagine the celestial lovers meeting on their bridge of magpies, their love shining brightly across the heavens.

Through the festival of Tanabata, the tale of Orihime and Hikoboshi is immortalized. It serves as a timeless reminder of love's enduring strength, the value of dedication, and the beauty of the stars that guide us.

The Harrowing Tale of Kiyohime and Anchin

Love, a powerful and beautiful emotion, can sometimes grow into an all-consuming obsession. When love turns into an unhealthy fixation, it can drive people to unimaginable lengths, causing pain and suffering for both the lover and the beloved. One such harrowing tale from Japanese folklore that vividly illustrates this transformation is the story of Anchin and Kiyohime. This legend reveals the dark side of love turned obsession.

The setting of this daunting legend was the ancient province of Kii, where there lived a beautiful young woman named Kiyohime. The daughter of an official of the Manago manor, she was known for her grace and beauty. One day, a traveling monk named Anchin arrived at her father's manor. Anchin was a handsome and devout monk on a pilgrimage to a sacred temple. When Kiyohime saw him, she immediately fell deeply in love.

"Welcome, honored monk," Kiyohime greeted, her eyes shining with admiration. "May I offer you food and rest for your journey?"

Anchin accepted her hospitality graciously, unaware of the growing affection Kiyohime harbored for him. During his stay at the manor, they spent time talking, and Kiyohime's feelings for Anchin intensified. When it was time for Anchin to continue his journey, Kiyohime pleaded with him to stay longer, but he gently refused.

"Kiyohime, I must fulfill my pilgrimage," Anchin explained, sensing her attachment. "It is my duty to the temple and to my faith. I will return to you the very moment I'm done with my responsibilities."

Heartbroken but hopeful, Kiyohime watched him leave, believing he would return. As Anchin continued his pilgrimage, he became increasingly aware of the inappropriateness of Kiyohime's affections. He resolved to avoid her on his return journey, fearing the consequences of her obsession.

Months later, Anchin returned to the province of Kii, taking a different route to avoid Kiyohime. However, she learned of his return and was determined to see him again. She waited by the roadside, hoping to intercept him. When Anchin saw her, he panicked and fled, seeking refuge in a nearby temple.

"Kiyohime, please understand," Anchin pleaded as he ran. "I am a monk, and I cannot return your love."

Kiyohime on the banks of the Hidaka River. [22]

Devastated by his rejection and consumed by her desire, Kiyohime's heartbreak twisted into rage. She pursued Anchin relentlessly. Anchin, on the other hand, had successfully crossed the Hidaka River and specifically told the boatman to not ferry Kiyohime. And so, when the enraged maiden arrived at the edge of the river, the boatman told her to turn back. Not ready to let the monk go, Kiyohime jumped into the river. It was at this moment that a harrowing transformation took place. The body of the once beautiful maiden contorted, and in the blink of an eye, she transformed into a monstrous serpent, driven by a single-minded obsession to get Anchin.

Anchin was beyond terrified. He ran as fast as he could to the Dōjō-ji. Wrestling with panic, Anchin sought help from the priest of Dōjō-ji. Here, sources vary; some claim that the priests at the temple did not believe Anchin's story, while others suggest they took his words seriously. Nevertheless, Anchin eventually found a hiding spot. He was said to have been hiding under the gigantic temple bell, hoping his life could be spared from the vengeful serpent. However, Kiyohime, in her new form, had a rather heightened sense of smell. She could easily smell the terrified monk's scent and pinpoint his hiding spot. Without wasting time, she coiled around the bell, her scales scraping against the metal. She breathed fire upon it, heating the bell until it glowed red-hot.

A section of a scroll depicting Kiyohime as a serpent, burning the bell. [88]

Anchin, trapped inside, slowly began to feel the searing heat and knew he could not escape his fate. The only thing he could do was to pray for the last time, his trembling voice mingling with the desperate hisses of the serpent outside. In a final agonizing moment, the flames consumed him, and the bell shattered from the intense heat. Kiyohime, realizing what she had done, let out a mournful wail that echoed through the temple grounds. Her monstrous form collapsed, and she wept bitterly over the charred remains of the monk she had loved. As she could no longer bear her sorrow, Kiyohime fled to the river, where she ended her own life.

Anchin and Kiyohime's tragic end serves as a reminder of the destructive power of unchecked emotions. Kiyohime's love, which turned into an all-consuming obsession, led to her transformation into a creature of wrath and vengeance. Anchin's attempts to escape only fueled her rage, culminating in a heartbreaking and fiery demise for both.

Chapter 5: Yokai and Supernatural Creatures

The streets of the Edo-period town were shrouded in an eerie silence as the moon cast its pale glow over the narrow lanes. The lanterns flickered softly, their light barely cutting through the thick darkness. A lone man—let us call him Sato—made his way home after a long day of work. The stillness of the night was unsettling, and the quiet was so profound that it seemed to amplify the sound of his own footsteps.

As Sato walked, a prickling sensation crawled up his spine. He felt the uncanny impression that he was being followed. Glancing around, he saw nothing but shadows dancing on the walls and the occasional rustling of leaves in the wind. The feeling persisted, growing stronger with each step, until he could no longer ignore it. Gathering his courage, he decided to turn around and confront whatever was behind him.

There, standing in the middle of the deserted street, was a small boy. The boy was more than half the size of an average man and wore a large bamboo hat that obscured much of his face. He looked lonely, a solitary figure in the night. In his hands, he held a dish with a large block of tofu, a Japanese maple leaf stamped on the side. The boy resembled a typical tofu seller, a common sight during the day, yet something about him filled Sato with unease.

"Good evening," the boy said in a soft voice, extending the dish towards Sato. "Would you like some tofu?"

Sato hesitated but then accepted the offering. The boy's eyes, barely visible under the brim of the hat, seemed to glimmer with a strange light. Thanking the boy, Sato quickly made his way home, eager to escape the unsettling encounter.

Once home, Sato examined the tofu. It appeared ordinary, and with a shrug, he decided to eat it. The tofu tasted rather bland and had no flavor at all. "Just an ordinary tofu," Sato thought to himself, feeling a sense of relief. Little did he know, he was lucky.

A depiction of Tōfu-kozō. [34]

In other circumstances, eating the tofu given by Tōfu-kozō could lead to far worse outcomes. For the unfortunate, mold would spread across the jiggly white surface of the tofu as they ate it. Sometimes, those who consumed the mold without noticing it would find it growing within their bodies, eventually leading to their demise. Such occurrences were rare, as Tōfu-kozō did not usually make humans their opponents. In fact, these yokai (supernatural creatures and spirits) were frequently depicted as amicable, timid, and humorous characters. They were often teased by other yokai for being weak and were known to serve as errand runners for stronger yokai.

Tōfu-kozō, with his endearing yet eerie presence, was a unique yokai. But, to understand him fully, it is essential to delve into what yokai represent in Japanese beliefs. Each type of yokai have their own unique characteristics and stories. They can be malevolent, benevolent, or merely mischievous, embodying the fears, curiosities, and the unknown aspects of human life. The origins of yokai are deeply rooted in ancient Japanese beliefs and the folklore of the countryside, where people lived in close harmony with nature.

However, the story of Tōfu-kozō is different. This yokai was born in the bustling cities during the Edo period. Tofu had arrived from China early in Japan's history during the Nara or Heian period, but it was not until the Edo period that tofu became popular. Initially enjoyed by the elites, tofu gradually became a staple food for all classes.

During this period, many reported encountering Tōfu-kozō. Each description varied slightly, but the essence remained the same. Some claimed that Tōfu-kozō was a shy creature, often tiptoeing behind those wandering the empty streets at night. Others said he preferred to appear during the rain. The drawings of Tōfu-kozō also varied. While many depicted him as a rather adorable young boy, others described him as having only one large eye or a long tongue. Despite these differences, most accounts agreed that Tōfu-kozō was neither malevolent nor evil.

Interestingly, Tōfu-kozō was often seen wearing red, a color believed by ancient Japanese to have the power to ward off evil. This detail connects him to other yokai and spirits in Japanese folklore, such as Hosogami, the smallpox spirit.

How the Ancient Japanese Warded Off the Smallpox Demon

The history of smallpox in Japan is as harrowing as it is fascinating. The disease first struck the archipelago in the eighth century during the Nara period. It is believed that smallpox arrived via trade routes from the Korean Peninsula and China, spreading rapidly through the population. The epidemic of 735-737 CE was particularly devastating, wiping out a significant portion of the Japanese population and altering the course of the nation's history.

Before the advent of medical science and the understanding of diseases, the ancient Japanese believed that smallpox was brought by a malevolent spirit known as Hosogami. This smallpox demon was thought to travel through the land, spreading the disease and wreaking havoc among the people. Hosogami was feared greatly, and various rituals and practices were developed to ward off this dreaded spirit.

One of the primary means of protection against Hosogami was the color red. It was widely believed that red had the power to repel evil spirits and negative influences. In the context of smallpox, families would dress their sick in red garments, decorate their homes with red objects, and even paint red symbols on their walls. The hope was that this vibrant color would drive away Hosogami and prevent the spread of disease.

In addition to the use of red, the ancient Japanese employed various other methods to protect themselves from Hosogami. Some believed that by pleasing the smallpox demon, they could avert the disease. As a result, they set up small shrines dedicated to Hosogami, offering prayers and sacrifices to pacify the spirit. These shrines were often adorned with red paper streamers called shide, which were believed to further enhance their protective power.

Another common practice involved tying straw ropes, known as shimenawa, around the house. These ropes, also adorned with shide, were traditionally used to mark sacred spaces and ward off evil spirits. By placing shimenawa around their homes, people hoped to create a protective barrier that would keep Hosogami at bay.

One of the most famous stories involving Hosogami is that of Minamoto no Tametomo. Tametomo was a legendary samurai of the late Heian period, renowned for his archery skills and adventurous life. According to folklore, Tametomo once encountered Hosogami and, using his extraordinary abilities, chased off the demon and protected the people from smallpox.

Minamoto no Tametomo was also a figure of great cultural significance. His actions against Hosogami were symbolic of the eternal struggle between humans and the supernatural forces that sought to harm them. By standing up to Hosogami, Tametomo became a symbol of hope and resilience.

The fear of smallpox and the reverence for Hosogami also led to various local festivals and rituals aimed at preventing outbreaks. In some regions, entire villages would participate in purification rites, offering prayers and performing

Minamoto no Tametomo casting off the smallpox demon.[85]

dances to appease the spirit. These communal activities not only served a spiritual purpose but also strengthened social bonds and provided a sense of collective security in the face of an invisible threat.

As medical knowledge advanced and the true nature of smallpox became understood, the belief in Hosogami gradually faded. However, the cultural practices and folklore surrounding the smallpox spirit left a lasting impact on Japanese society. The use of red as a protective color, the rituals of purification, and the stories of heroic figures like Minamoto no Tametomo remain embedded in the cultural memory. The tale of Hosogami illustrates the complex interplay between superstition, religion, and medicine in ancient Japan. It shows how people sought to make sense of the unknown and protect themselves through a blend of practical and spiritual means.

The Legend of the Nine-Tailed Fox

Another legendary figure in the world of yokai is the kitsune, a shape-shifting fox spirit renowned in Japanese folklore for its cunning and trickery. Among the most famous of these tales is that of Tamamo no Mae, the notorious Nine-Tailed Fox.

The story begins with a married couple who discover an abandoned baby girl. Some versions of the tale say they found her in the woods, while others claim she was left on the streets. The couple, childless and longing for a family, took the infant in and named her Mizukume. They showered her with love and care, and as the years passed, Mizukume grew into an extraordinarily beautiful and intelligent girl.

By the age of seven, Mizukume had already shown remarkable talent. She could read and compose poetry, charming everyone with her brilliance and grace. Her reputation soon spread, and she was invited to perform her poetry before the reigning emperor, Emperor Toba.

Mizukume's performance was nothing short of mesmerizing. The emperor was captivated by her eloquence and beauty. "Such a remarkable child," Emperor Toba mused, his eyes never leaving her. "She must be brought to court."

And so, Mizukume was taken to the imperial court, where she was given the name Tamamo no Mae. She quickly became a favorite among the courtiers. Mothers wished their children were more like her, and everyone in court adored her company. Her intelligence shone brightly, especially when scholars tested her knowledge with difficult questions, all of which she answered with ease. Her growing popularity caught the emperor's attention once more, and he spent every free moment in her presence.

As Tamamo no Mae grew into a fine maiden, she became the emperor's consort. They were inseparable, and Emperor Toba found great joy in her company. However, this happiness was not to last. Suddenly, the emperor fell mysteriously ill. His condition worsened day by day, baffling the court physicians, who could find no cure.

Only one thing seemed unusual: despite the emperor's grave condition, Tamamo no Mae did not appear particularly distressed. Her calm demeanor amidst the crisis raised suspicions among the courtiers.

In desperation, the court summoned Abe no Yasunari, an onmyōji known for his expertise in divination and the supernatural. Abe no Yasunari performed several rituals to diagnose the problem. He soon declared that the emperor was not suffering from a natural illness but was cursed by an evil spirit. Alarmed by this revelation, the court summoned priests from across the land to pray at the palace, hoping to ward off the malevolent force. Despite their efforts, the emperor's condition continued to deteriorate.

Growing ever more restless and desperate, the court pleaded with Abe no Yasunari to perform another ritual. This time, the onmyōji's findings shocked everyone: the culprit behind the emperor's illness was none other than Tamamo no Mae. He declared that she was a kitsune and was using her magic to slowly kill the emperor.

"Impossible!" the courtiers exclaimed. "Tamamo no Mae cannot be the cause of this!"

The emperor himself, though weakened, was deeply hurt by the accusation. "Tamamo," he whispered, "could this be true?"

The court agreed to perform a test devised by Abe no Yasunari to reveal Tamamo no Mae's true form. The onmyōji explained that during a sacred ritual, no evil spirit could maintain a disguise and would be forced to reveal itself. At first, Tamamo no Mae hesitated, but under pressure from the court, she agreed to participate.

Tamamo no Mae transforming into the nine-tailed fox. [86]

As the ritual commenced, the air grew tense. Chanting priests surrounded Tamamo no Mae, and the atmosphere crackled with spiritual energy. Suddenly, Tamamo no Mae began to writhe and twist, her form changing before their very eyes. In a horrifying transformation, the beautiful maiden morphed into a fearsome nine-tailed fox.

The courtiers gasped in terror, and the emperor's eyes widened in disbelief. The kitsune, now fully exposed, let out a fierce cry before leaping out of a nearby window and disappearing into the night. Heartbroken, the emperor knew he had to deal with the creature that had once been his beloved consort. Reports soon flooded in from across the country of women and children mysteriously disappearing, presumably taken by the vengeful fox. Determined to protect his people, the emperor summoned his two best warriors, Kazusanosuke and Miuranosuke, to hunt down and eliminate the kitsune.

The two warriors pursued Tamamo no Mae relentlessly. Despite her cunning and ability to outsmart them several times, Kazusanosuke and Miuranosuke's determination never wavered. After rigorous training and countless encounters, they finally managed to corner her. With precise aim, they fired two arrows that struck the kitsune.

This, however, was not the last of Tamamo no Mae. After her defeat, her spirit was said to be trapped in a boulder known as Sessho-seki, or the Killing Stone. Anyone foolish enough to touch the boulder was said to have faced death. This boulder existed for centuries, but in 2022, it mysteriously cracked open, leading many to believe that Tamamo no Mae's spirit had been freed.

Sessho-seki split in half. [87]

Despite her defeat, Emperor Toba's fate was also sealed: he succumbed to his illness not long after. The turmoil surrounding his court and the chaos following Tamamo no Mae's exposure contributed to the unrest that eventually led to the Genpei War, a civil war that changed the course of Japanese history.

The tale of Tamamo no Mae is a great lesson of how appearances can be deceiving and how power and beauty can mask darker intentions. This legendary kitsune, with her enchanting disguise and malevolent heart, remains one of the most captivating and cautionary figures in Japanese folklore. Today, her legend is referenced in movies, books, and various forms of media, keeping her story alive and relevant.

Her influence is not confined to Japan. In Chinese history, Tamamo no Mae appears as Da Ji, the notorious concubine of King Zhou of Shang.

Much like in Japan, Da Ji's beauty hid a cruel and malevolent nature that brought great misfortune to the Shang dynasty, leading to its downfall. Her story is eerily like that of Tamamo no Mae, highlighting the universal themes of deception and the destructive power of unchecked desires.

The Honorable Tanuki

Under the scorching sun, a merchant could be seen tirelessly walking through the bustling markets. He had hoped to sell at least one of his wares. However, his stock was meager and rather outdated, so none seemed interested in what he had to offer. Days turned into weeks, and the merchant's fortunes failed to improve. Each evening, he returned home with unsold goods and a heart heavy with worry about own future.

One day, as he walked along the foot of a mountain, he felt more disheartened than ever. The path took him past a dense forest, where the sounds of nature seemed to echo his melancholy. Suddenly, a series of desperate squeals pierced the air. Curious, the merchant ventured into the woods, following the sound until he found a tanuki—a raccoon-like creature—trapped in a hunter's snare. Its hind leg was caught in the sharp, shiny claw trap, and it squirmed in pain.

With a kind heart and swift hands, the merchant used all his might to pry open the trap and free the tanuki. The creature, scared and panicked, quickly darted into the thick bushes and disappeared. The merchant, relieved that the tanuki was safe, continued on his way, a small sense of satisfaction easing his burden.

Days passed, and the merchant's luck remained unchanged. As he trudged along his usual path, he stumbled upon an old, rusty tea kettle lying abandoned on the ground. Though it was in poor condition, the merchant saw potential in it. He picked up the kettle, hoping he might sell it to the monks at the nearby Morin-ji Temple. He cleaned and polished the kettle until it gleamed almost like new. Hope glimmered in his eyes as he made his way to the temple.

To his delight, the monks at Morin-ji Temple needed a tea kettle for an upcoming service. The head monk inspected the kettle and, satisfied with its appearance, purchased it from the merchant. For the first time in many days, the merchant left with a big smile on his face, grateful for the much-needed fortune.

During the ceremony, the monks soon noticed something peculiar as they poured tea from the kettle. The tea cooled almost instantly, and they had to frequently reheat the kettle. The peculiar kettle also seemed to twitch and squirm in the pourer's hand when it was hot—as if it was alive. The head monk was unhappy, believing that he had been cheated by the merchant. And so, the following day, he summoned the merchant back to the temple to explain himself.

The innocent merchant arrived and examined the kettle. "I promise you, honorable monk, I sold you an ordinary kettle," he said earnestly. "There is nothing unusual about it."

Letting out a defeated sigh, the monk chose not to make the issue any more serious. He then invited the merchant for tea. So, the kettle was placed on the fire once more. Within moments, the metal began to sweat. Suddenly, it sprouted a scrubby tail, furry paws, and a pointed nose. With just a glance, the merchant immediately recognized the creature; it was in fact the tanuki that he had saved days before.

The kettle-turned-tanuki glanced at them with a sweet smile. "Thank you for freeing me," the tanuki said. "I wanted to repay your kindness by becoming a kettle you could sell. But being burned and polished was unbearable. I could not maintain my form."

The tea kettle tanuki. [88]

The monk and the merchant laughed, impressed by the tanuki's attempt at honor. They had both heard tales of shape-shifting tanuki who were known for their mischievous pranks. However, this tanuki's story was different—he genuinely wanted to help. From that day on, the tanuki became an esteemed guest at Morin-ji Temple. He entertained the monks with his tales and tricks, bringing joy to even the grumpiest among them. The merchant, too, often visited, sharing tea brewed in an ordinary kettle, grateful for the friendship of the magical creature.

The tale of the tanuki spread far and wide, attracting visitors to Morin-ji Temple. People flocked to see the famous shape-shifting tanuki and hear the story of his kindness and transformation. Morin-ji Temple, located in Gunma Prefecture, became renowned for not only its historical significance but also this enchanting legend. The story passed down through generations, a timeless reminder of the unexpected rewards of kindness and the magical possibilities that reside in the heart of Japanese folklore.

The Myth of Shuten Doji, the King of Oni

This next myth took place during the reign of Emperor Ichijo (the sixty-sixth emperor of Japan). At this time, the Japanese had been plagued with news of young women disappearing mysteriously. These women, often known for their beauty and purity, vanished without a trace. As the number of disappearances grew, the court sought the counsel of the imperial Onmyōdō.

After performing intricate rituals, the diviner revealed a chilling truth: the women were not simply missing but had been taken by a group of fearsome demons known as oni. These oni had established their stronghold on Mount Oe, where they reveled in their evil deeds. Oni in Japanese mythology are often depicted as large, fearsome creatures with sharp claws, wild hair, and horns protruding from their heads. They are notorious for their strength and malevolence, often causing chaos and destruction wherever they go.

Determined to put an end to the abductions, the imperial court summoned their most powerful warriors, led by Minamoto no Raiko, a renowned hero of his time.

Without hesitation, Raiko and his band of warriors embarked on a journey to eliminate the oni threat on Mount Oe. Before beginning their hunt, they visited three important shrines in the Kansai region to seek the blessings of the gods. Raiko himself visited Iwashimizu Hachimangū in

Kyoto, the temple dedicated to Hachiman, the god of war and the patron deity of the popular Minamoto clan.

Understanding the danger of a direct assault on the oni, Raiko and his men chose to disguise themselves as yamabushi, ascetic monks or hermits who dwelled deep in the mountains. Yamabushi, practitioners of Shugendō, were respected for their spiritual prowess and lived harmoniously with nature and the supernatural. And so, dressed as monks, Raiko and his warriors made their way to Mount Oe, where they encountered three old men.

A statue of an oni in Japan. [89]

Without introducing themselves, the old men provided Raiko with valuable information about the oni's stronghold. They warned Raiko to be extremely cautious of the oni's leader, Shuten Doji, whose name literally means "Drunken Demon." Shuten Doji was the strongest and most fearsome of his kind, so defeating him would require divine intervention.

The old men then bestowed Raiko with a vial of magical sake and an unbreakable helmet. Raiko, looking at the items gifted by the mysterious old men, immediately knew that these wise men were not normal human beings but the deities that he and his men had prayed to previously. The warriors then bowed deeply, thanking the gods before continuing their mission.

As they approached the mountain, Raiko and his warriors encountered a young maiden by a river, washing a blood-stained cloth. The maiden, one of the oni's victims, revealed that the cloth belonged to another captive who had been devoured by the demons. Upon learning of the warriors' mission, she provided detailed directions to Shuten Doji's palace.

Upon reaching the palace, the warriors were almost immediately spotted by a group of oni. These monstrous demons were initially planning on devouring them whole. One oni, however, suggested that they present the strangers to Shuten Doji first, fearing their leader's wrath if they acted rashly. The disguised warriors were brought before the demon king, who expressed his surprise at their arrival.

"No human has ever found this place," Shuten Doji growled. "How did you get here?"

Raiko, seizing the opportunity, calmly responded, "We are followers of a great monk who once traveled these paths and laid down a way to your palace. Our teachings compel us to befriend demons."

Intrigued but still suspicious, Shuten Doji invited the warriors to stay the night. To test their sincerity, he offered them sake made from the blood of the noble maidens and a side of human flesh. Raiko and his men, though horrified, pretended to enjoy the offerings, explaining that their sect required them to accept any gifts from demons. Convinced by their act, Shuten Doji lowered his guard.

That night, Raiko saw his chance. He offered Shuten Doji and the others the magical sake gifted by the gods. To gain their trust, Raiko drank some first, knowing it was harmless to humans. Shuten Doji and his comrades, unable to resist, drank the sake eagerly. The enchanted drink rendered the demons impotent, causing them to pass out.

With the oni incapacitated, Raiko and his men shed their yamabushi disguises and unsheathed their weapons. They launched a fierce assault on the sleeping demons, slaying them one by one. Raiko, wearing the divine helmet, sneaked into Shuten Doji's chamber and aimed his blade at the demon king's throat. With a swift, clean slash, he severed Shuten Doji's head. However, the battle was not over. Shuten Doji's decapitated head, still clinging to the remainder of his life, flew toward Raiko in a desperate attempt to bite his head off. Thanks to the unbreakable helmet, Raiko was spared. The head finally fell lifeless, marking the end of the demon's reign of terror.

With Shuten Doji and his minions defeated, Raiko and his warriors freed the captive young women and led them back to Kyoto. In the city, they were celebrated as heroes. According to some sources, Raiko initially planned to bring Shuten Doji's severed head to the capital, but divine signs advised against bringing anything impure to the city, so he buried it instead.

Chapter 6: Sea Whispers and River Songs

Water has always held a deep significance in Japanese culture, revered as a source of life and sustenance. Since ancient times, the Japanese have valued water not only for its life-giving properties but also for its spiritual and symbolic meanings. This deep respect is evident in various aspects of their daily lives, rituals, and, most vividly, their folklore.

In the earliest days of Japan, water was worshiped as a divine element. The country's numerous rivers, lakes, and oceans were seen as the abodes of gods and spirits. Agriculture, the primary livelihood for many, depended heavily on the regular flow of water. The practice of rice farming, which became central to Japanese society, is a clear reflection of the dependence on water. The careful irrigation systems designed to cultivate rice paddies showcase the meticulous relationship the Japanese maintained with water sources.

This reverence for water is also evident in the traditional occupation of ama, often referred to as the "Mermaids of Mie." These remarkable women, known for their free-diving skills, have harvested seafood, seaweed, and, most famously, pearls from the ocean's depths for over two thousand years. The ama divers' intimate connection with the sea embodies the deep respect and symbiotic relationship the Japanese people have with water. Their ability to dive without modern equipment—even oxygen tanks—and rely on breath control and endurance is a mark of human resilience and an acknowledgment of the ocean's mysterious and life-giving properties.

Ama divers, c. 1921. [40]

However, water's significance extends beyond being a source of life. In Japanese culture, water also serves as a bridge between worlds. Many Japanese myths and legends revolve around water bodies as gateways to other realms, places of mystery, and zones of peril. Rivers, lakes, and oceans are not just physical entities but are imbued with spiritual and supernatural dimensions.

This duality of water as both life-giver and gateway to the unknown is central to many aquatic myths. Water is a domain where benevolent spirits dwell, offering protection and blessings, but also where malevolent creatures lurk, posing dangers to the unwary. The Japanese people's intimate relationship with water is reflected in their folklore, which is full of tales of sea gods, dragon kings, and spirits inhabiting the waters. The first legend we are about to delve into is the most popular one: The Tale of Urashima Taro.

The Two Versions of Urashima Taro, the Man Who Visited the Dragon Palace

The story begins in a peaceful coastal village, far from the never-ending noise of the busy cities of Japan. Here lived a kind-hearted fisherman known as Urashima Taro. He was well-loved by the villagers for his gentle nature and his willingness to help others. Every day, Taro would set out in his small boat to fish in the sparkling blue sea, providing for his family and neighbors with the bounties he caught.

One sunny morning, as Taro was walking along the beach, he saw a group of children gathered around something. As he approached, he realized they were tormenting a small turtle, poking it with sticks and laughing at its attempts to escape. Taro's heart ached for the poor creature, and he quickly intervened.

Urashima Taro stopping the children from toying with the turtle. "

"Stop that!" he shouted, waving his arms to scare the children away. "How can you be so cruel to this innocent turtle?" The children, startled by Taro's stern voice, scattered and ran off. Gently, Taro picked up the turtle, noticing its trembling body and frightened eyes.

"Don't worry, little one," he said softly. "You're safe now." He carried the turtle to the edge of the water and set it down gently on the sand. The turtle looked up at him, as if to say thank you, and slowly made its way back into the sea. Perhaps content with seeing the small turtle saved and free from harm, Urashima Taro smiled and went about his day as usual.

The very next day, Taro went fishing from his boat. Suddenly, he noticed a turtle swimming in his direction. He immediately recognized the creature: it was the same turtle he had saved yesterday. However, much to his astonishment, the turtle began to speak.

"Kind fisherman, I am the turtle you saved yesterday," it said. "I am grateful for your kindness and wish to repay you. Please, come with me to the Dragon Palace beneath the sea, where the beautiful Princess Otohime wishes to thank you personally."

Though surprised, Taro felt a sense of adventure and agreed. After giving the fisherman a set of gills, the turtle instructed him to climb onto its back. Then, with a magical swirl, they dove beneath the waves. Taro marveled at the underwater world around him, filled with coral reefs, schools of fish, and fantastical sea creatures.

Soon, they arrived at the Dragon Palace, a magnificent structure made of coral and pearls, glowing with an ethereal light. Taro was led inside, where he was greeted by Princess Otohime, the most beautiful woman he had ever seen. Her hair flowed like ebony, and her eyes sparkled like the great ocean.

"Welcome, Urashima Taro," she said with a warm smile. "Thank you for saving the turtle. Please, stay with us and enjoy the wonders of our palace."

Taro was treated to a grand feast, with the most delicious food and drink he had ever tasted. He was entertained by graceful dancers and enchanting music, and for what felt like days, he experienced the joys of the Dragon Palace. Princess Otohime spent much time with him, and Taro found himself falling in love with her gentle nature and beauty. However, despite the paradise around him, Taro began to miss his family and village. He approached Princess Otohime and expressed his desire to return home.

"I understand," she said, her eyes filled with sadness. "But before you leave, I wish to give you a gift." She handed him a beautiful lacquered box tied with a silk cord. "This is the tamatebako, a little something to remember me by. Keep it close to you, but please, do not open it."

Then, with a heavy heart, Taro thanked the princess and climbed onto the back of the turtle, who swiftly carried him back to shore. Taro stepped onto the same beach where he had saved the turtle, but something felt different. The village in which he had lived his entire life seemed altered, and the people were unfamiliar. After asking some strangers what had happened to his dear village, Taro soon realized that many years had passed since he had left—a few centuries, at the very least. His family and friends were long gone, and everything he had known had changed.

Distraught and confused, Taro remembered the tamatebako. Believing it might hold the answer to his predicament, he untied the silk cord and opened the box. As he did, a thick cloud of white smoke enveloped him, and he suddenly felt weak and tired. His hair turned white, and wrinkles appeared on his skin. When the smoke cleared, Taro found that he had aged rapidly, becoming an old man in an instant.

Urashima Taro turning old after opening the tamatebako. "

As it turned out, the magic of the Dragon Palace had kept him young, but once the box was opened, time caught up with him. Only now did he remember Princess Otohime's warning to not open the box, but it was too late. With a mixture of sorrow and acceptance, Taro sat by the shore, gazing out at the vast ocean. While his dream of an adventure had come true, he had also lost so much.

The legend of Urashima Taro is a folktale that points to the passage of time and the fleeting nature of life, urging us to cherish each moment and the people we love. However, there is an older version of the tale, recorded in the Otogi Bunko during the Muromachi period, that focuses more on the theme of love.

In this version, Urashima Taro is not just a kind-hearted fisherman but a young man who falls deeply in love with Otohime, the beautiful daughter of the Dragon King of the Sea. The story begins with Taro setting out to fish one morning. As he casts his line, he feels a strong tug and reels in a magnificent turtle. Amazed by its size and beauty, Taro contemplates his catch but ultimately decides to release it back into the ocean, showing compassion and respect for the creature.

The next day, when Taro went fishing again, he encountered a beautiful woman who claimed to be the turtle he had saved. Expressing her gratitude, and perhaps attracted to the kind-hearted man, she proposed they get married and invited Taro to come with her.

"Close your eyes," she said to the fisherman.

Urashima Taro and the princess. 48

A few moments later, Taro opened his eyes to see that they were nearing the legendary island of Mount Horai—the fabled mountain where the Chinese Emperor Qin Shi Huang once believed the elixir of life to be hidden. There, Taro realized that the woman was a princess known as Kamehime. From there, the princess took Taro to see her parents before throwing a ceremony in which they were wed.

From that point on, the story closely follows the modern version. Taro enjoyed a life of luxury with his wife for three years until he eventually grew homesick. As the feeling of missing home grew stronger, he decided to go home just for a little while to visit his parents. Princess Kamehime was angry at first. "How can you stand a day without my presence when I can't even live a second without seeing you?"

However, knowing that nothing could stop her husband, she relented. She gave Taro a jeweled comb box. "I hope you won't forget about me, and should you ever want to come back, hold this box tight. But remember to never open it."

The ending of this version, however, is the same. Engulfed in sadness as soon as he learned that three hundred years had passed and his once familiar village was but a thing of the past, Taro wandered through the village, mourning the loss of everything and everyone he had once known.

In his despair, Taro clutched the jeweled comb box Otohime had given him. He thought of her and how much he missed her. Overcome by his longing to see her again, he forgot his promise and decided to open the box.

Taro aged rapidly, his youth fading in an instant. Realizing his mistake, he understood that he would never see his beloved Otohime again. The box, meant to symbolize their eternal bond, had become the instrument of their final separation.

Kappa, a Turtle-Like Creature in Rivers

The origins of the kappa are as murky as the rivers they inhabit. Some believe the first mention of a kappa dates to a text from the eighth century, which described a "river deity." This suggests that kappa have been part of Japan's spiritual world for over a millennium. Another theory, however, is much darker. In ancient times, it was said that families who could not care for their stillborn babies, often due to poverty or disability, would cast them into the river. These abandoned souls were thought to transform into kappa, forever haunting the waters where they were discarded.

A depiction of kappa. "

Rivers, ponds, and lakes are kappa playgrounds, hunting grounds, and homes. Physically, kappa are about the size of a small child, but their appearance is anything but innocent. They have scaly—and at times, hairy—reptilian skin, webbed hands and feet, a beak as their mouth, and a shell-like carapace on their backs. Their most distinctive feature, however, is the hollow indentation on top of their heads, which holds water. If the water spills or dries out, the kappa becomes weak and powerless, almost unable to move until the cavity is refilled with water from its home.

Despite their vulnerability, kappa are known for their mischievous and often malevolent behavior. They lurk near water, waiting to pounce on unsuspecting victims. Their pranks can range from harmless—like peeking under women's kimonos—to deadly, such as drowning people and animals, kidnapping children, and even consuming human flesh. Kappa also have a reputation for tormenting animals, especially horses and cows. In one story, a kappa was caught stealing horses and was forced to write a vow never to harm humans again.

Kappa have a peculiar obsession with politeness. If you bow to a kappa, it feels compelled to return the gesture. This quirk has been used to outsmart them, as seen in the tale of a sumo wrestler who was challenged by a kappa. Knowing the kappa's weakness, the wrestler accepted its challenge to a sumo match. In sumo wrestling, it is customary to bow to your opponent at the beginning of a match, showing respect and acknowledging the forthcoming contest. And so, as they prepared to grapple, the wrestler performed a deep bow. The kappa, driven by its compulsion for politeness, instinctively returned the bow, causing the water in its head to spill out. Instantly weakened, the kappa lost its strength, allowing the wrestler to easily overpower and defeat it.

Kappa also have detachable arms, and if an arm is pulled off, the kappa will often perform favors or reveal valuable secrets to get it back. This characteristic highlights their paradoxical nature—powerful yet easily subdued by those who understand their quirks. Moreover, kappa have a strong dislike for iron. They become agitated when iron objects fall into the water and can be repelled by those carrying iron. Some tales recount kappa offering rewards to anyone who helps remove iron objects from their watery habitat. This peculiar combination of physical vulnerabilities and specific dislikes adds depth to the kappa's character, making them both fearsome and approachable entities, depending on one's knowledge and approach.

Interestingly, kappa have a particular fondness for cucumbers, which are often used to appease them. In ancient Tokyo, families would write their names on cucumbers and float them downriver to keep kappa at bay. Some even believed that eating cucumbers before swimming would protect them from kappa attacks, though opinions on this practice varied.

Despite their menacing reputation, kappa are not entirely malevolent. If treated kindly, a kappa can become a loyal ally. They might help farmers irrigate their fields or bring fresh fish as a gift, which is considered a sign of good fortune. Kappa are also said to possess great knowledge of medicine. According to legends, kappa were skilled in the art of treating broken bones and dislocated joints. They were said to have a deep understanding of human anatomy and the ability to realign bones with remarkable precision. Some even believe that the kappa were the ones who taught these skills to early practitioners of traditional Japanese medicine. This knowledge of bone setting, now known as sekkotsu, became an integral part of Japanese medical practices, particularly among village healers and those specializing in martial arts injuries.

Due to their complex nature, kappa are sometimes venerated as water deities. Shrines dedicated to kappa can be found in various regions, including Aomori and Miyagi Prefectures. Festivals aimed at appeasing kappa and ensuring a bountiful harvest continue to this day, reflecting their enduring significance in Japanese culture.

The Tale of Hoori and Toyotama-hime

In ancient times, when the land and sea worlds were closer than they are today, there lived a young hunter named Hoori. One day, Hoori lost his older brother Hoderi's precious fishhook while fishing. Desperate to find it, he decided to visit Ryūgū, the majestic underwater palace of the sea god, hoping to seek permission to search its grounds.

As Hoori wandered through the enchanting gardens of Ryūgū, he came across a beautiful woman by a well. This was Toyotama-hime, the daughter of the sea god. Their eyes met, and they found each other so captivating that they quickly fell in love and were soon married.

For three years, Hoori lived blissfully with Toyotama-hime in the underwater palace, but as time passed, he remembered his quest to find the lost fishhook. His longing for the hook grew, and he became increasingly despondent. Seeing her husband's sorrow, Toyotama-hime confided in her father about Hoori's plight.

The sea god then summoned Hoori and asked, "What troubles you, my son?"

"I have lost my brother's fishhook, and I cannot return without it," Hoori replied sadly.

Determined to help, the sea god called upon all the fish in the ocean. "Has any of you seen a lost fishhook?" he asked. A large tai fish immediately swam forward and confessed, "There is something lodged in my throat that has caused me great pain." When the sea god inspected it, he found Hoori's missing hook.

The sea god handed the fishhook to Hoori. "Here is what you seek. Take it and return to your world. But know this: I will also bless your fields with rain and prosperity while denying it to your brother."

The sea god gave Hoori two magical jewels, the tide-controlling manju and kanju. "These will protect you from your brother's wrath," he said. With that, the sea god set Hoori on the back of an enormous dragon, who carried him swiftly back to the surface world.

True to the sea god's word, Hoori's fields flourished, while Hoderi's harvests withered. Furious and envious, Hoderi attacked Hoori, but Hoori raised the tide with the magical jewels, drowning his brother. Only when Hoderi swore eternal submission did Hoori lower the tide, sparing his life.

During this time, Toyotama-hime became pregnant with Hoori's child. When her time came, she and her sister Tamayori-hime traveled to the surface on the back of a giant turtle. "Hoori, please build me a birthing hut thatched with cormorant feathers by the shore," she asked.

Hoori hastened to build the hut, but Toyotama-hime went into labor before it was completed. She entered the unfinished hut and turned to Hoori. "To give birth, I must return to my natural form. Promise me you will not look upon me," she pleaded.

Unsurprisingly, Hoori's curiosity got the better of him. Unable to resist, he peeked inside the hut and saw Toyotama-hime in her true form—an enormous wani, a sea dragon, writhing and creeping about.

Ashamed and heartbroken that her true form had been seen, Toyotama-hime decided she could no longer stay in the land of humans. Despite her love for Hoori, she returned to the sea, leaving their newborn son behind. Before she left, she closed the path between the land and sea, forever separating their worlds.

Toyotama-hime felt betrayed, yet her love for Hoori remained. And so, she asked her sister, Tamayori-hime, to care for the child. "Take care of him for me," she said, her voice tinged with sorrow.

Tamayori-hime raised the boy, who was named Ugayafukiaezu. When he grew up, he married Tamayori-hime, and together they had four children. One of their sons would become the legendary Emperor Jimmu, the first emperor of Japan, symbolizing the lasting bond between the worlds of land and sea.

The stories of Urashima Taro, the kappa, and Hoori and Toyotama-hime are full of lessons about respecting nature, the dangers of greed, and the virtues of compassion and bravery. Urashima Taro's journey reminds us that life is fleeting and that we should cherish the world around us. The kappa, with its mix of mischief and danger, shows that understanding and respecting nature can lead to harmony. The tale of Hoori and Toyotama-hime highlights how all living things are connected and the importance of respecting the mysteries of nature.

These stories also caution against greed. Urashima Taro's curiosity, which leads him to open the tamatebako and age instantly, serves as a warning against temptation. Hoori's use of the tide-controlling jewels to the point that he was willing to drown his brother, illustrates the destructive potential of greed. However, amidst these warnings, there are also stories of kindness and bravery. Urashima Taro's act of kindness earns him a magical journey, while the kappa can become a helpful ally when treated with respect. Hoori's brave journey and his love for Toyotama-hime also reflect the courage required to bridge different worlds.

These tales reflect how deeply Japanese culture reveres water. As an island nation, Japan's history, culture, and daily life are closely tied to the sea, rivers, and lakes. These stories remind us to maintain harmony with nature, live with compassion and bravery, and respect the waters that give us life.

Chapter 7: Adventures and Legends in the Wild

Two men, weary and lost, trudged through the dense forest as night descended. As the air grew colder and the sounds of the forest grew more eerie, the men's desperation for shelter intensified. They stumbled upon a small hut.

Knocking on the door, they were greeted by an old woman, her gnarled hands busy spinning thread.

"Please, good lady, may we shelter here for the night?" one of the men asked, his voice trembling.

The old woman squinted at them. "My hut is small and modest," she said. "It is not fit for men dressed as fine as yourselves."

"We beg of you," the other man implored. "The woods are dangerous, and we fear for our lives. We ask for nothing more than a corner to rest until dawn."

The old woman sighed, a deep, resigned sound. "Very well,' she said reluctantly. "But promise me one thing. Do not, under any circumstances, open the door to the inner room."

"You have our words," the men chorused, relief flooding their faces.

As the hours passed, the old woman went out, leaving the men alone in the dimly lit hut. Curiosity gnawed at them. What could be so precious that the old woman guarded it so fiercely? They exchanged furtive glances. Unable to resist, tiptoed to the forbidden door. Quietly, they opened it a crack and peered inside.

Their faces blanched with horror. Piles of bodies and ancient bones lay heaped in the room, the grisly remains of those who had come before them. The men quickly shut the door, their hearts pounding with fear. They gathered their belongings, but as they moved toward the door, they heard the old woman returning. She sensed their betrayal immediately. Her form began to change: horns sprouted from her forehead, and her fangs gleamed under the moonlight. The legendary Yamamba, the mountain witch, stood before them.

A depiction of Yamamba (also spelled Yama-uba). "

"You broke your promise," she snarled, her voice a guttural growl.

Terrified, the men bolted from the hut, running as fast as their legs could carry them. They recited sutras, hoping the benevolent power of the Buddha would protect them. Yamamba pursued them, her rage palpable, but the men's prayers seemed to slow her down.

As they neared the edge of the village, the witch was forced to retreat. The sacred ground of the village was beyond her reach, and she melted back into the shadows of the mountains.

Breathing heavily, the men collapsed at the village's edge, safe at last. They had narrowly escaped the witch's wrath.

Yamamba's nature was rather complex. She was neither purely evil nor kind. While she killed those who broke their promises, she was also known to help humans—like many other mythical creatures of Japanese beliefs. Farmers and weavers spoke of her assistance in their labor, a mysterious force that sometimes worked in their favor.

This tale, like many others, reveals Japan's untamed mountains, forests, and rural areas. These wild places were full of surprises, harboring spirits and supernatural beings that guarded or haunted the grounds. Some people avoided venturing too deep into the unknown, while others sought the thrill of adventure. Mothers would warn their children to steer clear of these places, and should they ever get lost in forests or the wild, to always respect their surroundings lest they anger the spirits (kami) dwelling within.

Another tale of the untamed written in the eleventh century provides a more heartwarming story. It begins in a small village called Kamiide, believed to be in the Suruga Province. The story centers around a young boy named Yosoji. His village had been plagued by a devastating smallpox epidemic, and among the afflicted was his mother. Her condition grew worse each day, and Yosoji's heart ached as he watched her suffer.

Desperate to find a cure, Yosoji sought out a fortune teller, hoping for a miracle. The old seer listened to his plight and, after a moment of deep thought, spoke. "There is a stream at the foot of Mount Fuji," he said. "Its waters have the power to cure disease. Bring this water to your mother, and she will recover."

Filled with hope, Yosoji set out on his journey the very next day. As he ventured into the woods, he came across three different paths. Each seemed equally likely, but he had no idea which one to take. The description given by the fortune teller had been vague, leaving Yosoji confused.

Just then, a young girl dressed in white emerged from the bushes and approached him. "Are you lost?" she asked, her voice gentle and soothing.

Yosoji, though puzzled by her sudden appearance, felt a glimmer of hope. "I need to find a stream at the foot of Mount Fuji," he explained. "It's for my mother; she's very ill."

The girl smiled softly. "Follow me," she said. "I know the way."

Yosoji followed her, and soon they arrived at the small stream the fortune teller had spoken of. The girl stood by as Yosoji carefully scooped some water into a flask. "Thank you," he said, his heart swelling with gratitude.

He hurried back to his village and gave the water to his mother. Days passed, and her condition began to improve. Yosoji's joy was boundless, but he knew his task was not yet complete. He returned to the forest, hoping to find the girl again.

At the crossroads of the three paths, he saw her once more. She greeted him with a serene smile. "Return here in three days," she instructed. "You must make five trips to the stream to cure the entire village."

Yosoji nodded and followed her instructions faithfully. On each trip, he collected more water, and each time, the villagers' health improved. By the end of the fifth journey, the smallpox epidemic had been vanquished, and the village was filled with celebration. The villagers thanked Yosoji for his bravery and determination.

The spirit showing Yosoji the stream. "

Knowing he owed his success to the girl in white, Yosoji went back to the forest, hoping to see her one last time. But when he arrived at the stream, he found it dried up, and the girl was nowhere to be seen. He knelt by the dry bed and prayed, asking for her to reveal herself so he could express his gratitude.

As if in answer to his prayers, the girl appeared. Yosoji's heart leaped with joy. "Thank you for everything," he said earnestly. "May I know your name so I can tell the villagers who our true savior is?"

The girl smiled, a mysterious glint in her eyes. "My name is not important," she replied gently. "Farewell, Yosoji."

With that, she swung a branch of camellia over her head. A magical scene unfolded before Yosoji's eyes: a cloud descended from Mount Fuji and enveloped her. The cloud lifted her into the sky, revealing her true identity. She was none other than Konohanasakuya-hime, the goddess of Mount Fuji.

Yosoji watched in awe as she ascended, her divine presence illuminating the night. He returned to the village, carrying the tale of their miraculous savior, forever grateful for the goddess's kindness.

Not all tales of the untamed were told to instill fear. This legend of Mount Fuji and the benevolent kami Konohanasakuya-hime exemplifies the wonders and surprises that nature holds.

The Tragic Legend of Yamato Takeru

From the early days of his youth, Prince Ousu, later known as Yamato Takeru, had been surrounded by a sense of destiny. As the youngest son of Emperor Keikō and the elder lady of Inabi, he was raised in the shadow of the Yamato clan's divine lineage, said to be descended from the sun goddess Amaterasu.

One fateful day, Prince Ousu committed an act that would forever alter his life. In a fit of rage or perhaps a twisted sense of justice, he killed his brother. This act of fratricide cast a dark shadow over his character and instilled a deep-seated fear in his father. Emperor Keikō, believing that his son harbored a dangerous and malevolent nature, chose not to punish him directly but sent him away on a dangerous mission.

"Go to the land of the Kumaso," the emperor decreed, his voice cold and unyielding. "Quell their rebellion or perish in the attempt."

The Kumaso people were fierce warriors who refused to submit to the central rule of the Yamato clan. Their chiefs were feared for their strength and brutality. It was a mission that seemed almost certain to fail, a task designed to rid the emperor of his troublesome son. Undeterred, Prince Ousu accepted the challenge, determined to prove his worth.

Before setting out, he journeyed to the sacred Ise Shrine to seek the blessing of Amaterasu. There, he met his aunt, the high priestess of the Ise

Shrine. She saw the turmoil in his eyes and the burden he carried. "Take this robe," she said, handing him an exquisite silk garment. "It will bring you luck and protect you on your journey."

With his wife, Princess Ototachibana, and a few loyal followers, Prince Ousu set out to confront the Kumaso. His journey was dangerous, but his cunning and bravery soon earned him a new name. He learned that the Kumaso were having a feast, and this was indeed a golden opportunity for the young prince to strike. Attacking head-on, however, was suicide. So, he planned to sneak into the banquet. Donning the robe his aunt had gifted him, the prince disguised himself as a female servant. He let down his hair, styled it with a comb, and adorned it with jewelry. His soft features made it easy to pass as a female servant. The prince entered the banquet without suspicion. The leader of the Kumaso is said to have called the disguised prince, demanding he pour wine faster, to which he gladly obliged. He was, after all, waiting for his enemies to get drunk.

Then, the moment the Kumaso were thoroughly drunk, the prince made his move. He unsheathed a small knife concealed beneath his robe and swiftly attacked the Kumaso chief. This daring feat earned him the name Yamato Takeru, which simply means "The Brave of Yamato." After quelling the rebellion just as his father had instructed, Yamato Takeru made his way home. On his way, the prince added more feats to his list of achievements, slaying several divine beings believed to be hostile to the Yamato rule.

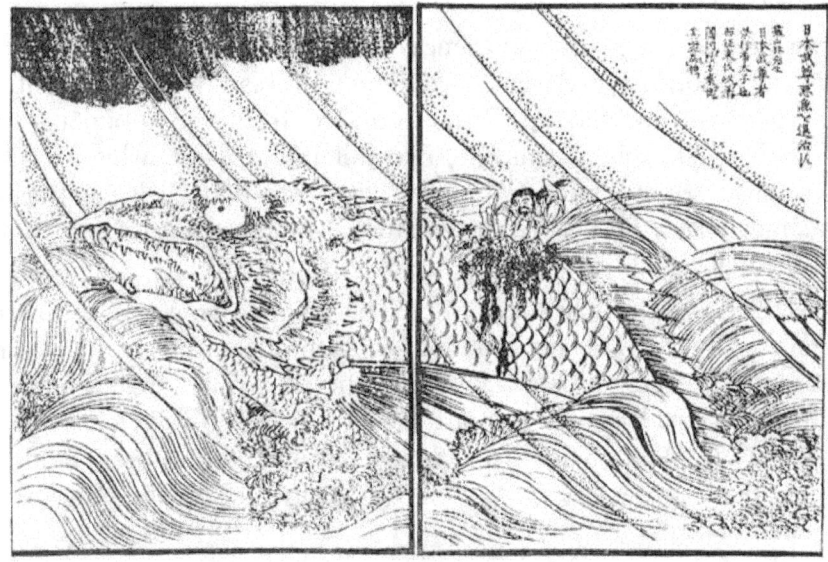

A depiction of Yamato Takeru battling a certain sea monster.[47]

However, despite his victory, Emperor Keikō remained unmoved. He viewed his son with the same suspicion and fear as before. "Go to the eastern lands and obliterate those who refuse to submit to my rule," he commanded, sending Yamato Takeru on yet another perilous mission.

At this, Takeru revealed his more vulnerable human side. The prince, aware of his father's intentions, confided in his aunt. "I know my father wishes for my demise," he said, his voice heavy with sorrow.

His aunt, touched by his plight, gave him the legendary sword Kusanagi. "This sword," she said, "was found in the tail of the great serpent slain by Susanoo, the great kami of storms. It will protect you as you face your destiny."

Yamato Takeru set out once more, accompanied by his faithful wife. However, their voyage was treacherous. As they crossed the sea, a violent storm threatened to capsize their vessel. Princess Ototachibana sacrificed herself to the god of the sea, soothing the divine being's anger and allowing her husband to continue his quest. Grieving but resolute, Yamato Takeru pressed on, conquering foes both mortal and divine.

His path led him to Ashigara Pass, where he encountered a deity in the form of a deer. Seeing through the disguise, he slew the deity, making the passage safe for future travelers. He also successfully subdued a deity in Shinano (modern-day Gunma Prefecture) before reaching Owari. It was also here that he married Princess Miyazu, finding a brief respite in his arduous journey.

Yamato Takeru's final challenge came at Mount Ibuki, a sacred mountain shrouded in legend. Confident in his strength, he left the Kusanagi sword behind and set out to confront the mountain deity barehanded. On his ascent, he encountered a large white boar—or according to some sources, a white snake—which he believed was the deity's messenger. Respecting the creature, he did not kill it, unaware that it was the deity itself.

The deity, enraged by the prince's blasphemy, conjured a powerful hailstorm. The icy winds howled through the mountains, battering Yamato Takeru with relentless force. Hailstones the size of fists pelted him, and the once clear path turned into a treacherous, frozen maze. Disoriented and exhausted, the brave prince staggered through the storm. The deity's curse seeped into his bones, sapping his vitality and leaving him feverish and weak.

He struggled to find his way and fortunately stumbled upon a spring at Samegai. He drank deeply, the refreshing liquid offering a momentary reprieve from his torment. For a brief period, the prince felt his former strength returning, but the respite was fleeting. The curse of the mountain deity was too potent. He knew his end was near.

Yamato Takeru and the sword Kusanagi. *

With his last breath, he gazed up at the sky, a profound peace washing over him. His spirit, unshackled from his mortal form, transformed into a majestic white bird. The bird took flight, soaring through the heavens, its pure form gliding gracefully back to his kin.

When the white bird reached the imperial palace, Emperor Keikō saw the spirit of his son. At that moment, the emperor's heart softened, and he finally understood the true worth and unparalleled bravery of Yamato Takeru. The fear and suspicion that had clouded his judgment lifted, replaced by a deep sense of loss and regret. To honor the valiant prince who had fought so bravely for the Yamato Kingdom, he erected a grand mausoleum, a lasting tribute to Yamato Takeru's courage and sacrifice.

Tengu, the Spirits of the Mountains

Tengu are one of the most enigmatic and formidable creatures in Japanese folklore. Often depicted as mountain goblins or warrior spirits, these supernatural beings are both revered and feared. They are typically portrayed with a combination of human and avian features: red-faced with sharp, piercing eyes and sometimes wings and the beak of a bird. As time passed, the depiction of tengu evolved, and they became more anthropomorphic. Sometimes they were shown with a long, prominent nose rather than a beak, hinting at their transformation from avian spirits to human-like warriors.

Tengu masks. *

Tengu are known for their martial prowess, often depicted as skilled swordsmen and masters of disguise. They are closely associated with yamabushi, or mountain ascetic monks, and frequently take on their appearance. These monks, who practiced a form of Shugendō—a belief system combining Shinto, Buddhism, and Taoism—were known for their rigorous training and mystical practices in the mountains.

One legend involving tengu begins with the Empress Dowager Fujiwara no Akirakeiko, also known as the Somedono Empress, the mother of

Emperor Seiwa. The empress was constantly afflicted by a spiritual ailment, frequently suffering from spirit possessions. Many prayers and rituals were conducted for her recovery, and numerous monks and priests were summoned to perform these rites, yet the empress remained tormented.

In search of a solution, the court heard of a monk living in a remote temple atop Mount Katsuragi in what is now Nara Prefecture. This monk had honed his magical rituals over many years and possessed extraordinary powers. It was said he could send his bowl flying to fetch food and his bottle to retrieve water, all without moving a muscle. Intrigued by these tales of his abilities, the emperor dispatched envoys to summon this monk to the palace, hoping he could cure the empress.

The monk agreed to help and commenced a ritual to expel the malicious spirit plaguing the empress. During the ritual, one of the empress's servants suddenly began to cry and laugh uncontrollably. She was restrained and beaten as the monk chanted his incantations. A fox then sprang out from her clothing, revealing itself to be a kitsune—the spirit responsible for haunting the empress. With additional rituals, the monk successfully dispersed the kitsune, and the empress began to recover.

Grateful for the monk's success, the emperor invited him to stay at the imperial palace. The monk enjoyed the comforts and luxuries of the palace, but his stay took a dark turn. One day, he glimpsed the empress in her private chambers, clad only in her undergarments. Consumed by desire and perhaps influenced by evil whispers, the monk attempted to assault her. The empress's cries alerted her ladies-in-waiting, who quickly summoned Taima no Kamotsugu, the court physician. Kamotsugu apprehended the monk and brought him before the emperor.

Furious and betrayed, the emperor had the monk imprisoned. The monk, however, did not regret his action. Instead, he declared his desire to see the empress again and vowed to become a demon after death if necessary. His sinister vow was reported to the emperor, who then ordered the monk's exile to the mountains.

In his mountain exile, the monk's obsession festered. Desperate to reunite with the empress, he starved himself to death, fully intent on transforming into a demon. His malevolent wish was granted, and he became a tengu. He turned into a figure eight feet tall with a bald head, skin as black as a crow, and eyes that gleamed with malice. Wielding a magical hammer and wearing only a loincloth, he descended upon the imperial palace, striking fear into the hearts of all who beheld him.

The tengu infiltrated the empress's bedchamber and possessed her, spending nights with her while she was entranced. Each morning, the maids found her with no memory of the encounters. Alarmed, they reported these events to the emperor. The emperor, more concerned for the empress's future than frightened by the tengu, ordered further rituals to banish the demon. The tengu also sought revenge against Kamotsugu, whose fear led to his untimely death, followed by the mysterious deaths of his sons.

For a time, the rituals succeeded, and the empress's condition improved. However, the respite was short-lived. The tengu soon returned to the empress's bedchamber, resuming his nightly visits. The story ends on a cliffhanger, leaving the fate of the empress and the tengu unresolved. The moral of the tale, as recounted by old storytellers, was a warning that noblewomen should avoid relationships with priests, as such liaisons could lead to disaster.

However, not all stories about tengu revolve around the creature being a malice to human beings.

The phenomenon of people disappearing mysteriously (generally known as kamikakushi) was often attributed to the handiwork of kami or other divine spirits, and tengu were frequently implicated. This mysterious abduction done specifically by a tengu is known as tengu sarai. Tengu were said to snatch people away, especially children, and take them to the mountains. These children often returned with fear and trauma, but in rare cases, they came back profoundly changed.

One of the most famous examples of a tengu abduction was a seven-year-old boy from the Edo period named Torakichi. His experience was meticulously documented by a Shinto scholar, Hirata Atsutane. According to the records, Torakichi was spirited away by tengu and spent five years with them. During this time, he traveled to different otherworldly places, saw the moon up close, and acquired many skills. He learned martial arts, medicine, calligraphy, and weapon-making under the guidance of the tengu. Upon his return, Torakichi exhibited extraordinary abilities and knowledge far beyond his years.

While they are often feared for their mischievous and sometimes malevolent actions, tengu also possess great wisdom and mastery of martial arts. This duality is reflected in the belief held by some that tengu are the reincarnated spirits of Buddhist priests who were proud and self-important in life. This notion explains why tengu frequently take the form of yamabushi, or mountain ascetic monks, as a reflection of their past lives and their connection to spiritual and martial disciplines.

Tengu have a reputation for being exceptional swordsmen. They also tend to mentor those they deem worthy in the skills of martial arts. This mentorship often involves rigorous training and the imparting of secret techniques that are otherwise inaccessible to ordinary humans. One of the most renowned examples of a tengu mentor is Sōjōbō, the king of the tengu, who is said to reside on Mount Kurama.

Minamoto no Yoshitsune, one of Japan's most celebrated warriors, is famously associated with Sōjōbō and the tengu. According to legend, Yoshitsune was sent to a temple on Mount Kurama after his father's demise in a war. There, he was trained by the king of the tengu.

Minamoto no Yoshitsune training under the tutelage of Sōjōbō.[50]

Under Sōjōbō's tutelage, Yoshitsune mastered the art of the sword, learning techniques that enabled him to move with extraordinary speed and agility. He also gained insights into military strategy and the use of magic in combat. These skills proved invaluable during the Genpei War, where Yoshitsune led the Minamoto clan to victory against the Taira clan, securing his place in Japanese history as a legendary warrior.

Chapter 8: Ghost Tales

The story of Okiku has many different variations, but the most popular one begins at Himeji Castle, where the legend is believed to have originated. Okiku was a servant at the castle, responsible for washing dishes. When she first entered the castle's service, she marveled at the many treasures it held, but none were as precious as the ten exquisite plates used by the lord to entertain high-ranking guests. Okiku knew she had to handle these plates with utmost care, for even a single chip could mean her death.

Okiku's beauty was renowned throughout the castle, attracting the attention of many, particularly the samurai retainers. Among them, one samurai named Aoyama became infatuated with her. His desire for Okiku grew so intense that he would do anything to have her.

One day, Aoyama approached her. "Okiku," he said, his eyes intense with longing, "I cannot hide my feelings any longer. I wish to marry you."

Okiku's heart pounded in her chest. She bowed respectfully and replied, "My lord, I am honored, but I do not share your feelings."

Aoyama's face darkened with disappointment. "You will come to love me in time," he insisted, but Okiku remained firm in her refusal.

Days turned into weeks, and Aoyama's frustration grew. He tried to woo her with gifts and kind words, but nothing swayed her. Finally, in a fit of desperation, he devised a sinister plan to force her into submission.

One evening, after the castle had quieted down, Aoyama crept into the room where the treasured plates were kept. With a sly grin, he took one of the ten plates and hid it. The next day, he confronted Okiku, his tone accusatory.

"One of the plates is missing," he said, his voice cold and threatening. "Do you know what this means?"

Okiku's eyes widened in horror. She rushed to count the plates, her hands trembling. "One, two, three, four, five, six, seven, eight, nine," she whispered, her heart sinking. She counted again and again, but there were only nine.

"Please, Aoyama. I swear I did not lose the plate!" she cried, tears streaming down her face.

Aoyama feigned concern, but his eyes gleamed with malice. "Okiku," he said softly, "I can tell the lord it wasn't your fault. But you must agree to be mine."

Despite her fear, Okiku stood her ground. "No, my lord. I cannot."

Her refusal ignited Aoyama's fury. He grabbed her roughly and beat her with a wooden sword. Okiku cried out in pain, but she did not relent. Enraged, Aoyama tied her and suspended her over a well in the courtyard.

"You will change your mind," he snarled, dunking her into the cold, dark water, "or you will die."

Each time he pulled her up, gasping for air, he demanded her compliance. Each time, she refused. Finally, in a fit of blind rage, Aoyama drew his katana and struck her down, her lifeless body falling into the well.

In Japanese folklore, spirits are believed to pass on to the afterlife unless held back by strong emotions. A person who dies unjustly may become an onryō, a vengeful spirit, driven by the need for retribution. Unlike yokai, which are supernatural creatures, yūrei are spirits of the dead (ghosts), and onryō are among the most feared, capable of causing great harm.

After her death, Okiku transformed into an onryō. One night, her mutilated form arose from the well to walk the castle halls, searching for the missing plate. "One, two, three, four, five, six, seven, eight, nine," she would count, her voice echoing through the halls. Then, a heart-wrenching scream would follow, chilling anyone who heard it. Those who heard part of her counting fell ill, while those who heard the full count died of fright. Aoyama, tormented by her nightly visits, was driven mad by lack of sleep.

The castle's lord, desperate to end the haunting, called upon a priest to cleanse the grounds. The priest, wise and cunning, awaited Okiku's nightly appearance. When she reached nine in her count, he quickly shouted, "Ten!" Okiku's spirit, seemingly satisfied that the missing plate was found, finally found peace. Her tormented expression softened, and she disappeared into the well, never to return again.

Yet, some say Okiku's spirit did not rest entirely. In 1795, a strange infestation of caterpillars plagued Japan's wells. These insects, resembling a tied-up woman, were believed to be Okiku's lingering spirit. The caterpillar became known as Okiku mushi. Today, this insect is commonly known as the jakō ageha, or the Chinese windmill (Byasa alcinous), a haunting reminder of her tragic fate.

Okiku's story became so famous that it has been adapted into various forms of media over the centuries. Her tale has inspired plays, books, and movies, capturing the imagination of audiences worldwide. Her story inspired the popular horror movie *The Ring*, known as *Ringu* in Japan. The film features a vengeful spirit with a similar tragic backstory, highlighting how deeply ingrained Okiku's legend is in Japanese culture and how it continues to inspire modern interpretations of ghost stories.

Indeed, Japan's rich folklore is home to countless ghost stories, but three stand out as the most famous and influential. They are known as Nihon san dai kaidan or Japan's Big Three Ghost Stories. Okiku's story is one of the three, and the second we are about to explore also revolves around revenge. Today, it remains one of the most chilling and compelling ghost stories in Japanese history.

Oiwa's Curse

The story takes place in the Edo period and follows a kind-hearted woman named Oiwa. She was married to Tamiya Iemon, a ronin. Unlike the legendary samurai of the past, Iemon was a wasteful man and a thief, notorious for his misdeeds. For the longest time, the couple did not live a happy married life; their days were often filled with Iemon throwing a fit and Oiwa absorbing his anger, hoping one day he would change for the better. That was, however, until one day when Oiwa sensed that Iemon would never improve himself. She made up her mind to finally leave him. Oiwa confided in her father, who was also a ronin at the time. And so, after listening to his daughter's laments, Oiwa's father confronted Iemon and demanded that he divorce Oiwa. He also knew that Iemon had lived a life far from the honorable path.

"You have disgraced our family enough, Iemon," he declared, his voice firm with authority. "Leave my daughter and never return."

Enraged by his father-in-law's ultimatum and fearing the exposure of his crimes, Iemon drew his sword and murdered Iowa's father in cold blood. Returning home, he lied to Oiwa, claiming that her father had been killed by bandits on the road. He begged her to reconcile with him, promising to avenge her father's death.

After the death of her father, Oiwa, grief-stricken and vulnerable, chose to remain with Iemon. In due course, she became pregnant and gave birth to a son. However, the family's financial struggles deepened, and Oiwa's health took a severe turn post-childbirth. As she grew weaker, Iemon's frustration and resentment toward her intensified.

During this turbulent period, Iemon crossed paths with Oume, the youthful and attractive granddaughter of Ito Kihei, a wealthy and influential doctor. Oume, captivated by Iemon despite his marital status, fell deeply in love with him. Her grandfather, cherishing Oume dearly, resolved to ensure her happiness at any cost. Together, they schemed to remove Oiwa from Iemon's life, allowing Oume to take her place.

Jealous of Oiwa's beauty and her position as Iemon's wife, Oume and her grandfather conspired to ruin her. Ito Kihei, feigning benevolence, provided Oiwa with an ointment he claimed would restore her health. In truth, it was a poison intended to disfigure her. As days passed, Oiwa's condition deteriorated. Her once beautiful face became grotesquely scarred, and her hair fell out in clumps. Witnessing Oiwa's transformation, Iemon's feelings turned from resentment to outright hatred.

"Iemon, my love, is the ointment working?" Oiwa asked, hoping that her condition was improving.

Iemon, unable to hide his revulsion, replied coldly, "Yes, Oiwa, keep using it."

Seeing his opportunity, Ito Kihei suggested that Iemon divorce Oiwa and marry Oume instead. "Marry my granddaughter, and you will inherit our family's wealth," he promised.

Entranced by Oume's beauty and repulsed by Oiwa's appearance, Iemon agreed. After all, Oume was younger than his wife, and her grandfather's wealth was indeed enticing. He began selling Oiwa's belongings, including her kimono and their son's clothes, to gather funds for his new marriage. However, another problem lingered: he needed a legitimate reason to divorce Oiwa. Desperate, Iemon enlisted his friend Takuetsu to assault Oiwa so he could accuse her of infidelity.

On the planned night, while Iemon was away, Takuetsu entered their home and approached Oiwa. But the sight of Oiwa's disfigured face surprised him, and he had a change of heart— Takuetsu could not carry on with the plan. And so, he chose to tell poor Oiwa the truth.

"Apologies will never be enough, Oiwa. But at the very least, let me tell you the truth," Takuetsu confessed, his voice trembling. "Iemon orchestrated this. He wanted me to violate you so he could claim you were unfaithful."

Devastated, Oiwa looked at herself in the mirror for the first time since using the ointment. She saw a monstrous reflection staring back at her. In a desperate attempt to cover her scars, she brushed her hair over her face, only for it to fall out in bloody clumps. Overwhelmed by betrayal and her horrific appearance, Oiwa grabbed Takuetsu's sword to take her own life. Takuetsu tried to stop her but failed. In just moments, Oiwa dropped to the floor, surrounded by a pool of blood.

As Oiwa lay dying, she cursed Iemon with her final breaths. Iemon's servant, Kohei, later discovered her body and reported the news. Instead of grief, Iemon felt relief and joy. Kohei, suspecting foul play, confronted Iemon but was killed and disposed of alongside Oiwa. Iemon fabricated a story that Kohei and Oiwa were lovers, freeing himself to marry Oume.

From there on, Oiwa's curse swiftly took effect. On the first night after marrying Oume, Iemon was plagued by a feeling of uneasiness. He had trouble sleeping, so he rolled on his side to look at his new wife. Much to his horror, it was not Oume by his side, but his disfigured late wife. In a panic, he slashed out with his sword, only to realize he had killed Oume and the sight of Oiwa was nothing more than an illusion. Terrified, he sought help from Ito Kihei but was confronted by Kohei's ghost. In his frenzy, Iemon swung his sword again. Once the illusion ended, he discovered that he had also killed Ito Kihei.

Haunted by Oiwa's vengeful spirit, Iemon fled into the night. She appeared everywhere—in his dreams, shadows, and even the lanterns

Iemon seeing Oiwa's ghostly face on lanterns.[51]

lighting his way. Driven mad by her relentless pursuit, Iemon sought refuge in the mountains, but even there, Oiwa's ghost found him. Unable to distinguish reality from nightmare, Iemon descended into madness.

The Peony Lantern Ghost Story

The third story of the Nihon san dai kaidan begins on the night of the Obon festival when the air is thick with the scent of incense and the soft glow of lanterns. This annual event, held to honor and welcome the spirits of ancestors back to Earth for a few days, is a deeply significant time in Japanese culture. Families prepare by cleaning their homes, offering food, and lighting lanterns to guide their loved ones' spirits. It is a time of reverence and reunion, where the boundary between the living and the dead blurs.

However, amidst the joyous reunions of one Obon festival, one man chose not to participate. Ogiwara Shinnojo, recently bereaved of his wife, remained in his house, enveloped in grief. As the festival carried on outside, Ogiwara sat alone, his heart heavy with sorrow.

In the distance, he noticed a faint light. As it drew nearer, he could see it was coming from a lantern. The lantern, adorned with painted peony flowers, was carried by a woman who appeared to be a servant. Beside her walked another woman whose beauty was so striking it left Ogiwara almost speechless. He rose to greet them, his curiosity piqued by their mysterious presence.

The beautiful woman introduced herself as Otsuyu, and the woman carrying the lantern was her servant. They explained that they had just come from a nearby temple. Enchanted by Otsuyu's beauty and the sense of calm she brought, Ogiwara invited them into his home. They talked, laughed, and enjoyed each other's company late into the night. When Otsuyu left before dawn, Ogiwara felt a pang of

Otsuyu and her servant.[53]

sadness at her departure.

To his surprise, Otsuyu returned the following night. Once again, they spent the night together, sharing stories, laughter, and eventually the bed. This routine continued for several nights, and Ogiwara found himself falling deeply in love. His days became a mere prelude to the nights he spent with Otsuyu. He barely left his home, consumed by anticipation for her next visit.

However, Ogiwara's peculiar behavior did not go unnoticed. Concerned, a neighbor decided to check on him one evening. Hearing eerie laughter from within, the neighbor peeked inside and was horrified by what he saw. Ogiwara was not with a beautiful woman but with a decomposing corpse, its skeletal form barely covered with decaying flesh.

The next day, the neighbor confronted Ogiwara, explaining the ghastly sight he had witnessed. Shocked and disbelieving, Ogiwara listened as the neighbor urged him to stop meeting Otsuyu. "She will drain your life away," the neighbor warned. "You must break free from her spell."

Determined to uncover the truth, Ogiwara recalled that Otsuyu had mentioned coming from a nearby temple. He ventured to the temple and, sure enough, found a peony lantern lying atop a grave. His heart sank as he realized that Otsuyu had died long ago, before they had met. Ogiwara recounted his experience to a Buddhist priest, who provided him with a spirit-repelling charm to place outside his home. That night, Otsuyu did not return.

Despite the charm's effectiveness, Ogiwara's longing for Otsuyu only grew. Consumed by sadness and desperation, he turned to alcohol for solace. One fateful night, in a drunken haze, Ogiwara stumbled to the temple and made his way to Otsuyu's grave. There, she appeared before him, as beautiful as ever. Otsuyu invited him to stay with her, and, overwhelmed by love and longing, Ogiwara agreed.

Ogiwara was never seen again. When the priest decided to open Otsuyu's grave, he discovered two bodies lying together: Ogiwara, embracing the decomposed remains of Otsuyu.

Legends say that on dark, cloudy nights, people would sometimes see Otsuyu, her servant, and Ogiwara Shinnojo walking together. Those who saw them would fall ill, prompting rituals to release the three spirits from the earthly realm forever.

The Peony Lantern stands apart from the other two ghost stories of the Nihon san dai kaidan in its emotional core. While the stories of Okiku and Oiwa are driven by fierce vengeance, Otsuyu's lingering spirit is fueled by profound loneliness.

These ghost tales hold deep cultural significance, reflecting societal norms, fears, and the collective psyche regarding death, loyalty, love, and retribution. They provide thrilling and chilling narratives that offer insights into traditional Japanese concepts of life and the afterlife, illustrating how the past continuously informs the present. Through these stories, we explore the consequences of betrayal, the power of love, and the inevitability of death.

Ghost stories are integral to festivals like Obon, where spirits are honored and remembered. These stories have also permeated literature, highlighting their enduring popularity and influence on Japanese art and entertainment.

Ghost Tales in Japanese Theaters

Ghost stories find a prominent place in theater, especially in Noh and Kabuki, where the haunting tales come to life on stage, captivating audiences with their eerie beauty. Kabuki is a classical Japanese dance-drama known for its highly stylized performances, vibrant costumes, and elaborate makeup. Originating in the early seventeenth century, Kabuki was initially performed by female dancers, but it evolved to become an all-male art form. Kabuki plays often include dramatic plots, historical events, and supernatural elements.

The story of Oiwa from *Tōkaidō Yotsuya Kaidan* is one of the most famous ghost stories performed in Kabuki, where the elaborate staging and intense acting bring the tragic and vengeful spirit to life, captivating audiences with its horror and emotional depth. The story of Oiwa is performed with dramatic flair, using special effects to create ghostly apparitions and chilling scenes. The elaborate sets, lighting, and makeup enhance the eerie atmosphere, making the audience feel the horror of Oiwa's vengeance.

Kabuki actors dressed as samurai.[58]

Noh, on the other hand, is a more refined and minimalist form of theater that dates to the fourteenth century. It combines music, dance, and acting to create a highly stylized performance. Noh plays often explore themes of the supernatural, with ghosts and spirits frequently taking center stage. The actors wear intricate masks and costumes, and the performances are accompanied by traditional music. The story of Okiku from *Banchō Sarayashiki* is a classic example of a ghost tale in Noh, where the haunting presence of Okiku, wronged in life, is portrayed with subtlety and grace, evoking a sense of melancholy and spiritual unrest. The use of masks and minimalist stage design helps to convey the tragic beauty of Okiku's spirit, creating a hauntingly poignant performance.

Both Kabuki and Noh have adapted the story of the Peony Lantern, highlighting the tragic love story between Ogiwara and the ghostly Otsuyu. In Kabuki, the costumes and acting emphasize the romantic and supernatural elements, while in Noh, the story is told with a more subdued and introspective approach.

The integration of these tales into festivals, literature, and theatrical performances like Noh and Kabuki illustrates their enduring popularity and influence on Japanese culture and art. Through these stories, audiences are reminded of the thin veil between life and death and the timeless emotions that bind humanity across generations.

Chapter 9: Wisdom of the Elders

An old man and his wife lived in a small village. Their life was one of simplicity and hardship, woven together by their daily labor. As the end of the year approached, the world around them was transformed by a blanket of thick snow. The air grew bitterly cold.

The old couple earned their meager living by weaving straw hats. Every day, they worked tirelessly, their hands moving deftly as they crafted the hats with care and skill. By the end of this particular day, they had managed to weave five straw hats, hoping to sell them in the town the next day. As the old man put down the last hat, he sighed deeply. "Wife," he lamented, "the new year is almost upon us, and yet we have no rice cakes to celebrate. It has been years since we've had any to mark the occasion."

An example of a Japanese straw hat. [4]

In Japan, the new year, or Oshōgatsu, is a time of great importance. It is a season for family, for renewing hope and joy, and for starting afresh. Rice cakes, or mochi, symbolize prosperity and good fortune.

The absence of these simple treats made the couple's poverty all the starker. The old woman, however, looked at her husband with gentle optimism. "Tomorrow, you will go to town and sell these straw hats," she said. "With the earnings, we shall buy rice cakes and welcome the new year properly."

Comforted by her words, the old man nodded, and they went to sleep, clinging to the fragile hope of a better tomorrow.

The next morning, the old man set off for the town, carrying the five straw hats. He trudged through the thick snow, braving the freezing air with each step. As he arrived in town, he called out to passersby, trying to sell the hats. Unfortunately, no one was interested.

With a heavy heart, the old man began his long journey back home, his hopes dashed. The snow seemed thicker and the cold more biting. As he walked along the foot of the mountain, he came across a row of six Jizo statues. The old man, known for his compassionate heart, stopped and looked at the statues.

A row of Jizo statues. [55]

"Ah, you poor things," he murmured. "Though you are statues, surely you must feel the cold as we do." He decided to use the straw hats to cover the heads of the Jizo statues. One by one, he placed the hats upon them until he came to the last statue. Realizing he only had five hats, he removed his own hat and placed it on the final statue. Smiling at his deed, he continued his journey home.

When he arrived, his wife was waiting for him, worry etched on her face. "Husband, where is your hat? You must be freezing!" she exclaimed.

The old man recounted his encounter with the Jizo statues and how he had given away their straw hats, along with his own. His wife listened, pride welling up in her heart. "Your compassion is admirable," she said. "We may not have rice cakes, but we have each other's company, and that is what truly matters."

They spent the new year's eve in the simplest of ways, without rice cakes, but with the warmth of their companionship. As they drifted off to sleep, they were content.

In the middle of the night, they were awakened by distant voices singing about the old man's kind act. The singing grew louder, and suddenly, there was a thud outside their door. The couple jumped out of bed and hurried to see what had happened. To their astonishment, they found the freshest rice cakes, neatly arranged on a straw mat, placed right in front of their door.

"Who could have done this?" the old man wondered aloud. He noticed tracks in the snow and decided to follow them. He traced the tracks back to the six Jizo statues, still wearing the hats he had given them. To his amazement, the statues were walking across the snow.

Delighted, he rushed back to his wife. "It was the Jizo statues! They have rewarded us for our kindness," he exclaimed.

His wife smiled, her eyes shining with happiness. "Thanks to your compassion, we can enjoy the rice cakes and have a wonderful new year celebration after all."

And so, the old couple enjoyed a joyous new year, their hearts warmed by the kindness and gratitude they had experienced.

In Japanese belief, Jizo statues are protectors of children, travelers, and the souls of the deceased. They are revered for their role as compassionate guardians. This tale of the grateful statues teaches us that acts of kindness, no matter how small, are never forgotten and often return to us in ways we least expect.

The wisdom of elders is a theme that runs deep in Japanese folktales. Rooted in centuries-old traditions, these moral tales have been passed down from generation to generation, serving not only as entertainment but as tools for teaching and reinforcing societal values. They highlight virtues like compassion, honesty, and humility, weaving them into the fabric of daily life. Through simple yet profound stories, elders impart wisdom, guiding the young and reminding the old of the principles that bind their community together.

There is also a tale that teaches the dangers of greed. This story, known as "The Tongue-Cut Sparrow," also took place in a quiet countryside village, where yet another couple lived. While the husband was kind-hearted and soft-spoken, his wife was a tempestuous woman, bad-tempered and with a tongue like a sword. Her words could pierce through anyone's spirit, leaving them bruised and battered.

The husband longed for a child, but his ill-tempered wife wished for none. Whenever he tried to persuade her, she would scold and shout at him until he relented. To soothe his yearning for a child, the man kept a sparrow as a pet. He cared for the bird with all his heart, feeding it by hand and spending time with it. His wife, seeing the affection her husband lavished on the sparrow, despised the bird terribly.

The wife was especially foul tempered on wash days. Her youth had long faded, and now her back and knees protested the arduous task of kneeling to wash clothes. One day, she mixed some starch and placed it in a bowl to cool, preparing to wash the clothes. Suddenly, the sparrow came and pecked at the starch. In a fit of rage, the wife grabbed the poor bird and cut off its tongue, then flung it into the air, shouting, "Never come back!"

When her husband returned, he searched the entire house for his beloved pet. With a heavy heart, he asked his wife what had happened. She recounted every detail, and the man's sadness deepened. He searched for the sparrow day and night, but when he couldn't find it, he gave up hope. One day, as he wandered the mountains, he came across his beloved sparrow. The bird recognized him, and after exchanging bows and greetings, the man expressed how much he had missed his pet. The sparrow invited him to its new home, and the man, delighted, agreed.

The sparrow had built a new life for itself, with a wife and two daughters. It introduced its family to the old man, who was overjoyed for his pet. They spent days together, talking, playing Go—a game of strategy played with black and white stones on a wooden board—and laughing. It was a wonderful time for both.

After several days, the man decided it was time to return home. The sparrow, though sad to see him go, was grateful for the visit. As a token of gratitude, the sparrow offered the man a parting gift. It placed two baskets before him—one heavier than the other—and asked him to choose. Aware of his age and limited strength, the man chose the lighter basket, saying it would be easier to carry down the mountain path. And so they parted, the man carrying the lighter basket home.

When he arrived, his wife greeted him with a barrage of angry words. She was furious that he had been gone for days. The man begged her to stop scolding, and she reluctantly obliged. He then recounted his visit to the sparrow's home and the kindness shown to him. When he opened the basket, they found it filled with gold, coral, precious gems, and other valuables. His wife's eyes gleamed with greed. She declared that she, too, would visit the sparrow to receive a gift.

The wife's visit was far from pleasant. The sparrow was not delighted to see her, but out of politeness, it invited her into its home. Unlike her husband, she did not receive the same hospitality. When she expressed her wish to leave, the sparrow did not offer any gift. Nevertheless, she insisted. The sparrow eventually presented her with two baskets—one heavier than the other. Greedily, she chose the heavier basket and began her journey home. Impatient, she opened the basket to see her treasures.

Instead of gold and gems, a swarm of goblins, a horned oni, and a serpent sprang from the basket. The serpent coiled around her, cracking her bones until she met her end.

The husband, after burying his wife, adopted a son. With the wealth he now possessed, the father and son lived happily ever after.

While the tale of the grateful Jizo statues tells the lesson of kindness, this tale about the tongue-cut sparrow teaches the peril of greed. In seeking more than one's share, one may find oneself entangled in misfortune and suffering.

Another lesson usually found in these age-old folktales is the peril of unbridled desire. Desires can drive people to reach for more than they need, often leading them away from true happiness and satisfaction. The constant yearning for something greater can blind one to the simple joys of their current life.

A Warning about Desire

Once upon a time, there lived a humble stonecutter. Every day, he would chisel away at large stones by the mountainside, shaping them into slabs for gravestones and houses. For the longest time, he was happy and content, asking for nothing more than what he had.

Unbeknownst to the stonecutter, the mountain where he worked was the dwelling of a spirit, who would occasionally appear before human eyes. The stonecutter had heard stories of this spirit, but he never believed them. That was about to change.

One day, as the stonecutter carried his stones to a house belonging to a rich man, he was overwhelmed by desire. He stared at the house, wondering, "How would it feel to live such an easy life?" From that day on, he lost interest in his work, thinking life would be easier if he did not have to do heavy labor yet still enjoyed luxury. "I wish I were a rich man," he muttered, believing he would be much happier.

The mountain spirit heard his wish and, with a distant voice, granted it. "Your wish is granted," the spirit intoned.

The stonecutter, finding no one around, shrugged it off and went home, only to find his house transformed into a grand mansion. Ecstatic, he indulged in his new life, forgetting his old ways.

Later, summer came, and with it, new desires. He saw a prince arriving in town, shaded by servants holding umbrellas. "How wonderful it would be to be a prince," he thought, "shielded from this scorching heat." So, he wished to be a prince, and the mountain spirit granted this wish as well.

Living as a prince, the stonecutter felt powerful, but his heart still yearned for more. Looking up, he saw the sun, which could dry rivers and scorch the earth. "The sun is mightier," he thought. "I wish to be the sun."

Again, the spirit granted his wish. As the sun, he scorched the land and tormented everyone until a cloud blocked his rays. Frustrated, he realized even the sun was not all-powerful. "I wish to be the cloud," he declared.

As a cloud, he blocked the sun and poured rain, causing floods that destroyed villages and palaces alike. Yet, a great rock by the mountainside remained unscathed. "That rock is mightier than I," he mused. "I wish to be the rock."

Transformed into the great rock, he felt invincible. But one day, another stonecutter approached. With his tools, the stonecutter chipped away at him, causing a huge slab to fall. Powerless, the rock could only watch. "How can this tiny man be more powerful than a rock?" he cried. "I wish to be my old self again!"

The mountain spirit, with a touch of amusement, granted this final wish.

Back in his humble form, the stonecutter realized the folly of his desires. "I do not need to wish to be something greater," he thought. "I must be satisfied and grateful for what I have."

From that day forward, he never wished for things he did not have. Instead, he cherished what he already possessed, understanding that true happiness comes from contentment and gratitude.

The Obasute: The Mythical Practice of Elderly Abandonment

In medieval Japan, there was a practice known as obasute (or ubasute), in which elderly people were taken to the mountains and abandoned. This cruel tradition was rooted in the belief that the elderly, unable to perform heavy labor, consumed precious resources without contributing significantly to the community.

One such tale of obasute involves a young farmer and his aged mother. They lived under the rule of a particularly heartless lord, who decreed that anyone who reached the age of seventy must be taken to the mountains and left to die. The elderly were seen as burdens, their wisdom undervalued compared to their daily consumption of rice.

When the farmer's mother turned seventy, she knew the time had come. "My dearest son," she said gently, "you must take me to the mountains. It is the lord's decree."

The young farmer's heart ached at the thought. "Mother, I cannot do such a thing. You have cared for me all my life."

"You must," she insisted, "for the lord's wrath will be severe if we disobey."

A depiction of a young man carrying his mother up Obasute Mountain.[56]

With great reluctance and a heavy heart, the young farmer agreed. He carried his mother on his back, ascending the steep, rocky path. Along the way, she quietly snapped twigs from the trees and dropped them behind them.

"Mother, why do you break the twigs?" he asked.

"So that you may find your way back home," she replied. Her words brought tears to his eyes. Moved by her selflessness even in the face of death, the young farmer could not bear to leave her. He turned back and brought his mother home, hiding her in a secret room he dug beneath their house.

The village soon faced a new threat. An ambitious lord sought to conquer their land, and he issued a challenge to the cruel village lord: produce a rope made of ash, and the village would be spared. If they failed, the village would fall.

Desperate to save his people and preserve his power, the cruel lord gathered the villagers and asked if anyone knew how to create such a rope. None could provide an answer. The young farmer, anxious to help, consulted his hidden mother.

The old woman thought for a moment and then said, "Wet some straw with salty water and weave it into a rope. Let it dry, then burn it carefully. The ash will hold the shape of the rope."

Following her instructions, the young farmer created the ash rope and presented it to the cruel lord. Astonished, the lord asked, "How did you, a mere farmer, come up with such wisdom?"

The young man confessed, "It was not my wisdom, but my mother's. She is still alive, hidden in my home."

Realizing the depth of his error, the cruel lord saw the invaluable wisdom of the elderly. He revoked the decree, declaring, "Now that our village is safe again, let it be known that no elder shall be abandoned again. Their knowledge and experience are treasures that we must honor and protect."

Chapter 10: Key Symbols of Japanese Folklore

Japanese folklore is full of symbols and motifs that reveal deeper truths about life, nature, and humanity. Usually, these symbols are intricately woven into stories, providing lessons and guidance to those who pay attention.

For example, most people cannot help but think of cherry blossoms when they hear the word Japan. This is fair, as cherry blossoms are more than just flowers in the eyes of the Japanese. These sakura flowers bloom in the spring, bringing joy to all who see them. But their beauty is fleeting, reminding us that life itself is short and precious. Every year, families and friends gather under the blooming trees, celebrating the tradition of hanami, or flower viewing. They laugh, share stories, and enjoy the moment, knowing that the blossoms will soon fall. Through these tales, the cherry blossoms teach us to cherish each day and appreciate the beauty around us.

This deep connection to the sakura is reflected in countless stories and poems in which the blossoms are celebrated for their beauty and the profound lessons they teach about the cycle of life.

Cherry blossoms at Mount Yoshino. [57]

One such story tells of a samurai who would sit beneath the cherry trees, contemplating the impermanence of life. The falling petals reminded him of the fragility of existence and the importance of living honorably and fully. This tale, like many others, illustrates how the cherry blossom is a powerful symbol of beauty and ephemerality, teaching the value of mindfulness and presence.

Meanwhile, in the rivers and streams, koi fish swim with all their might against the strong currents. The koi fish, or carp, is a symbol of luck, perseverance, and strength in Japanese culture. During festivals, people celebrate the koi's journey as it struggles upstream, symbolizing the ability to overcome life's challenges. On the annual Children's Day festival, families fly koi-shaped windsocks, called koinobori, to celebrate the hope that their children will grow up to be as strong and determined as the koi. There are stories of koi transforming into powerful dragons, showing that determination and hard work can lead to great transformation and success. These tales encourage us to be resilient no matter how difficult our path may be.

The folding fan, with its graceful curves and intricate designs, is another symbol with meaning. Known as sensu, or ogi, the folding fan symbolizes the unfolding of future possibilities and the elegance of life's journey. Fans are often given as gifts to convey good wishes and the hope for a bright future. The act of opening a fan is a metaphor for revealing hidden potential and embracing new opportunities.

The fan's delicate design and graceful movements in traditional Japanese dance and ceremonies tell stories of beauty, status, and good fortune. Each flick of the fan can reveal a new scene or emotion, making it a versatile tool for storytelling and expression.

A Japanese folding fan from the Heian period. [58]

In many folktales, a fan plays a crucial role. One popular story tells of a young maiden who, with the help of a magical fan, was able to reveal hidden treasures and secrets. This tale, like many others, shows the power of the fan as a symbol of guidance.

Mythical creatures also play a significant role in Japanese folklore. Dragons, revered for their power and strength, are seen as protectors and guardians of nature. The dragon's ability to control the weather and the seas highlights their role as powerful yet compassionate beings. In festivals, dragon dances celebrate their might and bring good fortune to communities. Stories of dragons emphasize their protective nature, showing us that true strength lies in safeguarding and nurturing those around us.

Nature itself is imbued with symbolism in Japanese folklore. Water, for instance, is a symbol of purity and change. It purifies and sustains life, and its flow represents the constant movement and transformation of existence. Rivers, lakes, and the sea are often depicted as homes to spirits like the kappa, who embody the dual nature of water—both life-giving and potentially dangerous. These stories teach us to respect and honor the natural world, understanding its vital role in our lives. The ever-changing nature of water reminds us that life is fluid and we must adapt to its flow.

Mountains hold a sacred place in Japanese culture. These towering peaks are worshiped and revered, as they are seen as abodes of gods and spirits. Pilgrimages to sacred mountains are common. Folktales often feature mountain deities who test the resolve of characters, guiding them toward personal growth and enlightenment.

Forests, with their dense foliage and hidden depths, symbolize mystery and life. They are home to spirits like the kodama, which inhabit trees and watch over the woods. Forests in folklore are places of both danger and refuge.

All of these symbols offer moral lessons, guiding characters to make ethical choices and embrace virtues like courage, compassion, and humility. They serve as cautionary elements, highlighting the perils of greed, pride, and disrespect for nature.

In Japanese folklore, symbols also play an important role in the concept of "mono no aware," the awareness of the impermanence of things. This concept is deeply ingrained in Japanese culture and is reflected in the appreciation of fleeting moments of beauty, such as the blooming of cherry blossoms or the passing of seasons. The symbols in these tales often evoke a sense of wistfulness and appreciation for the transient nature of life. They teach us to find beauty in impermanence and to live with a mindful awareness of the present.

In the end, these symbols and stories serve as bridges between the tangible and spiritual worlds. They connect us to the natural order and offer insights into human behavior. They remind us that we are part of a larger world, held together by shared experiences, values, and dreams. As we journey through life, these symbols guide us, teaching us to live with respect, gratitude, and awareness.

Conclusion

As our journey through Japanese folktales and legends draws to a close, it becomes clear that these stories are far more than echoes from an ancient past. In every tale, themes that resonate deeply with the human spirit emerge, touching upon the eternal values that bind humanity together.

These folktales reveal the profound respect held for nature in Japanese culture. Through tales of kami, spirits inhabiting everything from the mightiest mountains to the smallest streams, the natural world is shown to be sacred and alive. Stories of the kappa and the sacred camphor tree at Kayashima Station remind us that every element of nature is imbued with life and deserves respect.

Loyalty and honor shine through many of these tales, especially in the legends of samurai like Miyamoto Musashi and the forty-seven ronin. These stories of valor and sacrifice demonstrate that true strength lies not in might but in unwavering dedication to principles. The story of the forty-seven ronin, who avenged the death of their master at great personal cost, speaks to the timeless values of loyalty and courage.

The wisdom embedded in these folktales transcends time, offering insights into the human condition. Themes of love, sacrifice, courage, and cunning are explored. The tale of Urashima Taro, for instance, reflects on the fleeting nature of time and the consequences of actions, urging thoughtful choices and cherishing every moment. These stories encourage looking beyond the surface to seek the deeper truths that guide us toward a more meaningful existence.

In a fast-paced modern world, the lessons from these ancient stories emphasize slowing down and reflecting on life. These tales are guides that help us navigate the challenges of contemporary life, whether through respecting nature, upholding honor, or acting with kindness and empathy.

These stories also bridge the gap between cultures, offering a glimpse into Japan's rich heritage and the values that have shaped its society. The universal themes of love, honor, and the supernatural transcend cultural boundaries, allowing connections with others on a profound level. Through these tales, a broader perspective on traditions and values is gained, enriching our understanding of the world.

Japanese folktales also inspire creativity, influencing countless works of art, literature, and cinema. The imagery and profound themes found in these stories continue to captivate artists and writers, providing a wellspring of ideas that can be reimagined in new and innovative ways.

As the final pages of this book close, it becomes evident that Japanese folktales are timeless treasures, offering lessons that are as valuable today as they were in the past. They remind all to live in harmony with nature, to uphold honor and loyalty, and to seek wisdom in daily life. Let these stories inspire stewardship of the earth, actions of integrity, and cherishing the wisdom passed down through generations. The legacy of these folktales lives on, guiding with timeless truths and enriching lives in ways that are both profound and enduring. These stories will continue to captivate and inspire, showcasing the power of storytelling to shape our understanding of the world and humanity's place within it.

Here's another book by Enthralling History that you might like

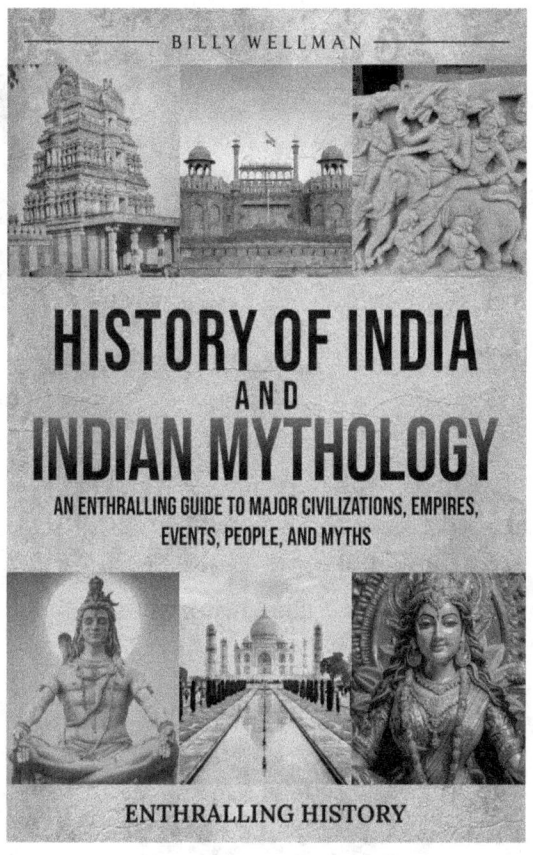

Free limited time bonus

Stop for a moment. We have a free bonus set up for you. The problem is this: we forget 90% of everything that we read after 7 days. Crazy fact, right? Here's the solution: we've created a printable, 1-page pdf summary for this book that you're reading now. All you have to do to get your free pdf summary is to go to the following website:
https://livetolearn.lpages.co/enthrallinghistory/

Or, Scan the QR code!

Once you do, it will be intuitive. Enjoy, and thank you!

Works Cited

Part 1: History of Japan

奈良文化財研究所ホームページ, https://www.nabunken.go.jp/. Accessed 25 August 2024.

Japanese Wiki Corpus, https://www.japanesewiki.com/. Accessed 25 August 2024.

4-7 The 2.26 Incident of 1936 | Modern Japan in archives, https://www.ndl.go.jp/modern/e/cha4/description07.html. Accessed 6 November 2024.

Benedict, Ruth. *The Chrysanthemum and the Sword: Patterns of Japanese Culture*. Houghton Mifflin, 2005.

Brown, Delmer M. "The Impact of Firearms on Japanese Warfare." *The Far Eastern Quarterly*, vol. 7, no. 3, 1948, pp. 236-53. *jstor*, https://doi.org/10.2307/2048846. Accessed 9 Oct 2024.

"Chapter Two." *A Bowl for a Coin: A Commodity History of Japanese Tea*, by William Wayne Farris, Knowledge Unlatched, 2019. Accessed 16 August 2024.

Clements, Jonathan. *A Brief History of Japan: Samurai, Shogun and Zen: The Extraordinary Story of the Land of the Rising Sun*. Tuttle Publishing, 2017.

Curry, Andrew. "Turning Japanese." *Archaeology*, vol. 61, no. 1, 2008, pp. 18-65. *jstor.org*, http://www.jstor.org/stable/41780320. Accessed 23 June 2024.

Duus, Peter, et al., editors. *The Japanese Wartime Empire, 1931-1945*. Princeton University Press, 1996.

"Emperor Hirohito and PM Yoshida | American Experience." *PBS*, https://www.pbs.org/wgbh/americanexperience/features/macarthur-emperor-hirohito-and-pm-yoshida/. Accessed 2 November 2024.

Farris, William W. "Trade, Money, and Merchants in Nara Japan." *Monumenta Nipponica*, vol. 53, no. 3, 1998, pp. 303-34. *jstor*, https://doi.org/10.2307/2385718. Accessed 9 July 2024.

"History of Zen Buddhism | International Zen Association." *Association Zen Internationale*, https://www.zen-azi.org/en/history-zen-buddhism. Accessed 13 August 2024.

"History - Tokugawa Ieyasu." *BBC*, https://www.bbc.co.uk/history/historic_figures/ieyasu_tokugawa.shtml. Accessed 16 October 2024.

Ishii, Mikiko. "The Noh Theater: Mirror, Mask, and Madness." *Comparative Drama*, vol. 28, no. 1, 1994, pp. 43-66. *jstor*. Accessed 20 Sept 2024.

Kazui, Tashiro, and Susan Downing Videen. "Foreign Relations during the Edo Period: Sakoku Reexamined." *Journal of Japanese Studies*, vol. 8, no. 2, 1982, pp. 283-306. *jstor*. Accessed 17 Oct 2024.

Pearson, Richard. "Debating Jomon Social Complexity." *Asian Perspectives*, vol. 46, no. 2, 2007, pp. 361-88. *JSTOR*, http://www.jstor.org/stable/42928722. Accessed 24 June 2024.

Spafford, David. "Emperor and Shogun, Pope and King: The Development of Japan's Warrior Aristocracy." *Bulletin of the Detroit Institute of Arts*, vol. 88, no. 1/4, 2014, pp. 10-19. *jstor*, http://www.jstor.org/stable/43493624. Accessed 12 July 2024.

Suzuki, Daisetz Teitaro. *Introduction to Zen Buddhism, Including a Manual of Zen Buddhism*. Causeway Books, 1974.

Takashi, Kato. "Edo in the Seventeenth Century: Aspects of Urban Development in a Segregated Society." *Urban History*, vol. 27, no. 2, 2000, pp. 189-210. *jstor*. Accessed 17 Oct 2024.

Turnbull, Stephen. "The Onin War: A Turning Point in Samurai History." *Medieval Warfare*, vol. 10, no. 2, 2020, pp. 38-45. *jstor*, https://www.jstor.org/stable/48683814. Accessed 29 09 2024.

Walker, Brett L. *A Concise History of Japan*. Cambridge University Press, 2015.

Yoshie, Akiko. "Gendered Interpretations of Female Rule: The Case of Himiko, Ruler of Yamatai." *U.S. - Japan Women's Journal*, vol. 44, no. 1, 2013, pp. 3-23. *JSTOR*, http://www.jstor.org/stable/42771843. Accessed 29 June 2024.

Part 2: Japanese Folktales and Legends

"About Inari-Okami," *Spirit Fox* (blog), May 31, 2022. https://spiritfoxtarot.wordpress.com/my-patron-inari/.

Barsotyi, Marty. "People From Japanese Lore: Yamato Takeru." *Wasshoi*, November 9, 2021. https://www.wasshoimagazine.org/blog/discovering-japan/yamato-takeru.

Cartwright, Mark, and Taku. "Izanami and Izanagi." *World History Encyclopedia*, July 2, 2024. https://www.worldhistory.org/Izanami_and_Izanagi/.

Cavendish, Richard. "The Forty-Seven Ronin Incident." *History Today*, December 12, 2002. https://www.historytoday.com/archive/months-past/forty-seven-ronin-incident.

Copeland, Rebecca. "Yamamba: The Japanese Mountain Witch." *Medium*, February 12, 2022. https://medium.com/japonica-publication/yamamba-the-japanese-mountain-witch-b1e13262300b.

De Lange, William. "Arima Kihei." *Miyamoto Musashi* (blog), accessed June 18, 2024. http://www.miyamotomusashi.eu/duels/arima-kihei.html.

"Fourth Century: The Legend of Prince Yamatotakeru: The Path He Took and Yamato's Expansion," *Heritage of Japan* (blog), February 4, 2009. https://heritageofjapan.wordpress.com/following-the-trail-of-tumuli/4th-century-the-legend-of-prince-yamatotakeru-the-path-he-took-and-yamatos-expansion/.

Frydman, Joshua. *The Japanese Myths: A Guide to Gods, Heroes and Spirits*. National Geographic Books, 2022.

Griffis, William Elliot. "The Tongue-Cut Sparrow: A Fairy Tale From Japan," Professor D.L. Ashliman (University of Pittsburgh), last modified April 5, 2015. https://sites.pitt.edu/~dash/sparrow.html.

Japonais, Katana. "Samurai and Their Relationship With the Katana: History and Anecdotes." *Katana Sword* (blog), April 7, 2023. https://katana-sword.com/blogs/katana-blog/samurai-and-their-relationship-with-the-katana-history-and-anecdotes.

Kimball, Donny. "The Myth Shuten Doji | Kyoto's Mt. Oe & the 'Drunken Demon.'" *A Different Side of Japan* (blog), December 2, 2023. https://donnykimball.com/shuten-doji-mt-oe-8334ec2dd479.

Kincaid, Chris. "The Stonecutter." *Japan Powered* (blog), May 23, 2016. https://www.japanpowered.com/folklore-and-urban-legends/stonecutter.

Kondo, Daniel. "Princess Kaguya | a Tale for the Ages." Japan House (Los Angeles), September 9, 2021. https://www.japanhousela.com/articles/princess-kaguya-a-tale-for-the-ages/.

Linfamy. "Yokai Explained: Tofu Boy (Don't Eat What He Gives You)." YouTube video, 4:33, November 27, 2021. https://www.youtube.com/watch?v=-s_vQ_W73qo.

Lye, Sian. "Volcanoes: What Are They?" Japan National Tourism Association, accessed June 11, 2024. https://www.japan.travel/national-parks/plan-your-visit/guides-and-stories/volcanoes-what-are-they/#:~:text=Japan's%20volcanoes%20are%20largely%20formed,by%2Dproduct%20of%20volcanic%20activity.

Masanobu, Kagawa. "'Tengu': The Birdlike Demons That Became Almost Divine." Nippon Communications Foundation, December 2, 2022. https://www.nippon.com/en/japan-topics/b02507/.

Matsui, Alana. "Scary Stories: 7 Japanese Tales That Will Chill You to the Bone." *Savvy Tokyo*, February 6, 2024. https://savvytokyo.com/scary-stories-7-japanese-tales-that-will-chill-you-to-the-bone/.

"Mt. Ibuki." Omi Tourism Board, February 21, 2020. https://visit-omi.com/poi/article/mt-ibuki.

Meyer, Matthew. "Hōsōgami." Yokai.com GK, accessed June 24, 2024. https://yokai.com/housougami/.

Meyer, Matthew. "Oiwa." Yokai.com GK, accessed June 25, 2024. https://yokai.com/oiwa/.

Meyer, Matthew. "Okiku." Yokai.com GK, accessed June 25, 2024. https://yokai.com/okiku/.

Meyer, Matthew. "Toyotama Hime." Yokai.com GK, accessed June 21, 2024. https://yokai.com/toyotamahime/.

Meyer, Matthew. "Yamabiko." Yokai.com GK, accessed June 27, 2024. https://yokai.com/yamabiko/.

Naoki, Matsumoto. "Amaterasu: The Japanese Sun Goddess." Nippon.com, July 1, 2023. https://www.nippon.com/en/japan-topics/g00748/amaterasu-the-japanese-sun-goddess.html.

Rinpoche, H.E. Tsem. "Kappa – the Japanese Water Demon | 河童－日本水怪," Tsem Rinpoche, February 21, 2024. https://www.tsemrinpoche.com/tsem-tulku-rinpoche/one-minute-story/kappa-the-japanese-water-demon.

Strusiewicz, Cezary Jan. "How Women Disappeared From Kabuki Theater | Tokyo Weekender." *Tokyo Weekender*, January 10, 2022. https://www.tokyoweekender.com/art_and_culture/japanese-culture/no-women-kabuki-theater-japan/.

"The Legendary Duel Between Sasaki Kojiro and Miyamoto Musashi." *The Archaeologist: Civilizations of the World* (blog), November 15, 2022. https://www.thearchaeologist.org/blog/the-legendary-duel-between-sasaki-kojiro-and-miyamoto-musashi.

"The History of Miyamoto Musashi." Niten Institute, accessed June 15, 2024. https://m.niten.org/english/instituto/miyamoto_musashi/musashi-biografia.

"The Myths of Japan: Into the Underworld." Miyazaki Prefecture Tourism Association, accessed June 13, 2024. https://visitmiyazaki.com/mythology/into-the-underworld/.

"The Story of Kiyohime." Tenabe International English Guide Association (TIEGA), accessed June 21, 2024. https://tekutekutb.kiiminpo.jp/cnts2/lw/?db=tiega&mode=tiega&id=241020&name=The+Story+of+Kiyohime.

"Tsuru No Ongaeshi – Japanese Folktale." *Kyuhoshi* (blog), updated April 9, 2024. https://www.kyuhoshi.com/tsuru-no-ongaeshi/.

Uchida, Yoskiko. "The Wise Old Woman." | *Kirkus Reviews*," October 1, 1994. https://www.kirkusreviews.com/book-reviews/yoshiko-uchida/the-wise-old-woman/.

Wright, Gregory. "Inari." Mythopedia, December 6, 2022. https://mythopedia.com/topics/inari.

Image Sources

1 https://commons.wikimedia.org/wiki/File:Sasaki_Toyokichi_-_Nihon_hana_zue_-_Walters_95208.jpg
2 Original: Ash Crow and Maximilian Dörrbecker (Chumwa) Vector: AntiCompositeNumber, CC BY-SA 3.0 <https://creativecommons.org/licenses/by-sa/3.0>, via Wikimedia Commons, https://commons.wikimedia.org/wiki/File:Gempei_war-battles.svg
3 https://commons.wikimedia.org/wiki/File:Emperor_Go-Daigo.jpg
4 https://commons.wikimedia.org/wiki/File:Ashikaga_Takauji.JPG
5 https://commons.wikimedia.org/wiki/File:Sengoku_period_battle.jpg
6 https://commons.wikimedia.org/wiki/File:Odanobunaga.jpg
7 https://commons.wikimedia.org/wiki/File:Tokugawa_Ieyasu2.JPG
8 https://commons.wikimedia.org/wiki/File:Meiji_Emperor_painted_by_Takagi_Haisui.jpg
9 https://commons.wikimedia.org/wiki/File:Emperor_Sh%C5%8Dwa_official_portrait_1_(cropped).jpg
10 Kokiri at English Wikipedia, modifications by Huhsunqu and Markalexander100., CC BY-SA 3.0 <http://creativecommons.org/licenses/by-sa/3.0/>, via Wikimedia Commons, https://commons.wikimedia.org/wiki/File:Japanese_Empire2.png
11 Boccaccio1, CC BY 2.0 <https://creativecommons.org/licenses/by/2.0>, via Wikimedia Commons: https://commons.wikimedia.org/wiki/File:Yotei_Volcano_on_Hokkaido_in_Japan_20101025.jpg
12 https://commons.wikimedia.org/wiki/File:Izanagi_and_Izanami_giving_birth_to_Japan_c1870_after_Kawanabe_Kyosai.jpg
13 https://commons.wikimedia.org/wiki/File:Japan_Map_CIA_2021.png

14 ChiefHira, CC BY-SA 3.0 <https://creativecommons.org/licenses/by-sa/3.0>, via Wikimedia Commons: https://commons.wikimedia.org/wiki/File: Yomotsu_Hirasaka.JPG

15 Brigham Young University, CC BY-SA 4.0 <https://creativecommons.org/licenses/by-sa/4.0>, via Wikimedia Commons: https://commons.wikimedia.org/wiki/File:30.Yukionna.jpg

16 A.Davey from Portland, Oregon, EE UU, CC BY 2.0 <https://creativecommons.org/licenses/by/2.0>, via Wikimedia Commons: https://commons.wikimedia.org/wiki/File:Two_Women_rinse_the_hands_(act_of_misogi_using_temizu)_(1915-04_by_Elstner_Hilton).jpg

17 I, KENPEI, CC BY-SA 3.0 <http://creativecommons.org/licenses/by-sa/3.0/>, via Wikimedia Commons: https://commons.wikimedia.org/wiki/File:Hushimi-inari-taisha_omotesando.jpg

18 DVMG, CC BY 3.0 <https://creativecommons.org/licenses/by/3.0>, via Wikimedia Commons: https://commons.wikimedia.org/wiki/File:Keihan_Kayashima_Station_platform_-_panoramio_(11).jpg

19 en.Wikipedia: Werewolf, CC BY-SA 3.0 <http://creativecommons.org/licenses/by-sa/3.0/>, via Wikimedia Commons: https://commons.wikimedia.org/wiki/File:Inuyama_inari_1.jpg

20 Marco Almbauer, CC BY-SA 4.0 <https://creativecommons.org/licenses/by-sa/4.0>, via Wikimedia Commons: https://commons.wikimedia.org/wiki/File:Torii,_Fushimi_Inari-Taisha.jpg

21 https://commons.wikimedia.org/wiki/File:Wind_God_and_Thunder_God_Screens_by_Tawaraya_Sotatsu_hi-res.png

22 https://commons.wikimedia.org/wiki/File:Installation_of_the_Sun_Goddess_(Amaterasu)_c1870_after_Kawanabe_Kyosai.jpg

23 https://commons.wikimedia.org/wiki/File:Origin_of_the_Cave_Door_Dance_(Amaterasu)_by_Shunsai_Toshimasa_1889.jpg

24 Douglas Perkins, CC BY 4.0 <https://creativecommons.org/licenses/by/4.0>, via Wikimedia Commons: https://commons.wikimedia.org/wiki/File:Ise_Jingu_02.jpg

25 SLIMHANNYA, CC BY-SA 4.0 <https://creativecommons.org/licenses/by-sa/4.0>, via Wikimedia Commons: https://commons.wikimedia.org/wiki/File:Daisho_Uesugi_clan_2.jpg

26 https://commons.wikimedia.org/wiki/File:Samurai-in-Armour-by-Kusakabe-Kimbei.png

27 https://commons.wikimedia.org/wiki/File:Miyamoto-Musashi-Fights-Sasaki-Kojiro-at-Ganryujima-Ukiyo-e.png

28 https://commons.wikimedia.org/wiki/File:Kanadehon-Chushingura-Stage-3-Utagawa-Kuniteru.png

29 https://commons.wikimedia.org/wiki/File:Sengakuji_Ronin_Graves.jpg

30 https://commons.wikimedia.org/wiki/File:Taketori_Monogatari_2.jpg

31 ★Kumiko★ from Tokyo, Japan, CC BY-SA 2.0 <https://creativecommons.org/licenses/by-sa/2.0>, via Wikimedia Commons: https://commons.wikimedia.org/wiki/File:%E4%B8%83%E5%A4%95_(19545533256).jpg

32 https://commons.wikimedia.org/wiki/File:Chikanobu_The_Boatman.jpg#filehistory

33 https://commons.wikimedia.org/wiki/File:Dojoji_engi_emaki_-_p4.png

34 https://commons.wikimedia.org/wiki/File:MasayoshiTofu-Kozo.jpg

35 https://commons.wikimedia.org/wiki/File:Yoshitoshi_Driving_away_the_Demons.jpg

36 https://commons.wikimedia.org/wiki/File:Hokusai_Sangoku_Yoko-den.jpg

37 Miyuki Meinaka, CC BY-SA 4.0 <https://creativecommons.org/licenses/by-sa/4.0>, via Wikimedia Commons: https://commons.wikimedia.org/wiki/File:Splited_Sessho-Seki.jpg

38 https://commons.wikimedia.org/wiki/File:Hokusai_tea-kettle_raccoon.jpg

39 https://commons.wikimedia.org/wiki/File:Oni.jpg

40 https://commons.wikimedia.org/wiki/File:Parelduikers_Pearl_divers.jpg

41 https://commons.wikimedia.org/wiki/File:Jinjyoshogakukokugotokuhon-v3-p040.jpg

42 https://commons.wikimedia.org/wiki/File:Matsuki_Heikichi(1899)-Urashima-p12.jpg

43 https://commons.wikimedia.org/wiki/File:Matsuki_Heikichi(1899)-Urashima-p03.jpg

44 https://commons.wikimedia.org/wiki/File:Kyoka_Hyaku-Monogatari_Kappa.jpg

45 https://commons.wikimedia.org/wiki/File:Suushi_Yama-uba.jpg

46 https://commons.wikimedia.org/wiki/File:YOSOJI%27S_CAMELLIA_TREE.jpg

47 https://commons.wikimedia.org/wiki/File:Kosa_Yamato_Takeru_and_monster_fish.jpg

48 https://commons.wikimedia.org/wiki/File:Yamato-Takeru-with-Sword-Kusanagi-no-Tsurugi-by-Ogata-Gekko.png

49 Motokoka, CC BY-SA 4.0 <https://creativecommons.org/licenses/by-sa/4.0>, via Wikimedia Commons: https://commons.wikimedia.org/wiki/File:Tengu_Masks,_Awashima_jinja_shrine_2.jpg

50 https://commons.wikimedia.org/wiki/File:Yoshitsune_Training_with_the_Tengu_Sojobo_LACMA_M.84.31.530a-c_(cropped).jpg

51 https://commons.wikimedia.org/wiki/File:Kuniyoshi_The_Ghost_in_the_Lantern.jpg

52 https://commons.wikimedia.org/wiki/File:Yoshitoshi_Botan_Doro.jpg

53 https://commons.wikimedia.org/wiki/File:Kabuki_actors_dressed_as_samurai_in_1880.jpg

54 https://commons.wikimedia.org/wiki/File:Japanese_buddhist_monk_hat_by_Arashiyama_cut.jpg

55 Naokijp, CC BY-SA 4.0 <https://creativecommons.org/licenses/by-sa/4.0>, via Wikimedia Commons: https://commons.wikimedia.org/wiki/File:Bandai-ji,_Jizo_Statue_001.jpg

56 https://commons.wikimedia.org/wiki/File:Yoshitoshi_-_100_Aspects_of_the_Moon_-_97.jpg

57 Luka Peternel, CC BY-SA 4.0 <https://creativecommons.org/licenses/by-sa/4.0>, via Wikimedia Commons: https://commons.wikimedia.org/wiki/File:Yoshino-yama-hills-cherry-blossom-2018-Luka-Peternel.jpg

58 https://commons.wikimedia.org/wiki/File:Fan_of_Japanese_Cypress_ITUKUSHIMA_shrine.JPG

www.ingramcontent.com/pod-product-compliance
Lightning Source LLC
Chambersburg PA
CBHW050334010526
44119CB00004B/139